Buster Keaton

Tempest in a Flat Hat

Buster Keaton

Tempest in a Flat Hat

EDWARD McPHERSON

Newmarket Press  New York

First U.S. edition by Newmarket Press, June 2005

Published by arrangement with Faber and Faber Limited, London

This book is published in the United States of America.

First Edition

10 9 8 7 6 5 4 3 2 1

Library of Congress Cataloging-in-Publication Data

McPherson, Edward.
  Buster Keaton : tempest in a flat hat / Edward McPherson. –1st ed.
    p. cm.
  Includes bibliographical references and index.
  ISBN 1-55704-664-6 (pbk. : alk. paper)–ISBN 1-55704-665-4 (hardcover : alk. paper)
  1. Keaton, Buster, 1895-1966. 2. Motion picture actors and actresses–United States–Biography. 3. Comedians–United States–Biography. I. Title.
  PN2287.K4M36 2005
  791.4302'8'092–dc22
2005006810

ISBN 1-55704-665-4

QUANTITY PURCHASES
Companies, professional groups, clubs, and other organizations may qualify for special terms when ordering quantities of this title. For information, write Special Sales Department, Newmarket Press, 18 East 48th Street, New York, NY 10017; call (212) 832-3575; fax (212) 832-3629; or e-mail info@newmarketpress.com.

www.newmarketpress.com

Manufactured in the United States of America.

Overleaf: Publicity photo from *The Navigator* (1924).

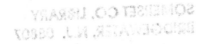

For my grandparents

Contents

List of Illustrations

20 The sleuth at his day job. Publicity photo from *Sherlock, Jr.* (1924).

21 The great detective at work. Publicity photo from *Sherlock, Jr.* (1924). From left: Kathryn McGuire, Joe Keaton, Buster, Jane Connelly, Ward Crane, Erwin Connelly.

22 Two swells at sea—Buster and Kathryn McGuire in a publicity photo from *The Navigator* (1924).

23 Keaton and his *Seven Chances* (1925).

24 Buster and his leading lady, Brown Eyes, in a publicity photo from *Go West* (1925).

25 Buster is the rope-a-dope, Sally O'Neil is the girl, and the sparring partner is unidentified in this publicity photo from *Battling Butler* (1926).

26 Keaton inspects a Civil War cannon in a publicity photo from his brilliant comedy of love and war, *The General* (1926).

27 Keaton rides the cowcatcher in a publicity photo from *The General* (1926).

28 *College* (1927)—Buster fitted out for baseball and track, looking like the athlete that he is.

29 Buster wakes to feel a draft in a publicity photo for the stormy comedy *Steamboat Bill, Jr.* (1928).

30 Buster and the inimitable Josephine on the set of *The Cameraman* (1928).

31 Buster and Josephine pose for a publicity photo for *The Cameraman* (1928).

32 Buster and Elmer at MGM, c. 1931.

33 Poster for *Spite Marriage* (1929).

34 Jimmy, Buster, and Bobby at the Villa, sitting in the American Austin roadster fated for destruction in *Parlor, Bedroom, and Bath* (1931).

35 Buster and his second wife, Mae Scriven.

36 Buster and his third wife, Eleanor Norris, arriving at New York's LaGuardia Airport from Paris, 1947.

37 Keaton and Chaplin in *Limelight* (1952).

38 Buster in *A Funny Thing Happened on the Way to the Forum* (1966).

Introduction: Four-thirty in the afternoon in Muskegon, Michigan

I am sitting in an auditorium, watching a woman rip the lining out of an expensive fur felt fedora and dunk it into a bucket of water. I am taking notes on this; the forty-odd people around me are taking notes on this. We have come from London, New York, Los Angeles, Boston, New Orleans, Cottage Grove. We have been here since eight-thirty this morning. It is a Buster Keaton convention. We're learning to make a porkpie hat.

The people around me are warm, gracious, and—as they will be the first to admit—unusual. They are all members of the Damfinos, the International Buster Keaton Society, some 700 members strong. They're the kind of people who know Buster's hat size ($6\,7/8$), people who sit around talking about projection speeds, people who have been *inside* the Italian Villa (Buster's former Hollywood mansion, not open to the public), people who recall which prints of which eighty-year-old movies are missing which scenes, people who get married in Keaton-specific locations, people with Buster tattoos, people who know whether Roscoe "Fatty" Arbuckle's suspenders buttoned on the inside or outside of his pants, people who will take five trains and brave two hurricanes to get to the convention, passionate people, people who take things personally. I am writing a book on Buster Keaton, and they make me nervous.

At the convention, I fail the trivia quiz miserably. They still let me attend the banquet, where we dine on Buster's favorite foods. There is an auction, and to the highest bidder go out-of-print books, a Keaton life mask, a portrait of Buster made out of 15,000 strung beads, original postcards, rare films, and the like. Later, I gain admittance to the costumed speakeasy, where someone shows up with Roscoe Arbuckle's actual scrapbook, full of never-before-seen clippings and photos; a huddle forms and lasts through the wee hours.

Why we're in Muskegon

It has nothing to do with nostalgia, or a discomfort with living in our own time, or a fascination with the esoteric. It's because of the movies. Keaton's films are witty, beautiful, unsentimental, moving, and—most of all—funny. As he scrambles onscreen, objects come to peculiar (yet pragmatic) ends, driven in an instant to the curious brink of comedic perfection: in his hurly-burly world, a car might serve as a sailboat, a violin could double as a paddle, and Keaton himself can turn into a monkey. Even when striking a minor key, a Keaton flick can't help but betray an excitement, an underpinning joy—the 1920s were a heady time, film was a new art, and society was in a terrible hurry to become something else. So houses fall, cars careen out of control, locomotives plunge into rivers—everything is on the verge of collapse or collision—and Keaton is there shooting it all, flinging down films from the high-wire act of modern life. The forces that stand between a man and love, happiness, and success are tremendous and well organized. It's all you can do but laugh.

And laugh hard. Keaton was a master of the streamlined gag. His precision, geometry, and grace register in your gut long before your mind can wrap itself around what he's doing. He once said, "A good comedy story can be written on a penny postcard," and the remark carries more than a whiff of Keaton's signature self-effacement.[1] To him, his films were nothing more than postcards: the disposable shorthand of someone on vacation. Indeed he would not have understood the point to such a book as this. He often insisted, "No man can be a genius in slap-shoes and a flat hat."[2] But he was more than a genius. He was a prodigious acrobat and brilliant writer, gagman, director, and editor—a 5'6" auteur masquerading as a clown.

And so people go to Muskegon, and to theaters across the world, because Keaton's work feels fiercely relevant. While his contemporaries wrote in strokes that today seem terribly broad, Keaton was a man who prized subtlety and understood meaning in the flick of an eye, a momentary hesitation, a shift in weight, a motion half-begun. He underscored the big-screen spectacle (cyclones, avalanches, stampedes) with the perfectly underplayed detail. His virtuosity most often is compared to that of Chaplin, but the two are birds of a decidedly different feather. Keaton put it this way: "Charlie's tramp was a bum with a bum's philosophy. Lovable as he was he would steal if he got the chance. My little fellow was a working man and honest."[3] Keaton was also the more honest storyteller—his films might be touching, but not in the determinedly sentimental mode of Chaplin. Keaton eschewed weepy close-ups, and his stories often don't end happily, but instead with a final nod to bitterness, dejection, or death—an unexpected final twist, the kind of flawless gesture that explodes the closure it purports to bring. Luckily for us, Keaton's little fellow had a habit of keeping his chin up, despite the fact that it seemed to attract punch after undeserved punch.

Why a book?

This book is merely a fan's notes. It is meant to celebrate an unbelievably fertile time in American cinema that was the result of an extraordinary man working under extraordinary circumstances—with absolute artistic freedom, in the fluidity of the silent medium, infused with the bravado of the machine age, supported by a crack team, fresh in the athletic vigor of his youth.

And for that, I will attempt to avoid the pitfall of the Stone Face. It was Keaton's greatest trademark, but over the years it unfortunately has served as an interpretative Rorschach for the thesis-laden biographer, an ambiguous nail on which to hang even the most ludicrous interpretation. Keaton's blank affect has led many critics to fixate on his "stoicism," to make him over as a sort of existential hero, or weep for him as a bruised and battered soul. Making matters worse, biographers have gotten bogged down in a sort of psychoanalytical quagmire—marking with relish each absent father that appears in his work, each instance of paternal abuse. Surely his father's alcoholism played a part in his own; certainly casting dear old Dad as a bruising monster is an act of aggression. But these approaches miss the joy in the films—they're funny!—and fail to recognize how a man can hold dignity in his face and still say it all with his eyes.

So with thanks to the Damfinos for their hospitality (and with apologies for any errors—I'm still working on the quiz), I submit this book to the generation just discovering Keaton, who find him not only at the art house, but in the video store—people who can partake in the relatively new pleasure of rewinding the scenes, dissecting the impossible pratfalls, and wondering over and over to themselves, *how did he do that?*

CHAPTER ONE

Cyclone Baby

Our hero came from *Nowhere*—he wasn't going *Anywhere* and got kicked off
Somewhere.

The High Sign (1921)

Friday, October 4, 1895. In Egypt, the Nile runs unusually high; Great
Britain is experiencing uncommonly cold weather after a period of
uncommon warmth; somewhere in Canada, a railroad superintendent
on the Chicago, Burlington, and Quincy Line mysteriously disappears
between stops; four men fall off a rope bridge some forty feet into a
riverbed in Sing Sing, New York; two Massachusetts balloonatics are
stranded aloft when their guide suddenly collapses. And in Piqua,
Kansas, population somewhere around 200, Joseph Frank Keaton is
born. His proud parents Myra, a 4′11″ ninety-pound whiskey-drinking
bull-fiddle player, and Joe, a brawling self-promoter with a prodigious
high kick, are traveling the vaudeville circuit with the Mohawk Indian
Medicine Show. When the show moves on, so does Joe, leaving his
wife and child to catch up with him some two weeks later. Throughout his life, Joe Jr. would claim that Piqua was blown off the map
shortly thereafter by a cyclone—a fictitious yet fitting bit of theatrical
kinetics for the boy who would weather tremendous storms, both real
and imaginary, as comedy's Great Stone Face.[1]

Myra and Joe were star-crossed lovers from the start. She was the
Iowa-born daughter of Frank L. Cutler, owner of the Cutler Comedy
Company, one of the Old West's many roving "medicine shows." A traveling nineteenth-century infomercial of sorts, the medicine show was a
marriage of entertainment and commerce, offering the public free outdoor variety acts while deriving revenue from the boozy tonic it aggressively hawked. The son of a miller, Joe Keaton hailed from a sober line
of Indiana Quakers, but—as his self-styled legend has it—he lit out for

1

the territories at age twenty-six with eight bucks and a Winchester rifle.[2] Somewhere in the great Oklahoma Territory, a landless and penniless Joe crossed paths with the Cutler Company, which was busy spreading the gospel of its "Kickapoo Elixir." He signed on with the show for three dollars a week as a bouncer, laborer, and "eccentric dancer." Thus Joe met sixteen-year-old Myra, and though he was a foot taller and ten years her senior, he began to woo.[3] "Doc" Cutler was not eager to have a yarn-spinning drifter for a son-in-law, and he sent Myra to live with relatives in Lincoln, Nebraska. But willful Myra was not to be denied; one day she showed up at Joe's boardinghouse, and on May 31, 1894, a Justice of the Peace married the young couple, even though they were a dime short of the two-dollar wedding fee.[4]

The Cutler Company had no place for its wayward daughter and her shiftless husband, so Myra and Joe were forced to find work with other outfits. It was a hard, vagabond life lived for paltry pay. Myra played three shows nightly while Joe pitched tents, canvassed the town to drum up business, and kept an ear out for the cry, "Hey, Rube!"—the carny distress signal, used when being set upon by resentful locals.[5] Rambunctious Joe was handy in a fight; his favorite on-stage bit was also his best brawling maneuver: a particularly nasty and sudden high kick. From a standstill he could whip his foot eight feet in the air with enough precision to knock a man's hat off his head—with or without harming the head. Joe was a bar-room braggadocio, an outgoing soul whose frequent black-eyes earned him the nickname "Dick Deadeye," after the scoundrel in Gilbert and Sullivan's *HMS Pinafore*.[6] Myra soon grew accustomed to her husband's scrapes with the local constabulary; she was a woman who rolled her own cigarettes and played a ruthless game of pinochle.

Then, eight months into her unruly union, in February 1895, Myra became pregnant.[7] That fall, in the whistle-stop town of Piqua, Kansas, she gave birth to a baby boy.

Most likely it wasn't until he was eighteen months old that Joseph Frank Keaton took his first pratfall, an ill-fated tumble down a full flight of stairs in a theatrical boardinghouse, from which he emerged unscathed—though he himself would later maintain he was aged just six months on the auspicious day.[8] Regardless, the act was witnessed by another guest, who picked up the infant and proclaimed to Joe something along the lines of, "My, what a buster!" The name—show-biz slang for a fall—stuck. In early versions of the story, the witness is George Pardey, a vaudeville comedian; a later, and less likely, account has the great Houdini himself unwittingly baptizing the lad.[9] The moniker even precedes the work of R. F. Outcault, originator of the "Buster Brown" comic strip.[10] This boy Buster was clearly an original.

Buster's tumble was a brisk introduction to what would amount to a lifetime of odd occurrences, fantastic mishaps, and propitious near-calamities. One summer day before he was three, young Buster sat behind his family's current boardinghouse, watching a washerwoman dry the laundry with an old-fashioned clothes wringer. The woman had turned her back on Buster, and he was gamely poking at the mysterious contraption when suddenly it sucked his right index finger into its solid-rubber maw. The machine was taken apart, but the finger couldn't be saved—a local doctor sliced it off at the first joint. Then, as legend has it, the day went from bad to worse. Baby Buster slept off the pain, and awoke that afternoon to toddle out into the yard. There he spied a peach, hanging from a tree, and attempted to dislodge it by tossing a brick. The projectile came down squarely on his head, resulting in another visit from the doctor and three stitches in the boy's scalp. Down but not out, Buster took another nap. This time he awoke to a howling wind. Curious, he went to the window, where he was immediately picked up by a raging Kansas twister that carried him for about a block before a local man could nab the flying youngster and deposit him in a storm cellar.[11] The boy was indestructible.

Such tall tales were surely the work of Joe Keaton, a one-man PR firm, who churned out countless dispatches from the Keaton family front on his great Blickensderfer typewriter, sending them off to any newspaperman who would take the time to read them.[12] From Joe, Buster learned the value of a good story; given a chance to set the record straight in his 1960 autobiography, he perpetuated many a family myth, including the one about his very bad day.

But if Buster developed an early taste for embellishment, perhaps it was because the vaudeville stage was populated by people who truly seemed larger than life. While Harry Houdini probably wasn't on hand to name the boy, the great magician and escape artist struck up with the Keatons shortly thereafter in Pittsburg, Kansas. Harry and Bess Houdini quickly became close friends of Joe and Myra. In December of 1897, the four of them—all fledgling vaudevillians—took on with the California Concert Company, a medicine show run by Doc Thomas B. Hill. The company didn't last the winter.[13] But Houdini stayed in touch with Joe, and Buster later would learn sleight-of-hand from the master.[14]

Joe and Myra were having a hard time making a go of it in the small-time world of medicine-show theatrics. The towns were poor, the audiences small, and the money scarce; when the show moved on, Myra and the baby would take the train, leaving Joe to cover the distance on foot.[15] Joe grew tired of tents, walking, and selling elixirs—he dreamed of a life in legitimate vaudeville. No more Kickapoos for them. The East beckoned.

So in November of 1899, the Keatons arrived in New York City. And like others before them, they found the streets didn't flow with milk and honey. The vaudeville season was booked in advance; there was little work to be had, even had Joe possessed an "act"—which he didn't. Joe underwent a period of self-invention. "The Man Who Broke Chairs" failed to win anyone over, and eventually he came up with a billing that left more to the imagination: "The Man With a Table." In this more realized act, Joe, in a clown suit, performed acrobatics on and around the eponymous table, managing to do damage to a chair, the floor, and his shins. Myra played the cornet and had her hat kicked off.[16] "The Two Keatons" passed a bitter month.

Then, as luck would have it, Joe ran into Tony Pastor, a vaudeville producer who gave him an audition. Remarkably, on December 18, 1899, Joe and Myra took the stage as the penultimate act at Pastor's Union Square Theater. The duo was the final human act; they were followed by a Vitagraph projection, a short film novelty that signaled the end of the show. By then, the audience usually had cleared out. It was the lowest rung on the ladder, but they had made it.[17] These were paying customers. The Keatons were in vaudeville.

At Pastor's, Joe and Myra performed three or four shows a day. Joe talked up the act, and soon they got other gigs. On the first day of 1900, when the Keatons played the Pleasure Palace, they must have felt they had reached the big time—the enormous theater, at 58th Street and Third Avenue, seated 4,900. That spring and summer, they took their routine beyond Manhattan to Brooklyn beer gardens, New Jersey theaters, the pier at Atlantic City.[18] Their act, while perhaps generic, was passable. Then, one week in mid-October, everything changed.

No one really cares much about a matinee. It's a good time to exercise the muscles, vary the routine, keep things fresh. The Keatons were in Delaware, starting a week at William Lee Dockstader's Wonderland Theater, when Joe got an itch. He put his boy, just turned five, in a red wig, vest, big shoes, and baggy trousers—a miniature version of his own theatrical costume—and set the kid onstage. No one laughed. Later that week, Joe tried again at the kiddie matinee, and this time there were titters—from the adults. Dockstader offered the Keatons an extra $10 a week to keep the boy in the act, day and night. The Keatons allayed their concerns over Buster's bedtime by letting him sleep through the morning, and thus "The Two Keatons" became three.[19]

Buster's official vaudeville debut owed less to good showmanship than simple pragmatism, for in fact the boy had been wandering onstage and interrupting his parents' act for years—since he was nine months old, if vaudeville legend is to be trusted. His distressed parents were forced to corral him into a stage trunk, which caused them further worry when an inattentive stagehand shut the lid and almost suffocated the child while his parents were performing.[20] As Buster grew older, Joe and Myra resorted to tying him to an offstage pole.[21] Eventually it seemed the best way to keep an eye on the boy was to put him in the act.

The routine started out as an improvised bit of familial roughhouse, but quickly evolved into an unscripted, helter-skelter drama concerning a father's epic battle to discipline his rambunctious son—the action consisting mainly of Buster being tossed about by a hidden suitcase handle strapped to his back. "The Man With a Table" was father to "The Human Mop," a boy whose many uses included wiping the floor and getting thrown through backdrops, into the orchestra pit, and off the stage.[22] Buster would earn this punishment with his insolent tongue and repeated disruptions of Joe's stage sermon, which instructed the audience in the best ways to make their children mind. Buster would flatten Joe with a basketball; Joe would throw him to the wings; Myra would play the alto sax.[23] Audiences squirmed, then laughed to see the impish boy reappear, unharmed. "The Three Keatons" had their gimmick.

To modern eyes, the act might seem to border on abuse, but Buster always denied such allegations. He was born a ham; such demonstrations came instinctually to him—and what boy doesn't enjoy playing rough?[24] Furthermore, Buster was a natural acrobat who grew up surrounded by professionals. His innate talent, his elastic, durable young bones, and the boldness of being under four feet tall made him an early, quick study of the comedy pratfall. Before he knew it, Buster was cultivating a stage personality. Buster and Joe got the biggest laughs when the boy didn't react to his success or failure. Realizing there is nothing funny about a comedian who laughs at his own jokes, Joe instilled in his boy a deadpan expression, hissing "Face! Face!" under his breath if—amidst the hilarity—Buster began to crack a smile.[25] Thus was born the impassive stone face, a Buster Keaton trademark that he would put to comedic effect for the rest of his life. He came to assert that it wasn't an act, that he was wholly incapable of laughter. To the public, this seemed true; Buster learned the discipline of comedy young, and he learned it well.

"The Little Boy Who Can't Be Damaged" was unique among his peers. The vaudeville stage saw countless cute and well-mannered "Little Lord Fauntleroys," but few irascible hellions. There was good reason for this. Few children could pull off what Buster did: the act was physically grueling, and he and Joe took some hard knocks. Once, Buster was thrown into a backdrop that happened to be hiding a brick wall; later, when Buster was about eight, Joe knocked him out for eighteen hours with a high kick. (With a showman's pride, Buster later remembered it as the only time the Keatons missed a performance due to an onstage injury.) Many vaudeville stages were rough-hewn affairs, and one day Joe—falling from a table—took a four-inch splinter to the head that speared his wig to his scalp.[26] Audience members, too, could be at risk. The Keatons were playing to a packed Syracuse house when Myra's saxophone solo aroused the ire of a particularly vociferous critic. Joe immediately hoisted Buster by the handle under his overcoat and threw him—feet-first—at the heckler, breaking three of the offender's ribs and smashing two of the adjacent man's front teeth. Buster, naturally, was just fine.[27]

After their historic Delaware engagement, The Three Keatons took a brief tour of the Midwest. By early spring they were back East, and on March 11, 1901, Buster made his triumphant New York debut at Proctor's 125th Street Theater. The family then signed on for a stint at Tony Pastor's, where it had all begun for Joe and Myra. But this time things were different: the act was held over after its initial run; the Keatons had to go on only twice a day; their weekly salary more than quadrupled, to about $225; the family was able to take an apartment on 21st Street.[28] Under a good-sized picture of Buster, a page-two story in the *New York Clipper* proclaimed, "The tiny comedian is perfectly at ease in his work, natural, finished and artistic, and his specialties have proved a fetching addition to the favorite act of the Keatons that is known all over the land by its title, 'The Man With the Table.'"[29] The kid was a hit.

1 "The Man With a Table," with wife and child, San Francisco, 1901.

7

2 A dapper young Buster, dressed to fool the Gerries, date unknown.

CHAPTER TWO

Meet the Keatons

All of my life I have been happiest when the folks watching me said to each other, "Look at the poor dope, wilya?"[1]

Buster Keaton

The article in the *Clipper* contains an interesting detail. It puts the tiny comedian's birth on October 4, 1893—two years before Buster's actual birthday. Chances are, Joe planted the misinformation. The willful error seems counterintuitive; why downplay the precocity of the boy's debut? The reason was simple: the Gerries had caught wind of the Keatons.

The Society for the Prevention of Cruelty to Children was known—in some circles less than affectionately—as The Gerry Society, after its founder Elbridge T. Gerry.[2] The well-intentioned, somewhat radical (for its time) group crusaded to rescue minors from New York City's streets, sweatshops, and theaters. By the time of Buster's debut, child-labor laws strictly prohibited a child under the age of seven from stepping foot on a stage, and in order to *do* anything—sing, dance, strum, tumble—a youth had to be at least sixteen. So Joe "aged" Buster by two years to make him stage legal, and then took the rather weak line of argument that what Buster did didn't really constitute a performance—he was merely a prop being thrown about. Various theater managers would further obfuscate things by spreading word that Buster was in fact a midget, a rumor that Joe did little to quell by dressing his son in pint-sized suits, accessorized with cane, case, and derby.[3]

And so the Keatons began a nine-year game of cat and mouse with the various agents of the Gerry Society. A typical week's engagement would begin with a Monday matinee, during which Joe and Buster— under the watchful eye of the Gerry scout planted somewhere in the

9

audience—would keep the mayhem in careful check. The inspector would rarely come by again, and suffice it to say by the weekend the show was another thing altogether.[4] The routine worked more often than not, yet there were times when the society thought it had gotten the better of the Keatons. Buster rather fondly remembered being hauled into the office of more than one New York City Mayor to be stripped and searched for bruises. None were ever found.[5] The theater was a game the Keatons were winning.

Not that the Gerry Society didn't have reason to come calling. Buster was becoming the family breadwinner, and he wasn't exactly like other children. For one thing, he didn't go to school. He had tried it once, at the age of six, but it didn't take. Buster had been indignant to be woken at 8 a.m. by his father, and packed off to school with the other children, but he found his Jersey City classmates to be a generous audience for his wisecracks, which he lifted from a schoolroom comedy routine he had seen more than once at the theater. The poor teacher was no match for Buster's borrowed wit, and the principal sent the young comedian home with a note asking that he never return. It was the only day of formal schooling he would attend in his entire life; after that, Myra took up the boy's education.[6]

The Keatons' act was getting bigger, and what was attracting the attention of Gerry and non-Gerry alike was its particular brand of bedlam—fast gaining fame as the roughest roughhousing in vaudeville. In 1900, America could still be a pretty polite place; theatergoers delighted in a good beaning, and the Keatons were happy to oblige. While the sequence of events differed from show to show, the act was a variation on the theme of mutual abuse. The boy picks up a broom and starts to pester his dad, who lightly swipes back. An exchange of playful little taps soon escalates into full-on whacks, which suddenly fall in time with the band, now blasting "The Anvil Chorus." Later, Myra toots on her sax while, in the background, Joe begins to lather up his face for a shave. Buster wanders in with a basketball attached to a rubber tube. He surreptitiously fixes one end above the mirror Joe is using, and walks across the stage, stretching the tube taut. When the long blade of the straight razor is poised above Joe's neck,

Buster releases the basketball, which whizzes towards the back of Joe's unsuspecting head. The audience gasps. Joe's face smashes into the mirror. Myra plays on.[7]

Thus the abuse clearly went both ways, and as Buster grew older, Joe took to wearing a steel cap underneath his wig to shield his pate from Buster's ever-stronger blows. One night, after a few too many drinks, Joe forgot his cap, and Buster knocked him unconscious with a broom handle; another time, Buster accidentally shot Joe in the face with a blank, leaving him lacerated and powder-burnt (but all right).[8] Each performance had its surprises, and Buster learned to be on the lookout for anything—especially once Joe began to channel all of his parenting, real and make-believe, through the family act. Offstage actions could earn onstage punishment, such as the time, years later, when Joe—himself a smoker—discovered a pipe in Buster's jacket. Buster knew he was in for it, but he went down swinging, and that night the duo broke three brooms, two chairs, the house set, and a table.[9]

When Buster was still little, the stage combat was punctuated by a rather humdrum, not-so-witty repartee:

"Son, can you read your A, B, C's?"

"I have never read them."

"What have you read?"

"I have red hair."[10]

Still, the kid was a charmer. Joe proudly advertised his boy as "the cutest little bundle of jollity that ever wriggled into the hearts of audiences."[11] A 1903 article in *The New York Times* begins, "Buster Keaton, who assists Papa Keaton and Mamma Keaton at Keith's this week, says that on the trains he is four years old, but in New York he is ten." (In reality, he was seven.) The pint-sized comedian goes on to relate, "When we travel daddy puts a short skirt on mamma. He buys a full-fare ticket for himself, a half-fare for mamma, and as for me—well, it's into the dog basket." The well-smitten reviewer brands Buster an "excruciatingly funny little chap."[12]

Soon, the little chap got some company. Despite what Buster said on the record, the family could now afford to travel by sleeper car—Mom and Dad below, with Buster relegated to the top berth (beside

Myra's saxophone).[13] And so, in his words, "the Pullman babies began arriving."[14] On August 25, 1904, Myra gave birth to Harry Stanley Keaton. The baby was named after family friend Harry Houdini, but quickly earned the nickname "Jingles" for the ruckus he made with his toys. On the day before Halloween 1906, Buster and Jingles got a sister, christened Louise Dresser Keaton, after the vaudeville and silent film actress of the same name.[15]

To be fair, Joe displayed an evenhanded parenting style, playing it equally cavalier with all of his children. With Myra out of the act (pregnant with Louise), Joe was desperate to keep the Keatons in the headlines, and he cooked up a publicity stunt in Portland, Maine, which involved having a local prop man kidnap eighteen-month-old Jingles outside of a grocery store. The stunt went awry when a gang of day laborers witnessed the baby-snatching and gave chase. Eventually Jingles was found at the train station, alone and eating candy.[16]

So The Man With a Table now had a wife and three kids, and, as was to be expected, strange and fascinating tales began cropping up about the unlucky family's miraculous resilience. Buster enthusiastically recalls the many fires, train wrecks, and freak accidents that plagued the Keatons' vaudeville days. Baby Louise walked through a French window. Jingles' pram rolled down the street, unmanned. So many boardinghouses burnt down that Joe instituted fire drills. The family always came through without a scratch.[17]

During Myra's absence from the stage, Buster's career had taken a brief dramatic detour, and The Little Boy Who Couldn't Be Damaged took on additional straight roles in melodramas such as *Little Lord Fauntleroy* and *East Lynne*.[18] Buster, tired of playing tragic, prematurely doomed children, was anxious to get back to the family's bread-and-butter act. True to form, it wasn't long before The Three Keatons became five.

The new members weren't much good in the knockabout game, so Jingles and Louise only appeared onstage at the very end, a cute coda to an act that professed to have its heart in family values. It was a bold move for a troupe on the Gerries' short list, but for the most part Joe kept the littlest ones off the stage in New York, and the family was left alone.[19] Then, one November day in 1907, Joe went too far.

The ultimate irony to the story is that it was all done for the children. The Keatons were in New York City, and Joe had agreed to exhibit all five of them at a concert at the Grand Opera House on 23rd Street and Eighth Avenue. The theater manager had promised no trouble from the Gerry Society—after all, it was a Thanksgiving benefit for the city's needy children. The acts were performing gratis. Joe was pitching a feature story about The Five Keatons to the *Dramatic Mirror*, a leading theatrical trade, and the paper was sending someone to the show. The family seemed on the verge of another breakthrough. That night Joe, Buster, and Myra did their usual routine, then Buster chased Jingles, and Louise, twelve months old, tried to "dance." The next day, the entire family made an encore appearance—in New York City court. *The New York Times* reported a sad tale of repeated offense: "The Keaton children, Joseph, Jr., fourteen years old, George, three, and Vera, one, have performed in several theatres in this city. The father has been arrested a number of times, and on each occasion has been fined." In his testimony, the theater manager refused to confirm that he was the theater manager, on the grounds that it "might tend to degrade and incriminate him." And so, while confused about Buster's age and his siblings' names, the paper did get one thing right: the Keatons were in trouble. Joe was fined and the family banned from appearing on the New York stage for two years—when Buster supposedly would turn sixteen. The Gerry Society had finally won.[20]

The sentence dealt the act a serious blow, for it kept the Keatons out of the country's most important vaudeville houses, such as Hammerstein's Victoria, Tony Pastor's, and the Palace. It put the family back where they had started: on the road, touring the theatrical hinterland of America and dreaming of a triumphant return East.

In exile, Buster gained something he'd never had before: a home. As the Keatons swung up, down, and through the country, they would return each summer to pass the vaudeville off-season in a modest upper-Michigan settlement sandwiched between two lakes—one Great, one small—called Bluffton.

Years earlier, the Keatons had played an amusement park outside of Muskegon, Michigan, a former logging town whose lake fed into Lake Michigan. The area's sandy beaches, deep woods, and fresh waters took fervent hold of Joe's imagination. In 1908, Joe and some of his associates founded what would become known as the Bluffton Actors' Colony. Across the lake from the town of Muskegon, it was a haven for the songwriters, musicians, comedians, comic heavies, performing dogs, educated zebras, and bowling elephants that kept the rest of the country in perpetual delight. By the cool, blue waters of Muskegon Lake, a handful of vaudeville's favorite sons and daughters settled down to while the summer away gossiping, trading secrets, retouching routines, playing pranks, one-upping each other, relaxing, cutting loose. Word of the colony spread, and soon Bluffton claimed over 200 residents.[21] It was vaudeville's bucolic playground, a vibrant fellowship of the performative spirit that lasted the span of a summer, and it was one of Buster's favorite places in the world.

A year after creating the Actors' Colony, Joe purchased his family a bona fide residence. Christened "Jingles' Jungle," the clapboard summerhouse had three bedrooms, a porch, and a gas stove.[22] In Bluffton, Myra played endless games of pinochle, Joe spun yarns at Bullhead Pascoe's saloon, and Buster took to being a kid.[23] In the more than seven summers the family lived in Michigan, Buster became an avid outdoorsman, spending the long days swimming, duck hunting, and fishing. He also began a lifelong devotion to the game of baseball, and Buster introduced many of his stage acrobatics to the sandlot, flipping head over heels before catching an infield fly, or traveling by cartwheels to pick up a lazy grounder. He was the flashiest if not the most enthusiastic shortstop Bluffton had ever seen.[24]

While surely a serene, idyllic retreat, underneath Bluffton's resort-town composure beat a wildly anarchic heart. Its inhabitants were free to fill their days with rocking-chair philosophizing and cards before dinner, but it was more likely that they were feverishly dreaming up the next big gag. Life was something performed for and *on* your neighbors, and Buster was fast becoming the town's clown prince of practical jokes. Some were simple sight gags: for instance, if Buster was riding his bike by the colony clubhouse and spied a stranger sitting on the porch, he would immediately barrel down the dock and launch himself into the water, bike and all. Other hapless visitors would row past the Keaton house and suddenly find themselves in the midst of an astonishing domestic scene. Pots and pans were being tossed off the porch with wild abandon—then came the children: first a boy, then a little girl, then the oldest would come flying off the porch, high, arms-flailing, and upside down. The poor sap would row madly off to report the abuse to the nearest authority, never aware that Buster had thrown his siblings and then himself off the porch, where they had landed safe and sound on the sand hill that sloped down thirty feet, perfectly soft and perfectly invisible from the water.[25]

While Buster's stunts were always shrewd, visually eloquent affairs, the ones that gained him the most fame came to involve increasingly intricate mechanics. It all started with the Clown Pole. A bamboo fishing pole stood wedged between two boards in the town pier, as if momentarily abandoned. The line was attached to a red cork, which bobbed innocently on the lake. Underwater, the line ran along the dock and through a pulley; it surfaced out of view and stretched all the way up to the clubhouse, where it came in through a window. An outsider would stop to puzzle at the unmanned pole, when all of a sudden the bobber would take a monstrous dive. Invariably the man would leap for the pole and begin a heroic battle to land the "fish," which would be one or more of the actors laughing—and tugging—from above. A crowd would materialize to cheer on the victim. The gag ended with the pole being wrenched out of the hands of the stranger, who eventually would get wise to the prank and come up to the clubhouse, where he received a medal and was encouraged to buy drinks for the house.

The Clown Pole was Buster's gift to the community. But one of his neighbors had difficulties of a very personal nature, and Buster next put his skills in the service of a friend. Ed Gray was an overweight, lethargic monologist who was plagued by two afflictions: an inability to get up in the morning, and a steady stream of picnickers and hikers who used his outhouse. To solve the first difficulty, Buster rigged Gray's entire house to his alarm clock. At ten o'clock every morning, the alarm went off and, if left unanswered, put into action machinations of devilish sophistication: the stove was lit, the covers rudely snatched off the late-riser, the bed canted abruptly by means of cams and an electric motor. The waking of Ed Gray became a popular daily attraction, much like Old Faithful, and, after a period of behavioral conditioning, Gray learned to anticipate the machine.[26]

The aggressive alarm clock was received with great fanfare, but Buster's pièce de résistance was Ed Gray's hilltop outhouse. The facility was being strained to the limits of its capacity by uninvited visitors too prim to do their business in the woods and too rude to knock and ask permission. So Buster dismantled the wooden structure and attached spring hinges to each of the four walls. He split the roof down the middle, nailing the halves to opposite walls. He then buried a pipe under the outhouse. What appeared to be a clothesline emerged from one end of the pipe and stretched to Ed Gray's kitchen window; underwear and shirts hung on the line. It was an inspired setup. When someone was bold enough to make himself at home in the outhouse, all Gray had to do was tug on the line and the roof and four walls fell outward, revealing the interloper, in all of his enthroned glory, to the town below.[27]

Buster was a practical help to his father as well. He fiddled endlessly with the innards of the family car, and when Joe—deciding he was in need of nautical transport—bought a used twenty-five-foot cruiser (which he dubbed *Battleship*), Buster converted the steam engine to a gasoline-powered two-cylinder. Joe fished from the boat in an admiral's hat; he kept his son onboard as helmsman and mechanic.[28] The boy displayed a keen aptitude and appreciation for tinkering, and in his autobiography, Buster muses, "I was so successful as a child performer that it occurred to no one to ask me if there was something else I'd like to do when I grew up. If someone had asked me I would have said, 'Civil engineer.' I imagine I would have been a good one. But even fifty years ago you could not qualify for a

16

degree with a one-day school education."[29] As it turns out, Keaton would develop his natural mechanical inclination by trial and error, and his engineer's mind would serve him remarkably well in his career as a filmmaker.

Bluffton was also where Buster became a teenager; there he took his first drink of whiskey, with fellow actor and life-long chum Lex Neal, and together the boys began to tackle—with mixed success—the mystery of girls. Buster's life fell into a comfortable rhythm: summer idylls by the lake, winter performances on the circuit.[30] Throughout his years, Buster would re-create the fried fish he ate those summers at Pascoe's: lake perch hand-rolled in cornmeal and flour and fried in half-butter, half-lard.[31] Buster was ever at heart a country boy.

CHAPTER THREE

Steamships, a Corpse, and Broken Furniture

The empty seats get you.[1]

Buster Keaton

In the summer of 1909, with the Keatons nearing the end of their two-year exile from New York, Joe received a unique offer, one that would allow the family act—in its entirety—to return to a legitimate vaudeville stage. Alfred Butt, the manager of London's Palace Theatre, invited the Keatons for a week's engagement, with the possibility of an indefinite extension should the act prove popular. The salary, £40 or roughly $200, was below average, but the prestige of the music hall and the convenience of the situation more than compensated.[2] The booking seemed a pleasurable way for the family to pass the remainder of the Gerry sentence, and a stint at the famed Palace was the perfect preface to a proud return to their native boards. On July 1, 1909, the entire family set sail on the SS *George Washington*.[3] The Keatons were going international.

The trip quickly became a cross-cultural comedy of errors, which Joe—a staunchly boorish patriot—lovingly detailed in a long, pointed sermon in *Variety*. Immediately upon booking his passage, Joe began to regret the decision to take his family abroad. Friends told horror stories about life in the British Isles, and Joe's cultural unease manifested itself promptly. The Keatons had only just boarded the ship when Joe picked up Louise and bellowed, "Before the boat sails I am authorized to sell this orphan child. What am I offered?" The girl went to an entrepreneurial little boy, for seventy-five cents, but the stunt failed to get the family thrown off the boat. Joe was simply barred from holding any further auctions. On landing in London, Joe claims he was set upon by hordes of opportunistic cabbies, footmen, Sherpas, and such—to the point that he had to employ a man simply to handle the tipping. The first night, the family was put up in a brothel. The following day, Joe reported to the Palace to find the Keatons unbilled and, adding insult to injury, without props. The theater expected them to supply their own incidentals: brooms, guns, chairs—but all the Keatons had brought was a table. It was a case of cultural misunderstanding—British acts carried all of their own props—but Joe took it personally.[4] Still, the show had to go on and, according to Joe, the family surmounted this and other obstacles—warm beer, an uneven, splintery stage, poor billing, an orchestra that balked at the idea of a woman on a saxophone. Then the impossible happened: the act bombed. Joe figured something was getting lost in the translation, but the fact was that the English assumed he truly was abusing the boy.[5] The next night, the Keatons were bumped earlier in the line-up and played to an essentially empty house. In the morning, Alfred Butt asked Joe if Buster was adopted; he presumed no father could treat his own son like that.[6]

Joe's cautionary tale ends with the family sailing off on the next available ship, exasperated, humiliated, anxious to get home to a country with a sense of humor. Buster, not half as pernickety as his father, mentions how he enjoyed seeing new acts, including the celebrated Peter the Great, a headlining chimpanzee whose behavior was perfectly human: he ate with utensils, rode a bike, and undressed for bed.[7] Joe avowed no such appreciation for the simian superstar; for him, the trip only served to make him a better Yankee.[8]

In October of that year, newspaper ads trumpeted, BUSTER IS SIXTEEN![9] Truthfully he was fourteen, but in a birthday announcement in *Variety*, Buster bid adieu to the Gerries.[10] In the eyes of the law, he was finally fully stage legal. As for Jingles and Louise, Joe wasn't going to take any more chances; as soon as the children could handle it, they were put in Michigan boarding schools.[11] This time there would be no interruptions.

Naturally, The Three Keatons' routine had evolved over the years. Buster grew too heavy to serve as a human projectile, and he took to interspersing the slapstick with wicked burlesques of other acts on the bill. For him, it was the most enjoyable kind of comedy.[12] He parodied the popular songs of the day, and the facility with which he did so made him a constant source of amusement, on and off the stage.[13] Vaudeville was fueled by a showman's good will, and the Keatons' victims understood the satire to be a warped form of flattery. Still, they often felt a need to settle the score—or start a fresh rivalry—all in the name of fun.

In a new routine, Joe comes downstage to recite a "beautiful poem," while his son appears in the background, sweeping. Soon Buster spots something on the floor, which he begins to stab at repeatedly with the broom handle, effectively drowning out Joe's poetry. Suddenly Buster strikes his target—a knothole—and the broom is hilt-buried in the stage, sending Buster's feet where his head was. Joe halts his recitation and comes to the aid of his son, and together they extricate the broom. Thus ends the skit—or so they thought. At the time Buster and Joe were still polishing the routine, The Three Leightons, whose stage trunk Buster had filled with wild cats, were demanding satisfaction. Buster waited and waited for the retribution, but none came. Then one day in New York City, at the end of the broom routine, the handle came up with a rope tied to it. After 175 feet of ad-libbing, Joe and Buster finally cleared the rope from the hole. At the end was tied an American flag; the band burst into "The Star Spangled Banner." Word of the gag spread, and soon the broom was surfacing with the strangest attachments—an eel, some mustard, the Keatons' two-weeks' notice. Once the broom was slingshot completely off the stage. The final installment was witnessed by a packed Canadian house. A rumor went out that the broom would emerge flying a German flag, a dicey proposition given that it was during the early days of the First World War and Canada was mourning a recently defeated regiment. That night, Buster peered down the hole and spied a flag. He hissed a warning to his father, and Joe, ever quick on his feet, told him to hoist it up and destroy it. When the flag surfaced, the two thrashed at it with abandon—until they realized it was the Union Jack. The silence was absolute; Joe and Buster raced for the wings, and then came the roar. Laughter. The audience had taken one look at the pair's frightened faces and gotten the joke. Nonetheless, the episode signaled the end of the broom-handle pranks.[14]

Mischievous cronies weren't the Keatons' only competition for the spotlight. Vaudeville houses occupied a curious intersection of polite society and popular incivility; within their walls it seemed anything could happen, and it often did. Theatergoers were rowdy, unafraid to make their presence known, and didn't always draw the line at simple heckling. Once The Three Keatons were upstaged by a dead body. They were in Philadelphia; the headlining diva had only just launched into her second song when a man stood up in the balcony, brandished a gun, and when the woman ran offstage, shot himself in the head. The remains were removed, the singer finished her song, and the Keatons took the stage. Buster drolly noted that, in the competition for the audience's attention, the corpse won.[15]

The Three Keatons had found considerable success; they were well known and they made good money. As early as 1909 the family could afford to purchase luxury items, such as a $250 kiddie car for Buster, which came from Macy's with three horsepower under the hood and could do eighteen miles per hour. By 1913, Buster had owned two real cars—a Peerless Phaeton and a Palmer Singer.[16]

Still, the act had a few problems, not the least of which was Joe. Age and success had only made the Keaton patriarch more ornery. In those days xenophobia was just one of many faults: Joe's loutish behavior was becoming more frequent, as was his drinking—and the man was a bad drunk. Joe had never shied from a confrontation, and now that the family was in a position of some renown, he saw little need to curb his tongue—or foot. Buster claims that Joe was at his best when fighting more than one opponent, such as the three California health officials who one day knocked on the door of the Keatons' hotel room. They were offering vaccinations for the family; Joe floored the trio with a single kick.[17] Another time, in Providence, Rhode Island, a cheap house manager provided the Keatons with substandard stage furniture—and then billed them when the pieces broke. Joe went into a rage, smashing all of the theater's prop furnishings. Word of Joe's tantrum spread to New York.[18]

But in Joe's mind, he had one true nemesis: Martin Beck, the manager of Broadway's illustrious Palace Theater who also ran the sprawling Orpheum vaudeville circuit, which covered Chicago and everything west. In his role as booking manager, Beck controlled the fate—and purse strings—of most acts in vaudeville. In the deregulated dealings of the day, he ran a viciously pro-management shop, bullying acts into submission by rewarding deferential troupes with lucrative, convenient routes and punishing troublemakers with unrewarding and geographically challenging bookings. One can imagine Joe Keaton easily falling into the troublemaking category—it was Beck's way or the high way, and Joe rightfully resented it. Joe was a longtime member of the White Rats, vaudeville's first union, and enmity between the two men went back as far as 1901. In 1907, Joe bravely signed with a fledgling competitor circuit, which went under after only three months. The Keatons were accepted back into the fold, but only out of necessity. Beck's memory was long—he employed spies across the country and kept detailed files on his performers—and when war broke out on the continent, the influx of European talent gave him the freedom to let "disloyal" acts go. Rather than immediately releasing the Keatons, however, Beck chose to harass them.[19]

In April of 1916, The Three Keatons—still smarting from the Rhode Island furniture incident—suffered the indignity of having to open the show at Beck's New York Palace. To go first on the program was a considerable insult to such a well-known act; the audience, usually only partially seated, was dead cold and—worse—completely inattentive. Joe was furious. At a matinee, he spied the devil himself. From the wings Beck hissed, "Okay, Keaton. Make *me* laugh!" That was it—with murder in his eyes, Joe leapt offstage and took after the tubby, frightened mogul, who ran out of the theater and into the street. Joe eventually lost him in a Sixth Avenue crowd. Beck retaliated by whittling down the Keatons' running time to a mere twelve minutes. Ever defiant, Joe and Buster stuck to their usual routine; they simply placed a large alarm clock at the foot of the stage, and when it signaled twelve minutes were up, they ended the act—regardless of what they were doing. The family finished the week, but it was the last time The Three Keatons ever played legitimate vaudeville. They were summarily banished to the boondocks, to appear in three-a-day houses on small-time circuits.[20]

After passing the summer in Muskegon, the only gig the Keatons could get was on the Pantages western circuit.[21] The family performed three shows a day in minor-league theaters before sparse crowds. Joe, primarily a beer man, took to liquor.[22] That fall, Buster turned twenty-one; he was 5'4", 140 pounds, and growing tired of his father's alcoholic slide.[23] Theirs was an act that depended on crack timing and agility—and with a half-soused partner, performing took on a new, dangerous edge. Even in its prime, the Keatons' routine was too physically taxing to lend itself to a thrice-daily schedule. Now with Joe off-step and out-of-sync, Buster had no choice. In January of 1917, after a week in San Francisco, he informed Myra he was breaking up the act. She didn't object; rather, she packed her things and followed her son. When the decision was made, Joe was out at a bar; they didn't even leave him a note.[24]

After arriving at the next gig in Los Angeles and finding neither son nor wife, Joe went to Muskegon, where he eventually reconciled with Myra. Buster, however, was not there. He had boarded a train—alone—to New York.[25]

3 Buster on the shoulders of Arbuckle, with two Comique ladies, date unknown.

CHAPTER FOUR

Le Cirque Cumeeky

Not long ago a friend asked me what was the greatest pleasure I got from spending my whole life as an actor. There have been so many that I had to think about that for a moment. Then I said, "Like everyone else, I like to be with a happy crowd."[1]

Buster Keaton

One blustery mid-March day, Buster made his way through the congested thrum of Times Square. He had been lonely in New York for over a month; he was eating a lot of pancakes. He had landed a part in *The Passing Show*, a popular Broadway musical comedy revue beginning its sixth season at the Winter Garden Theater. His agent—rather, his family's agent, who happened to be one of the best in the business—had gotten him the plum role. The pay was excellent, as high as $250 a week, according to Buster, and the show marked the young comedian's first break from vaudeville. Over the course of its run, *The Passing Show* would showcase the talents of such luminaries as Fred and Adele Astaire, Marie Dressler, and Joan Crawford. Buster seemed poised to travel the Great White Way. Then, on that rainy trip through Times Square, he bumped into a family friend.

Lou Anger was an old vaudeville chum, a comedian who had shared the bill with the Keatons. He since had quit the stage game and gone into the movie business as a studio manager. He worked for a man named Joe Schenck who was now producing the two-reel comedies of a 280-pound, blue-eyed, blond-haired, almost-thirty-year-old screen star beloved by all as Roscoe "Fatty" Arbuckle. In some versions of that encounter in Times Square, Anger is accompanied by Arbuckle himself—but whatever the case, Buster received an invitation to drop by the film studio and watch the proceedings.[2] The invitation would change his life.

Schenck's Colony Studio filled a former warehouse a block from the river on East 48th Street. On the first floor, Norma Talmadge, a dark-haired ingénue Schenck recently had married, made dramatic features; the second story was devoted to the work of Norma's youngest sister, Constance, who had made her name the year before in D. W. Griffith's landmark film *Intolerance* and was fast becoming a popular comedian; and above them all was Fatty Arbuckle and his newly minted Comique comedy unit, hard at work on its first slapstick short—a riotous bit of business called *The Butcher Boy*. Buster knew the comedian from the many movies he had made for the Keystone Film Company. Arbuckle was a fan of The Three Keatons; in fact, he had previously "borrowed" a few of their top gags and memorialized them on celluloid. When Buster showed up on the set with Anger, Arbuckle was dressed to work in his signature derby, bow tie, plaid shirt, suspenders, and voluminous trousers that fit his body like a barrel and which invariably stopped short to reveal a good four-inch swath of white sock. He invited the young comedian to join in the scene they were shooting, which happened to take place in a general store. Buster initially declined, and so Arbuckle, ever the gracious host, suspended production and gave the newcomer a tour of the facility. Arbuckle demonstrated his wonderful mechanical toys: movie cameras, klieg lights, tools for the cutting room—an array of gadgets the likes of which Buster had never seen. Sometime during the tour, Buster changed his mind. When Arbuckle finished showing him around, he disappeared into Wardrobe to assemble a costume.[3]

Buster saunters into the store from the right of the screen, unheralded, just another customer, seen from behind in baggy overalls and a curiously flat hat. He goes straight for that trusty vaudeville prop, the broom, and selects one or two from a barrel for inspection. With his foot, he nonchalantly flicks one off the floor and into his hands, then tosses it with the others. After sampling the molasses on the sly, he approaches Fatty and requests a pailful. While Fatty is filling the bucket, Buster busies himself with interrupting a board game; the crusty old men shoo him away. Fatty returns with the molasses, demands payment, and learns the money was left at the bottom of the bucket he just filled. The pail gets emptied into Buster's hat, which, when it comes time for parting formalities, sticks to his head in an impolite way. Soon his head is free but his foot is caught in a gooey mess. Fatty extricates Buster with some boiling water and a kick to the chest, which sends our hapless customer tumbling out the door and into the street. With a backwards somersault, Buster rights himself and exits his first scene ever to appear on the silver screen.

Amazingly, Buster nailed his film debut in one take.[4] His vaudeville talents made him a movie natural, something Arbuckle recognized on the spot. The two did additional scenes that day, one of which required Buster, as an innocent bystander, to get hit by a bag of flour meant for Arbuckle's nephew and number-two funnyman Al St. John. Buster fondly would recall his introduction to Arbuckle's working methods. To prevent flinching, the direction Arbuckle gave his new recruit was not to turn around until the moment Arbuckle shouted, "Turn!"[5] It's a brave sequence in the film: Fatty throws, St. John ducks, and Buster turns and takes it full in the face—in an explosion of flour, all that can be seen are his feet whipping a sorry arc, heels over head. The pair didn't leave the studio until midnight. When it came time to go, Buster asked Arbuckle if he could take one of the company's Bell & Howell movie cameras home, where he would later pick it apart and reassemble it in a night. Arbuckle said yes. He had only one question for Buster: Would he see him in the morning?[6]

The next morning, Buster informed his agent he was quitting *The Passing Show* to take a job with Comique.[7] He wasn't sure what his salary would be, but he was dying to be in movies, not theater. When he appeared at the studio, Arbuckle looked up and said, "You're late."[8]

At the end of the week Buster received his pay. He was a bit surprised to see the envelope contained only $40, all that Lou Anger said the studio could afford—a far cry from what Buster would have been making with *The Passing Show*. But it wasn't about the money. After six weeks of long days and nights at Comique, his salary would jump to $75 and then $125 a week.[9] Buster told Myra he was in the movies, but she held off from immediately informing her husband.[10] Joe Keaton wasn't keen on this new moving-picture business—to him, a fad was a fad; nothing could trump a live performance. When

William Randolph Hearst suggested that vaudeville's first family make some two-reelers for him based on *Bringing Up Father*, one of his papers' popular comic strips, Joe sniffed, "We work for years perfecting an act, and you want to show it, a nickel a head, on a dirty sheet?"[11]

By 1917, Father Keaton should have known better; signs were everywhere that movies were there to stay. Edison's fin de siècle Kinetoscope had spawned the first nickelodeons, which by 1905 were being visited regularly by 10 to 20 million Americans. The next year, New York's *Dramatic Mirror* opened a film department; in January of 1907, *Variety* ran its first movie review. And there must have been waves in the vaudeville circuit when on December 6, 1907, Proctor's 23rd Street Theater—a perennial New York destination for The Three Keatons—reopened its doors as the Bijou Dream and began projecting movies full-time. Tickets cost a dime or a nickel. In 1909, *The New York Times* was reporting 45 million people were going to the movies each week; by 1917, it estimated that number had grown to 15 million a day. Films were becoming big business: a theater would pay as much as $3,500 a week to rent a negative that might have cost $30,000 to make. The biggest stars drew fantastic salaries; Hollywood was led by a Mary Pickford/Douglas Fairbanks/Charlie Chaplin triumvirate, each member of which reportedly earned around $1 million a year.[12] To the man on the street, this new popular industry seemed to run on the unreal economics of dreams. The next round of screen hopefuls spent their days loitering outside production offices, eager for work as extras. The industry appeared wide-open, the kind of business where being in the right place with the right look—a cowboy hat and bandanna, a fancy dress suit—might get you past the studio gates, and after that anything was possible. Movies had begun their saturation of the culture, and so Buster wasn't exactly a cinematic naïf the day he bumped into Arbuckle. As a kid he had loved watching "chasers," the short bits of film that signaled the close of an evening's vaudeville show. Recently he had been floored by two films in particular: Mack Sennett's *Tillie's Punctured Romance* (1914), the first feature-length comedy film (which brought Charlie Chaplin fame), and D. W. Griffith's controversial epic *The Birth of a Nation*

(1915), which he watched three times during the forty-four weeks it played in New York theaters.[13]

Both films were black and white and gloriously silent, which isn't to say that all was quiet in the theaters that screened them. Early cinemas employed musicians—perhaps a pianist and violinist, perhaps a full orchestra—to drown out the noise of the projector and set the mood, and most films arrived from the distributor with a cue sheet that suggested the appropriate musical accompaniment. Soon sophisticated organs supplied not only the music, but the sound effects—loud bangs, whistles, whizzes, beeps, and claps. The words on the screen filled in the narrative gaps, and film titles were taken as a boon, not a nuisance. A new kind of writing emerged. Moviegoers expected a smart snappy read, and the studios tried hard not to disappoint. Fiction—at best—paid a dime a word, while that same word on a movie screen earned a title-writer $2.20. This is not to say that audiences ignored what the actors actually said; in fact, the general public grew quite adept at reading lips and complained if the titles didn't match. Even more vexing—or thrilling, depending on one's point of view— were the four-letter tidbits that might escape an actor's mouth but never made the title. The public could read between the lines; the name for the racy new pastime: "the cuss word puzzle."[14]

The films themselves were visually striking. While black and white was predominant, it did not represent the limit of the filmmaker's palette. Film could be tinted and toned to produce various effects. The earliest tints were produced by fixing colored gelatin sheets in front of the camera. They tinted the whole scene: suddenly nights became blue, fires raged red, and suns set pink. As the tinting process grew more sophisticated, it could be done post facto in the lab. Toning colored only the black parts of an image—the tone was a chemical property of the film stock itself. Eventually, through tinting and toning, two different colors could be achieved. Often nighttime scenes were shot during the day (to accommodate the light requirements of the era's slow film stock), and then tinted and toned to subtle effect. ("Blue-tone pink" was one popular combination.) In some cases, these day-for-night shots have been preserved on modern, untinted stock, and thus look conspicuously unnatural—helping perpetuate the myth that silent films were technologically unsophisticated efforts produced for easily amused audiences that didn't demand much in the way of realism.[15] Not so. With considerable finesse, the film industry was providing the greatest spectacles the world had ever seen.

The crew of *The Butcher Boy* had a modest, singular aim to which they stuck with unswerving devotion: make 'em laugh, no matter how. The film's slapstick pads what is at best a slapdash plot. Fatty, as the titular meat-cutter, adroitly juggles a machete, handles a good deal of meat without washing his hands, and infiltrates an all-girls' boarding school (in drag), where he dances about, displays a fondness for flashing his enormous bloomers, and gets spanked a lot. He eventually defeats his rival, Al St. John (also in drag), and—thanks to a conveniently placed clergyman—marries his sweetheart. Buster gets a good amount of solo time on screen, and he distinguishes himself with his pratfalls. In one instance, he gives a particularly brilliant example of what a break-dancer would call a head spin.

The movie was a simple comedy short—one of a handful of titles that might be included on a bill, a two-reel twenty-odd-minute film that would precede the bulk of the night's entertainment, usually a full-length dramatic feature. *The Butcher Boy* more or less typifies the genre; shorts offered audiences a standard triangulated affair: there's a boy, chasing a girl, who is being inconvenienced by a villain (often a romantic rival). Our hero usually has a compatriot or two, who—after much comic commotion—help him wind the story to some sort of happy end. The popular short form flourished; two-reelers often were better films than the features they accompanied. Comique's frenzied raison d'être was to churn out just such a comedy every two weeks.[16] The studio was a big, rowdy movie family in which everyone pulled his own weight—including Luke, the studio dog. The three-and-a-half-year-old bull pup, which belonged to Arbuckle's wife Minta Durfee, was a gifted film veteran; when his master had been with Keystone, Luke had been on the company payroll for $150 a week.[17] In *The Butcher Boy*, he and Buster probably share equal prominence, which says a lot about the role the newcomer played. Luke grinds pepper in the store, assists with the girls'-school break-in, bites a fair number of people, and generally drives the ruckus. He and Buster display the first signs of a working rapport the two would exploit for many films to come.

Though it is uncertain what, if anything, Luke taught Buster, the twenty-one-year-old apprentice got a hands-on crash course in on-the-fly filmmaking from Arbuckle. He was the perfect teacher. Born a whopping fourteen pounds, Arbuckle had gone into vaudeville as a youngster, though he left the stage for the screen as early as 1909. In 1913, he joined producer Mack Sennett's pioneer comedy unit as a Keystone Kop, and that year he made about thirty one-reel comedies. The Keystone Film Company was becoming a comedy power-house; during Arbuckle's tenure, its stable would boast the fun-making gifts of such comedians as Charlie Chaplin, Mabel Normand, and Chester Conklin. At Keystone, Arbuckle kept busy. In 1914, he appeared in a staggering forty-six films, many of which he directed; by 1916, he was making successful two-reelers.[18] The next year, Joe Schenck persuaded Arbuckle to leave Sennett—and California—to sign with him; the offer: $250,000 a year, bonuses, his own studio in the East, artistic freedom, and a new Rolls-Royce. Schenck gave the studio the upscale name Comique, which Arbuckle pronounced "Cumeeky."[19]

Arbuckle's prodigious output bespoke a fertile comic mind, and in his heyday the round comedian's popularity was second only to Chaplin's. While films had long held the national attention, only relatively recently were the stars themselves coming to the fore. Early studios resisted the cult of the celebrity; in 1910, Biograph Studios pointedly neglected to include the names of its actors in the credits, which sent many a star looking elsewhere for work and recognition. When America's curly haired sweetheart, Mary Pickford, signed with Adolph Zukor's Famous Players-Lasky Studios in 1913, the public was astonished by her $1,000 weekly salary; by 1916, she was making $10,000 a week plus percentages of the profits. In 1914, Charlie Chaplin joined Keystone at $150 a week; in two years, the Little

Tramp sold his services to the Mutual Film Corporation for $10,000 a week and $150,000 cash.[20]

And now there was another star clown, Arbuckle, hailed everywhere as "Fatty"—though only by his public; his friends called him Roscoe.[21] The papers cited him as the best-known proof "that everybody loves a fat comedian," but the affable man-child had a less than jolly home life.[22] Arbuckle had come east with the remnants of a morphine addiction and a faltering marriage. His wife Minta had been Chaplin's costar at Keystone; after only a week in New York, Arbuckle left her at the Cumberland Hotel, taking up residence at the Friar's Club, then at Joseph Schenck's house in Queens. Fortunately he wasn't alone in the new city—his nephew also had made the trip with him. Al St. John was a lesser comedian with a penchant for grimacing and high-knee hopping; at Comique, he was to become Arbuckle's most frequent screen nemesis.[23]

Whatever his personal struggles, Arbuckle was a riot to work with. He was lord over his very own funhouse, with the resources and manpower to realize whatever particular madness appealed to the collective imagination that day. Arbuckle found in Buster a kindred spirit; the two friends shared many a trait, not the least of which was a fondness for practical jokes. They approached these pranks with the same giddy devotion they brought to their work. The Comique crew was a larger-than-life presence at the Colony Studio. The racket that issued from their third of the warehouse day and night—a thrilling cacophony of grunts, bangs, guffaws, and shouts—was a great distraction to the violinists the neighboring units employed to seduce their actors into the appropriate dramatic moods.[24] The atmosphere of many a soggy love scene or heart-wrenching tragedy was undercut by the boys on the third floor.

That summer, perhaps in a backhanded bit of industry sabotage, Schenck moved the boisterous unit uptown, renting them space in Biograph's 176th Street studio in the Bronx. The carnival never skipped a beat. It was lunchtime, and most of the studio was eating in the fourth-floor commissary. The windows were ajar in an attempt to beat the heat. Suddenly the honk of a horn came from below in repeated, obnoxious bursts. Al St. John shot to his feet and announced, "That's my new Hudson Super Six!" He raced to the window and shouted, "Get the hell away from there!" Apparently satisfied, he sat back down. Then he heard the horn again. From the window he warned, "If you damn kids don't get away, I'm coming down!" When the horn disturbed his meal for the third time, he simply stood up and took a fuming, flying leap out the window. Women shrieked. Then everyone noticed a single hand clutching the sill, rapidly losing its grip. Men called for assistance; Arbuckle stirred, saying to no one in particular, "We don't need him anymore. Picture's finished." Nonetheless, Buster sped to the rescue, hopping on the windowsill at the very moment it seemed St. John was getting a handle on the situation. With agonizing precision, all of Buster's helpful efforts backfired—he crushed his friend's only supporting hand, pushed on his head, pulled his hair. Then he too slipped, and suddenly two men hung one-handed from a four-story death. The room was frantic. Someone swooned. Then Arbuckle rose and shouted, "Break!" The two jokers stopped their struggling, climbed inside, and resumed their lunch.[25]

The lunchroom antics are a fair representation of the Comique working method—equal parts collaboration and chaos. Boss Joe Schenck stayed out of the way, leaving the comedy to the professionals.[26] Arbuckle, as star, director, and most valuable comic prop, called the shots; it was up to his retainers to improvise along. They worked around the clock sans script, sans schedule—it was a freeform comedy jam in which gags simply sprang from whatever the day's ludicrous premise happened to be: Fatty at the beach, at Coney Island, out West, in a garage. The Comique circus was just the kind of place Buster was looking for. He had been making it up all his life.

Buster's new gang was an assorted lot. Atop the bunch was Joseph M. Schenck, the oldest of two Russian-born brothers who had come to America and worked their way up from selling newspapers to peddling beer to running a drug store to investing in amusement parks—one of which, the Palisades Park in New Jersey, had hosted The Three Keatons. In 1913 Joe Schenck, ever the savvy businessman, declared himself an independent movie producer. He would pro-

duce the films and then release them through an established distributor, such as Paramount or Metro.[27] A movie mogul on the make,
Schenck was also responsible for booking the attractions at Marcus
Loew's ever-growing chain of theaters. The position made him a prominent citizen. Then, in 1916, he married an up-and-coming screen idol
named Norma Talmadge, and—overnight—he had a star to produce.[28]

Norma, twenty-two, called her thirty-seven-year-old husband
"Daddy"; he called her "Child." Physically, she was the better off of
the pair. Nevertheless, one October night, after telling her mother
(with whom she lived) that it looked to be a late night on the set, she
eloped with Schenck to Connecticut. That Christmas, during a successful preview of Norma's breakout film, her mother, Peg, turned
to the producer and said she imagined he wouldn't make such a terrible son-in-law. He looked at her and said he was glad she felt that
way—he had occupied the position for the past two months.[29]

Peg was flabbergasted. She was a large, overbearing stage mother-
hen who took her tea with whiskey and ruled her family—three
daughters and a wayward, inconsequential husband—with a sharp
tongue and an iron hand. The Talmadges lived in Park Avenue's
Ambassador Hotel and—after Joe and Norma took over the honeymoon suite—the extended family passed their weekends at
Schenck's house in Bayside, Queens. The Ambassador was a long
way from the outskirts of Brooklyn, where the family had begun. It
was opportunistic Peg who drove the careers—and lives—of her
daughters; she had gotten her photogenic firstborn into modeling
and then, eventually, the movies—where Norma would flourish as a
striking, oft-tormented tragedienne.[30] Now Peg's youngest daughter,
Constance, was in the business. The blond, blue-eyed eighteen-year-
old, known to her friends and family as Dutch, was making light
comedies. She would become a popular fixture of the 1920s, attracting the attention of such men as F. Scott Fitzgerald, who would write
a screenplay for her in 1927, and studio genius Irving Thalberg, who
courted her to no avail.[31]

Most men overlooked Natalie, the middle daughter, who worked for Comique as a script girl. As there were no scripts, she mostly spent her time replying to fans and forging autographs. She was twenty the day Buster met her. Buster recalls that the willowy 5'2", 100-pound brunette, "seemed a meek, mild girl who had much warmth and feminine sweetness."[32] She would eventually become his wife. The marriage would make him part of the Talmadge–Schenck film family, a household of considerable power that would influence Buster's screen career, for better and for worse, for much of his life. Meeting Lou Anger on the street had set in motion a remarkable chain of events.

But Buster wouldn't know all this for quite a while—and even if he had, the young comic hadn't the time, or necessarily the inclination, for such pensive self-romance. On April 23, 1917, *The Butcher Boy* premiered in over 200 theaters.[33] There were glowing reviews for everyone. Fatty was a "winner"; the premise was "hilariously realized"; the film was an "epoch-making laugh-getter"; Luke was "eager and active" and "took his role very seriously"; and "Newcomer Keaton can take a fall and still come up swinging for laughs."[34] The troupe was a hit. Even "script" girl Natalie must have gotten a taste of the success: The *Dramatic Mirror* noted, "With characteristic gallantry 'Fatty' has refused to make public the exact number of feminine fans who have put their opinions of his ability to wear girl's clothes into writing, but those who are close to him admit that the figures run well up into the hundreds."[35]

*Truly yours
Buster Keaton.*

4 Buster with his porkpie hat.

CHAPTER FIVE

Up Through the Ranks

Roscoe loved all the world, and the whole world loved him in those days.[1]

Buster Keaton

Perhaps the most notable—and in the end enduring—feature of Buster's debut was his costume. On the day he met his future mentor, wife, and calling, he also found his future trademark—the porkpie hat. It was as if the comedian had sprung fully formed from the genius of a single day. Through the years Buster would refine his onscreen persona, but in *The Butcher Boy* his head is topped by what would remain his signature flat hat. The porkpie was a throwback to the nineteenth century, when it was a ladies' accessory, and while it's unclear whether Buster first picked out the hat himself, he quickly made it his own.[2] At the time, screen comedians wore derbies. Buster's choice—usually gray with a dark ribbon—separated him from the crowd. He manufactured the unique hats himself, often as many as twelve a year, as the rigors of slapstick (particularly the wet ones) necessitated frequent replacements. He would buy size $6\,^7/_8$ Stetson felt fedoras, remove the lining, punch in the crown, and trim and flatten the brim.[3] In the course of his breakneck antics, the thin, somewhat flimsy hat had a tendency to fly off. Buster would attach it with an unseen string. The flat hat was an outward manifestation of Keaton's interior cool, a measure of poise ever maintained in an off-kilter, runaway world.

And indeed, in the spring of 1917 Buster's world was spinning. He was caught up in Comique's whirlwind production cycle. His next turn came in a caper called *The Rough House*, which stars Arbuckle as Mr. Rough, a genial dolt whose home suffers from a mother-in-law infestation. Before he's even awake, the harried head of the household accidentally sets fire to his own bed; he then tries to douse the inferno with water, one teacup at a time. Over breakfast, in an attempt to amuse his nearly burnt maid, he sticks forks in a pair of rolls and walks them about in a two-handed Tramp-ish gait—a parody of Charlie Chaplin's wonky shuffle, which Chaplin so enjoyed that he recast the bit as the famous "dance of the dinner rolls" in *The Gold Rush*. Buster plays the moony delivery boy who arrives on a bike only to be clotheslined by a clothesline—a spill reminiscent of his two-wheel pratfalls off the Bluffton pier. He quickly becomes embroiled in combat with Al St. John (as the maniacal cook), and— as tends to happen—objects are thrown about with a widening sphere of casualties. Buster performs some excellent acrobatics in his battle with Fatty and St. John, and he spends much of the rest of the film falling down. Many of these pratfalls are silly, gratuitous, and poorly set up—but it is hard to fault Arbuckle for being overeager to exploit his new protégé's remarkable anti-gravitational abilities. Buster was always up for a fall. And contrary to the persistent rumor that he never smiled in front of the camera, he exhibits a wide range of facial expressions. Anyone familiar with him only as The Great Stone Face will get a pleasant jolt to see him smiling, then clapping his hands and hooting uproariously. The Little Boy Who Couldn't Be Damaged finally was getting a chance to laugh.

He was also beginning to learn the elliptical grammar of cinema. In the film, Buster and Al St. John join the police force; in their first assignment, they're sent to rescue the Rough household from two devious dukes—one a vegetarian, the other a thief. The boys (decked out in badges and bobby hats) take the long way, and their epic journey—from the 242nd Street subway stop—is a marvelous, Richard Lester-like homage to the powers of cinematic compression: in quick shots the cops exit the subway, crest a hill, scamper down a cliff, flip-flop over each other, scale a fence, and arrive downtown to save the day.

While the plot is typically thin, *The Rough House* employs a sophisticated set of special effects. When Fatty gets beaned by a plaster bust, he sees stars—literally. (The shifting constellations are drawn onto the film.) Many other effects are achieved through clever editing. Later in the mêlée, Buster throws a knife at Al St. John, who catches it in his teeth. Most likely, the actual shot was of the knife being yanked out of St. John's mouth (by means of an invisible string)—the sequence simply appears in the film in reverse. When patrolmen Keaton and St. John are summoned before the police chief, they appear and disappear instantaneously—as if by magic—thanks to some inventive stop-action camerawork. The chief rings for his men, filming stops, the chief freezes while the cops take their place, then the camera rolls and voilà—men appear from thin air. At one point, St. John picks up a broom and begins to take spinning swings at Buster, who ducks every time. The two become a comic blur—the swinging and ducking beating an impossibly allegro tempo. In the silent days, film was cranked through the camera by hand. To create the illusion of fast action, all a cameraman had to do was to under-crank the film. Slow-motion was created by over-cranking. Motors were available that produced uniform cranking, but no one used them—a good hand-grinding cameraman was just as consistent and more flexible; he could shift speeds as the action unfolded before him. When movies were young there was no industry-wide agreement on shooting speed. To further complicate matters, not only was the cranking up to the cameramen, but the projectionist in the theater could vary the rate at which he ran the projector. With time, the official rate was set at sixteen frames per second, but in actuality film was shot closer to eighteen to twenty-two frames per second and then exhibited at anywhere between twenty and twenty-six frames per second. It wasn't until sound came to the movies that speed became universally standardized—the audio tracks were recorded on the film and needed to run everywhere at a uniform pace, so as not to distort the sound.[4]

Buster was fascinated by the tricks of the film trade. When Arbuckle walked him through the editing process (mark film with wax pencil, cut, glue), Buster intuitively grasped the power of the medium.[5] In his autobiography, he recalls the thrilling revelation: "On the stage, even one as immense as the New York Hippodrome stage, one could show only so much. The camera had no such limitations. The whole world was its stage. If you wanted cities, deserts, the Atlantic Ocean, Persia, or the Rocky Mountains for your scenery and

41

background, you merely took your camera to them."[6] While Buster would become a filmmaker and performer who would stretch the physical limits of the medium as well as the technological, he immediately got the picture—the camera broke down time and space, leaving everything up to the director. Broad horizons beckoned as Buster became Arbuckle's right-hand man in every aspect of production— assistant director, gag writer, onscreen sidekick.[7] On Joe Keaton's dirty sheet you could project the world.

After settling into their new Bronx digs, Comique released *His Wedding Night* in late August. Fatty is Koff & Kramp Druggists' slightly seedy salesclerk. (When a woman loses consciousness in the store, he's not afraid to sneak a smooch or two.) Buster reprises his role as a delivery boy. Through a curious turn of events, he spends much of the film in Fatty's fiancée's wedding dress, and he nearly is wed to Al St. John.[8] While perhaps not ready for matrimony, in real life the two men were becoming close friends. One day on the set, after a standard knockdown drag-out comedic bout, St. John didn't get up. He spent five minutes blacked out on the floor. After coming to, he remembered nothing of what had happened. Injuries were common on the set, but the next day, he and Buster reviewed the morning rushes with a careful eye. In the midst of the scuffle, they saw it: one of the extras in the scene intentionally blindsided St. John with a cheap kick to the head. After watching the scene a few times, Buster told Arbuckle that he thought it needed to be re-shot. Lou Anger said no problem—the extras were still on hand and the set hadn't been struck. That day Buster and St. John high-lowed the mysteriously hostile extra—and it was his turn to lie on the floor. After the scene Arbuckle told his two pals to relax, but surely he appreciated the sentiment.[9] They were in this together.

Next up was *Oh, Doctor!* Fatty, a boozy physician, is hot to cheat on his wife. Buster, as his dainty abused son, has to cry a lot and look ridiculous in a kiddie suit, enormous bow tie, and plus fours. At one point, his father shoves him and he executes an impressive backwards somersault across a table into a chair. Dad needs to recoup his gambling losses, so—in a blatant Hippocratic violation—the good doctor drums up business by mowing down a crowd of pedestrians with his car. Gagman Jean Havez is credited for the scenario, which is unnecessarily convoluted, involving a thieving Al St. John, a traitorous moll, off-track betting, a stolen necklace, and Romeo, a horse that pays 500 to 1.

Fatty at Coney Island is an affectionate time capsule for Brooklyn's oceanfront playground as it existed in the late summer and early fall of 1917. The film opens with striking nighttime shots of Luna Park—the bygone amusement park of light, a radiant stretch of spires and domes outlined by a million glowing bulbs. Actual footage of parades and park-goers is sprinkled into staged scenes, which for the modern viewer satisfies a certain ethnographic interest in period details. But even at the time Coney Island was an interesting sight—film fans across the country (a bigger, less familiar place then than now) were curious to see the famed boardwalk, and from Arbuckle, Keaton learned the value of shooting on location. Most of the sequences in *Coney Island* were shot at the park itself; the film features real rides such as "The Witching Waves" and "The Chute."[10] It is a while before Fatty makes his entrance—the first character we meet is Buster, watching a parade with a girl. Soon a three-way race begins between Buster, Al St. John, and Fatty (who's married); the struggle to woo the girl takes the suitors on a wild romp through the park. Again, Buster laughs and cries—repeatedly. For his part, Arbuckle displays an unfortunate fondness for breaking the fourth wall; he makes sure we're in on the joke, winking and mugging for all he's worth. In a strange and noteworthy sequence in a bathhouse dressing room, he "talks" to the camera, asking it to tilt up so he can take off his pants; giggling and blushing, Fatty undresses. In contrast, Buster displays a charming straightforwardness, a more mature, consistent character—that is, compared to Arbuckle's awkwardly schizophrenic man-child persona. Buster's is usually the stronger, funnier choice. For example, when confronted by the sight of the girl (the lithe Alice Mann) in a black unitard, Buster faints; Fatty—who's in drag—leers and giggles. Buster's acting is also the most believably spontaneous. At one point he does a completely unmotivated, completely wonderful standing back-flip—he simply jumps, lands, and goes on his way—which stands in sharp contrast to Al St. John's counterproductive, tediously exaggerated high-hopping. With our three rivals and two women loose on the boardwalk, the film heads to a quick comedic dénouement. Al St. John hits on Fatty, Fatty does a funny porpoise-like swim, Buster gets the girl, and Fatty locks his wife in jail. In the final scene, he and St. John swear off women—but it doesn't take.

Fatty at Coney Island debuted a few days before Halloween. Buster had mostly completed his crash-course film education; roughly six months after dissecting his first Bell & Howell, there he was, standing alongside the camera, directing the scenes Arbuckle could not (namely, those he was in).[11] The two men were very much in synch; together they shared a comic vision—with one notable exception. While Arbuckle's fans included adults and children alike, for the most part he pitched his comedy to the lowest common denominator. He had come through the ranks of the Keystone machine, and while inarguably an innovator in his own right, Arbuckle never lost his taste for the Sennett all-pie, all-bumbling slapstick style. He insisted to Buster that the most important thing to keep in mind was that their audience had the mindset of a twelve-year-old. Buster disagreed, advising Arbuckle that one who held such beliefs was not long for the business.[12] Moviegoers were as clever as you or I—to treat them as anything less would be an imprudent insult—and even a simple comedy could tell an honest story. There were more and better jokes to be had than in Arbuckle's philosophy.

Still, the pair agreed on everything else. They were the best of friends, inseparable men-about-town in dashing suits and Arbuckle's flashy Rolls. They listened to jazz, started black-tie food fights at Reisenweber's—a swank Columbus Circle eatery—and spent weekends sailing and playing lawn games at Schenck's lavish Bayside barbecues. They socialized with the Talmadge girls, the Talmadge dog (Dinky the Pomeranian), Irving Berlin, Broadway stars, industry tycoons, flappers, wannabe starlets, and the social detritus that fame and wealth attracts.[13] But their work always came first—making movies: now that was the high life.

That October Comique closed shop and left the big city. The crew boarded the *Twentieth Century Limited* and headed west to a quiet seaside town with cheap rents and plenty of clear sunny days good for shooting—Long Beach, California, only twenty miles down the road from the rural film community they called Hollywood.

5 The Comique crew—Buster, Roscoe, Luke, and Al—in California, c.1918.

The company took up residence at the Balboa Amusement Producing Company on Sixth and Alamitos Streets.[14] Upon receiving word of their son's relocation, Joe and Myra Keaton found an apartment in Long Beach. They left Jingles and Louise in Michigan schools and took in Buster and a boarder—Natalie Talmadge, who was at that time more their son's friend and co-worker than girlfriend. In fact, Buster began dating (on and off) a different Brooklyn girl from the Comique family—Alice Lake, an extroverted ex-Keystone comedian with fetching eyes of different colors (one brown, one gray) and a habit of wandering the studio in the buff. Natalie was promoted to secretary-treasurer.[15]

Long Beach not only afforded Arbuckle Southern California's mythically fair weather but also a spectacular and diverse geography perfect for filming. At its disposal the company had miles of beach, calm waters off Catalina Island, and nearby scrub brush hills—it was a location manager's paradise. California also provided Comique with a new talent pool, and Arbuckle was quick to snap up a few more gag-men. Herbert Warren, the company scenario editor, and Jean Havez, a former songwriter, had made the trip west. Now they were joined by

45

Clyde Bruckman, a former Los Angeles sportswriter, and Mario Bianchi, a man who would later become known as Monty Banks.[16] The company also gained the services of a veteran actor new to the film game: the reluctant stage-snob himself, Joe Keaton.

A Country Hero was Comique's first California production. A lost film, it featured a schoolmarm (Alice Lake) pursued by a blacksmith (Arbuckle) who clashes with her father, the owner of the town garage—Joe Keaton.[17] Vaudeville was dying out, giving Joe satisfactory motivation to fill the hours with boozy reminiscing. From time to time, Buster or Roscoe or Natalie would succeed in coaxing him down to the studio. In all, Joe would take part in four Arbuckle films, but Buster recalls that working with his curmudgeonly father required certain directorial finesse. Joe's film debut called for him to send his son into a water trough with his trusty—and still formidable—high kick; the scene was going perfectly except that Joe kept using the wrong foot. After a few wasted takes, Arbuckle offered Joe some encouraging words. Joe barked, "I've been kicking that boy's ass ever since he was born, and now you tell me how." When the cameras rolled, he sent Buster in with the right foot, then dunked Arbuckle, for good measure. Even Alice Lake got a boot in the rear. Joe proved he was still as quick as the youngsters when it came to clowning on the fly.[18]

A Country Hero also featured a $20,000 sequence involving the destruction of two Fords by a locomotive. In Long Beach, Arbuckle was finding he had room to stretch his slapstick muscles. *Out West*, which wrapped that winter and came out in January 1918, was shot on location in the San Gabriel Canyon.[19] An over-the-top western parody with a high body-count, the film features Buster as the trigger-happy sheriff, Al St. John as Black-hearted Bill, and Fatty as the lone drifter. In keeping with the Arbuckle comic model (in which the theater was packed with mental twelve-year-olds), Fatty's backside gets significant screen time—he first appears submerged in a water tank, his hat slowly surfacing atop his expansive rump; later, hostile Indians lodge a few arrows in his rear. The film starts with a nice bit of business on a train, a prop that would become a Keaton favorite.

46

6 Publicity photos for *The Bellboy* (1918)—Arbuckle grabbing an over-attentive Buster by the seat of his pants—and for *Out West* (1918)—Arbuckle gets the drop on a battling Buster and Al St. John.

47

The exterior shots are beautiful—the bleak, rocky canyon provides a lunarscape as unforgiving as the tough cowboy code Arbuckle is lampooning. The narrative is typically feeble: Fatty gets a horse drunk, battles some outlaws, and rescues the girl, during the course of which a lot of people get shot in the behind. Buster gives a fine performance as the callous, wily sheriff; interestingly, Natalie received a screen credit for the scenario.

The Bell Boy actually stars two bellboys—Buster and Fatty—as the much put-upon porters of the Elk's Head Hotel. St. John is relegated to playing their vicious boss, while Joe Keaton takes a turn as a grouchy guest. Early in the film, Buster is cleaning the window of the lobby phone booth; he fixates on a particularly stubborn spot, fogging it with his breath and giving it a good scrub. Unsatisfied, he leans through the "glass" to get at it from the other side, revealing that it was all just a pantomime—he was polishing air. It's a modest, classic gag he would recycle multiple times. (Arbuckle himself used it two years later in his and Buster's last Comique two-reeler, *The Garage.*) The Elk's Head is a cut-rate joint, complete with a horse-drawn elevator that soon goes berserk (naturally). The boys again vie for the heart of Alice Lake (Cutie Cuticle, manicurist), and at the Saturday dance (charmingly packed with line dancers) Fatty spins Lake across floor with surprising grace. Arbuckle was an agile man and a fine dancer; the 280-pound comedian was so light on his feet that screen siren Louise Brooks said dancing with him was "like floating in the arms of a huge doughnut—really delightful."[20] Buster himself does some fancy flops around a partitioned bank set.

In April, the Balboa lot was renamed the Comique Film Corporation Studio.[21] By the conclusion of *Moonshine*, the studio's May release, Buster was bringing home $250 a week, and while he spends much of the film hanging from a tree, he is introduced as Arbuckle's co-star.[22] The film is a parody gone wild, a kind of meta-comedy in which titles pop up to praise the director's inventiveness and call attention to holes in the plot. Fatty is a federal agent hot on the trail of some backwoods bootleggers. The film crew returned to the San Gabriel Canyon, where they used Mad Dog Gulch to stand in for the Virginia sticks.[23]

Alice Lake reprises her role as the love interest, and as a bootlegger's daughter gives Al St. John a wonderful beating, showing herself to be as rough and tough a physical comedian as any of the guys. With *The Bell Boy*'s glass-polishing bit, Buster had proven his ability to sell the quiet, unadorned gag. Now, as Fatty's lieutenant, he gets another small solo when cornered by a leering, decidedly inbred-looking St. John. Inexplicably, Buster begins to mock the bootlegger's facial tics—fidgety brow, gaping jaw—and before you know it, he has metamorphosed into a monkey in expression, posture, and gait. Buster scampers up a tree, where he swings from one arm. It's an amazing performance, simple and riveting.

Not only a first-rate actor, Buster began to single himself out as a skilled technician. Early in the film, Fatty and Buster pull up in their car. After the two get out, Fatty orders Buster to assemble the men. In a long shot that displays the car head on, Buster opens the passenger door and out come (by my count) forty-nine men; they fall into rank behind Buster, who leads off the small army. The clown-car setup was Buster's idea. He taped off the camera lens, splitting the car down the middle. When the camera rolled, the men filed straight through the vehicle, entering (unseen) through one passenger door and emerging (on film) out the other side. After they were all "out of the car," the film was rewound, the lens re-masked to expose only the opposite side of the car (with its door closed), and the camera cranked through to the end. While the trick shot wasn't hard to figure out, the execution was flawless. When another studio decided to one-up the Comique team by having 108 cops exit a single taxi, they were sorely disappointed with the result—one half of the cab sat perfectly still, while the other rocked up and down with each departing passenger. They hadn't taken into account the bouncing of the shocks. Buster had; behind each of the four wheels of his car was a jack, propping up the entire vehicle.[24]

Moonshine is a delight in that it demonstrates just how codified film genres already had become by 1918. First Fatty throttles Alice Lake and pitches her into a river; she emerges instantly, madly in love with him. When her father questions the logic of this, Fatty informs him it's only a

49

two-reeler—there's no time to build up the love scenes. Soon Arbuckle is captured by the bootleggers and taken to their ritzy "nouveau riche" hideout where they dine in tuxedos. After pulling off a storybook escape (from *The Count of Monte Cristo*, to be exact), he surfaces in the river, climbs a rock, and declares, "And now . . . the world is mine! Mine!" From below, Buster applauds his performance. In hindsight it's a small bittersweet moment; in a few short years circumstances—some happy, some tragic—would tear Arbuckle down from that rock and place Buster atop it. The real fun of the film is its ending, in which the cast of thousands—on their lunch break—miss the grand finale, leaving only Fatty and Buster to take part in the big scene. St. John's cabin explodes with a hog-tied Fatty inside, only to then reassemble itself onscreen and have Arbuckle stroll out the door. (The explosion is run forwards and backwards in the film.) The heroes shoot the baddies, and Arbuckle wins the girl—whereupon he informs everyone that he can't have her, because he's already married. So Alice Lake defaults to Buster, and Fatty kicks at a rock and trundles off, alone, the pathos thick with hilarity.

Good Night, Nurse! is somewhat more standard fare. Fatty is a determined drunk whose wife—after her husband brings home some gypsies and a monkey—commits him to the No Hope Sanitarium. Buster is the blood-spattered surgeon whose treatment for alcoholism appears quite invasive. He quickly puts Fatty under with a large jug of ether. There is a nice shot from Fatty's point of view in which the doctors go out of focus before the scene dissolves. Soon after waking, the patient is up to his usual hijinks: he cheats on his wife, hops into drag, and instigates the most phenomenal pillow-fight ever seen. Eventually he escapes the hospital only unwittingly to enter—and win—something called "The Great Heavyweight Race." As Fatty is wrestled to the ground by sanitarium attendants, there is another dissolving point-of-view shot and we end with Fatty still on the operating table—it all having been an ether dream. The film's highlights include Joe Keaton—bandaged head to toe—throwing a high kick, Fatty presenting a drunken dance solo, and Buster executing a pratfall involving a lasso. Still, the film is a disappointment, interesting mostly in comparison to

Keaton's independent work. The it-was-all-just-a-dream ending is clumsy—an indication that Arbuckle simply didn't have the narrative dexterity that Buster would later exhibit. When Buster relies on the convenience of a dream in his own shorts and features, the device adds a suggestive layer—perhaps unsettling, perhaps humorous—to the overall proceedings. A Keaton-directed short almost always ends with an approximation of closure (no matter how slippery); *Good Night, Nurse!* simply ends.

For the most part, Comique was a world unto itself. The country had declared war on Germany the very month the studio released its first film, but politics rarely intruded on the serious business of fun-making. In the summer of 1918, that changed. *The Cook*, a recently found film, would be Buster's last for a while—Uncle Sam had given him a part in his latest epic, The Great War.

Buster always claimed that he was drafted; one biographer reports that he had tried to enlist but was turned away because of flat feet and his missing fingertip.[25] Military records suggest he did enlist, but not until the summer of 1918.[26] Whatever the case, Buster was going to war, and on the eve of his departure the studio threw him a memorable farewell bash. His friends performed and presented him with a money-filled wallet—a reminder that as a private, his salary would soon drop to $30 a week. Arbuckle was staying put; the army deemed him too overweight for combat. (He would do his part by amusing the troops and contributing tobacco to the cause.)[27] Joe and Myra went back to Michigan, where Joe found work in a munitions factory. On every artillery shell that passed through his hands, he wrote, "Give 'em hell, Buster!"—despite the fact that his son had joined the infantry. Natalie returned to her home in New York.[28] Buster left Comique and headed to Camp Kearney, not far from San Diego, where he signed with another company: Company C of the 159th Infantry, 40th (Sunshine) Division.[29]

After an abbreviated quarantine and boot camp, Buster's division was sent to Camp Upton in Yaphank, Long Island, for a brief lay-over before they were to ship overseas. It was August 1918, and

Upton was hot, muggy, and teeming with bugs.[30] After Buster placed a strategic phone call, Natalie was kind enough to drive over from Bayside in Schenck's gorgeous, chauffeured Packard. With such rarified transportation—well beyond the means of any enlisted man—Buster had no trouble slipping out of camp for a few hours. The pair went dancing and dining at Castles in the Air, an upscale Long Beach club. Natalie footed the bill, and a few days after Buster's heady AWOL adventure, he was sent across the ocean.[31]

From England Buster crossed the channel to France. Marching through the countryside, he found France cold, rainy, and curiously full of hills that sloped only upward, but he enjoyed the wild blackberries. Sleeping in tents, inside drafty barns, and on the ground took a toll on the doughboys; Buster suffered a fierce ear infection that never went away, resulting in him spending his war partially deaf. He remembers returning to camp one night after a card game and not hearing the sentry's repeated challenges; only the loud nearby click of a shell being chambered made Buster stop short and identify himself as "friend." His hearing loss had almost cost him his life.[32]

Eventually his outfit was stationed at Amiens. Officially, Buster was an army cryptographer; he took his role seriously, becoming so facile in Morse code that he could annotate his diary in it. He recalls studying cartography and semaphore signaling—the rigors of which perhaps appealed to his engineering nature. But before long, his other side— Buster the performer—came to the fore. He had demonstrated considerable success in locating scarce goods; his silent training enabled him to bridge language barriers and convincingly convey what he wanted—usually food and wine—to French-speaking shopkeepers. Soon he was putting those skills to more public use, clowning around after the daily drilling for the benefit of his fellow soldiers and the local townspeople. Then came the 11th of November, and with it the glorious Armistice. Buster, now a corporal, hadn't even set a foot in a trench.[33]

With the war over, the army now faced a different logistical battle: getting everyone home. Transportation bottlenecked, and entertainment troupes were formed to keep the homeward-bound companies cheerful. Naturally, Buster volunteered to form his division's group, the Sunshine Players; they flung together a variety show and took to the stage. Buster's bit was the "Princess Rajah" routine, a parody of an old vaudeville staple: the belly dancer. As a sultry snake-charmer, Buster wears a dog-tag bra and a skirt fashioned from standard issue utensils (knives, spoons, mess kits); he charms a hot dog. Just before shipping out, Buster had performed a version of the dance with Roscoe in *The Cook*; perhaps the skit was fresh in his mind. The act certainly was a hit, and Buster would revive his Princess in more than one film. Her rag-tag appearance was a riff on the realities of military distribution. Upon joining the army, Buster was issued a joke of a uniform: shoes two and a half sizes too big, overlong pants, and a coat that could swallow him whole. It was a suit ready-made for clowning.[34]

Unfortunately for Buster, he danced too well. Because of his morale-boosting abilities, he was kept in Europe through March—some four months after the peace.[35] Buster landed in New York and—still half deaf—was sent first to the veterans hospital, then to Johns Hopkins in Baltimore. The doctors told him his hearing would return in time. While laid up in New York, Buster happily received his first visitor—Joe Schenck, who was shaken by how thin and ragged his friend looked. He gave Buster all the money in his wallet. Buster went out and bought himself a respectable, well-fitting uniform, then he paid a visit to Natalie and Peg.[36]

Schenck's generosity is not surprising. While Buster had been drawing measly army pay overseas, the producer had sent Joe and Myra $25 a week. Buster was forever grateful to Schenck. That April he was released from the army; though he had joined up in California, Buster had listed Muskegon as his hometown, so the confused clerk discharged him through Michigan. While there, Buster paid a visit to his family. He stayed just three days, after which he returned, at last, to Los Angeles.[37]

When Buster had been in Baltimore, his doctors had allowed him to go for a walk. His first instinct was to drop by the local vaudeville house that had hosted The Three Keatons so many times in the past. He was moved by the reception he received—everyone in the theater, cast and crew alike, stopped to welcome him. From backstage, Buster watched an old pal run through his act. The stage lights threw shadows across the wings; you could hear the hum of a plugged-in audience; he was surrounded by a thick knot of friends. Buster finally felt home again, and as he watched he fervently wished that nothing would ever again take him away from the extraordinary, big-hearted fellowship they called show business.[38]

7 Publicity photo—Keaton, back from France, in California, 1919.

8 Buster hears no evil, sees no evil, and speaks no evil, c. 1921.

CHAPTER SIX

Back From the Back

I sometimes wonder if the world will ever seem as carefree and exciting a place as it did to us in Hollywood during 1919 and the early twenties. We were all young, the air in southern California was like wine. Our business was also young and growing like nothing ever seen.[1]

Buster Keaton

In the early spring of 1919, America bustled with new beginnings. The Great War was over; certainly no one could imagine another. The boys were home, their faith shaken, but all right. Many a doughboy brought back with him a taste for the exotic and a desire to live outside of commitments (after all, commitments had led them into war, hadn't they?); these returning sons strove to lose themselves in the detailed elations of life—to live in peace at a wartime pitch—in cars, at the movies, inside bars, across the wide lawns and in the cool shade of a nation at rest. Post-war society found itself in a moral tumult. Hemlines were shooting dangerously upward, and everywhere young ladies could be seen sporting their hair cropped short in that radical and chirpy cut—which carried with it the dizzy innuendo of casual intimacy—the bob. On Saturday night the gals donned form-fitting sheaths and painted their faces with blunt determination; they were a year away from getting the vote. Cars were mainly open-topped, often hand-cranked, and irrevocably transforming relations between the unwed sexes. The tabloid press was starting to catch on; the New York *Daily News* would debut in June. An unknown Babe Ruth was playing outfield in Boston; Charles A. Lindbergh didn't yet know how to fly, though the transatlantic gauntlet had been tossed. Broadcast radio was just around the corner. So was national Prohibition—it was slated to take effect on July 1st—but the country would hardly stay dry. America was on its way to becoming a land of flappers and sheiks, of parlor Bolsheviks and bearded bomb-throwers, of captains of industry and bull-market barons, of gangsters and molls, of stars and scandals, a country of excess dreams and excess disillusion—a nation spinning faster and faster on a herky-jerk treadmill called modernity. Society roared along to the visceral virtuosity of a blaring new tune; it was the dawn of that riotous, restless Jazz Age.[2]

About eight months had passed and Buster, now a war veteran, was "back from the back," as he liked to quip.[3] He had served mainly on the entertainment front, and he sought no glory for himself. Still, the war had taken a toll—despite what the doctors said, his hearing would never fully return (and would get worse when he caught cold), and Buster returned from overseas to find a town that had gone and changed without him.[4] Hollywood still clung to its rural roots—there were citrus orchards in East Hollywood and oil wells in Wilshire—but the movie business was booming, and down the road from such grounded pursuits Roscoe Arbuckle had established himself in a pleasuredome fit for a star: it featured twenty rooms, gilded baths, and parking space for his Rolls-Royce, Stevens-Duryea, Cadillac, White, and Renault Roadster. Arbuckle had paid for the home in cash.[5] Buster's head spun—since when did clowns live in castles?

In that heady fiscal climate, Buster recalls, "Combines were forming and re-forming with skullduggery on a scale to make a Ponzi or a George Graham Rice sick with wistfulness."[6] By 1917, the year Arbuckle relocated to California, the bulk of the film industry's east–west migration was long complete; Hollywood, not New York, was the established seat of the American movie business. By the time Buster returned in 1919, the twenty-five-year-old rural suburb found itself to be an international capital—80 percent of the movies *in the world* were being made in Southern California.[7] The picture industry was giddy with its own promise; talent was being paid an unheard-of premium. Upon setting foot in Hollywood, Buster received twin $1,000-a-week offers from rival company heads Jack Warner and William Fox. He turned both down and rejoined Joe Schenck at $250 a week; he was devoted to the man who had so graciously supported his family through the war.[8] In Buster's absence, Comique had moved from Long Beach to Edendale, down the street from the Mack Sennett studios. Arbuckle was thrilled to welcome back his best friend; Buster's studio pals presented him with a silver box, which promptly exploded upon opening.[9] It was good to be home.

The gang wasn't all there, though. Alice Lake had gone to Metro Pictures to do drama; Al St. John was trying to make it on his own at Warner Brothers. With his parents still in Muskegon, Buster took a room in the Hollywood Hotel with an actor from upstate New York named Ward Crane. The two bachelors were regulars at the packed dances in the downstairs lobby.[10] Romantically, Buster seesawed between Alice Lake and a new flame, Viola Dana. Dana, née Flugrath, was a mesmeric twenty-two-year-old widow from Brooklyn whose casting-director husband, John Hancock Collins, had died the year before of influenza. "Vi," as she was known, was a popular tomboyish comedian at Metro; soon Buster and the willful brunette began turning up together in fan magazines. He grew close to Vi and her two sisters, frequenting their Beverly Hills home in his off-duty hours. Perhaps the down-to-earth Flugraths served as an agreeable foil to the posturing Talmadges. As for Natalie, she was still in New York, living with her mother and being prepped by the family publicist for a debut in her sister Norma's next film, *The Isle of Conquest.* In Peg's eyes, Buster was not suitable marital material; her daughter would do better than a mere rough-and-tumble screen clown. Nonetheless, Buster kept in touch with Natalie through the mail.[11]

Buster didn't really have time for love, at least not for the offscreen kind. His devotion to the movies was absolute; he joined the Comique production frenzy as never before, logging at least six long days a week.[12] His post-war debut was the September release *Back Stage*, one of the finest Arbuckle–Keaton collaborations. Perhaps the success of the film has to do with its subject matter, a fitting choice for Buster's homecoming effort—vaudeville. *Back Stage* begins with Buster and another man dragging off furniture from a room—perhaps they're repo men? Only when they grab hold of the side walls and pull those down, too, is it clear that this is a set they're dismantling, not a real room. The back wall is hoisted up to reveal Arbuckle pulling on a rope. They're stagehands! The gag only lasts a few seconds, but it is an eloquent introduction to the illusory authority of cinema, a brief celebration of the filmmaker's power to fool us—at our pleasure. It is an oft-imitated opening, one with a noble pedigree that harkens back to the first acts of Shakespeare's *Tempest* and beyond. Buster loved the joke; he would reuse it—with significantly better execution—in one of his finest shorts, *The Playhouse.*

Back Stage details the trials and triumphs of a small vaudeville house with the good fortune to employ Fatty and Buster. The two spend their days clowning around in the wings. Buster does a clever pretend "walking-down-stairs" routine (an often repeated bit, most recently seen in an Austin Powers movie) and Fatty eats some glue. The real star of the first reel, however, is a mincing, high-kicking, inconceivably plastic "novelty dancer": the great and inimitable (even by Buster and Fatty) John Coogan. All legs and eccentric rhythm, Coogan goes into his vaudeville routine; the film simply grinds to a halt and lets him dance. His absurd kinetics are a thing of riveting beauty; even the stagehands linger to watch, bearing celluloid witness to a vanishing art. Eventually the plot winds up again, and we get an evil strongman, his toothsome assistant, and a mutinous troupe that walks out on the eve of the performance—leaving the boys to put on their own show. The duo stages an operetta (*The Falling Reign*), with Fatty as king (in lion skins) and Buster as queen (in drag, complete with thick tresses and beauty mark). The perky assistant (Molly Malone) stars as the courtesan and performs a wonderfully silly and perfectly modest dance of seduction. Not to be outdone, Buster himself succumbs to a dance craze; he whirls about the stage in a spectacular batch of hands-free cartwheels, then collapses into a hurdler's stretch. The novelty dancer comes to heckle, and Fatty takes a page out of Joe Keaton's playbook, letting Buster sail into the audience, knocking over the jeering critic. Once things settle again, the king dumps his queen for the girl, a jilted Buster stabs Fatty, and the curtain falls. Next up on the program, the "Snowflake Serenade," in which Arbuckle sings and plays ukulele, Buster does a funny shimmy, and the house façade falls forward onto Fatty, leaving him standing (unharmed) in the upstairs window. The gag was a Keaton favorite, one he replayed throughout his career, with increasingly dangerous stakes. Eventually the strong man shows up—there is a fight, the girl gets shot, Buster swings from the balcony, and the heavy is crushed by his own trunk of weights. *Back Stage* never suffers for any of its staged set pieces; the two reels zip along with the energy and dynamism of vaudeville. The jokes come faster and smarter than ever before, and for once Buster essentially shares equal prominence with Fatty (who indulges in considerably less mugging than usual). The apprentice now really was a co-star.

Surprisingly, Comique's next film, *The Hayseed*, is a largely forgettable caper, which suffers in comparison to what precedes (*Back Stage*) and follows it (*The Garage*). *The Hayseed* was shot the summer of Prohibition, and Fatty takes pause to administer last rites to an empty bottle of booze. (It is a proper burial, with flowers and a headstone.) The boys play a pair of country rubes and again put John Coogan on the payroll, this time as Fatty's rival, the village constable. Buster ruefully recalled that Coogan would bring to work his young son Jackie; the cute little imp would ham it up for the company between scenes.[13] Little did they know the boy would soon become the silver screen's first blockbuster child star, thanks to his performance in the title role in Charlie Chaplin's popular feature, *The Kid* (1921). No one at Comique thought to give Jackie a part. Naturally, *The Hayseed* works in a little line dancing and a talent show, giving Coogan Sr. a chance to strut his stuff. Other standouts in the cast include Luke the dog, who demonstrates a remarkable ability to climb ladders. But perhaps Buster's is the most notable performance of all. With only one or two exceptions, he maintains a perfect stone face.

In the summer of 1919, the Comique unit moved again, this time to Culver City. Labor Day came and went, and then the crew began shooting what was to be the last, and arguably best, Arbuckle–Keaton two-reeler—*The Garage*.[14] Jean Havez gets credit for the writing, the photographer was Elgin Lessley, and Arbuckle directed, but the film is closer to Buster's brand of comedy than to anyone else's. He and Fatty star as jovial jacks-of-all-trades, pulling quadruple duty as the town's only mechanics, cops, firemen, and dogcatchers. Inevitably the fire alarm sounds. Towing their enormous fire cart, the two shoot out of the garage and rush down the street. They're arguing over directions when they crash the cart into a post at a crossroads, each of them having tried to take a different path. They continue to bicker before realizing they're wearing the wrong hats—the point is moot until they go home and switch them. Without forcing interpretation too far, the scene reads as nicely (though certainly unintentionally) prescient; the men indeed were heading in different directions—stylistically. Their difference of opinion pitted Keaton's understated, wry, often mechanical sense of humor against Arbuckle's broader slapstick. Before long, the friends would go their separate ways, but for now it was time to change hats—they had fires to fight! Our heroes battle the town Casanova (Harry McCoy), who is after Arbuckle's girl, the garage owner's daughter (Molly Malone). In an inspired extended bit, the boys are set upon by Luke, a vaudeville dog under the sway of the rival. Luke gets hold of Buster's trousers (while they're still on his body) and rips them to shreds. A pantless Buster briefly seeks refuge in a barrel, but when it breaks—thereby scandalizing a forty-five-year-old maid—he is forced to extreme levels of invention. From a giant billboard advertising a Scottish entertainer, he cuts out the outline of a kilt and cap. When the woman returns with a patrolman, Buster (in his two-dimensional disguise) does a Highland jig. The ruse only lasts so long, and with the cop hot in pursuit, Buster hides behind Fatty. The two walk in synch, and when the officer passes them, Buster steps around in front. The policeman turns only to see Arbuckle's receding silhouette.

While the film is full of other simple yet effective bits—such as a bouquet of oil-dipped roses that wreaks messy havoc—*The Garage* boasts perhaps the most complex mechanical gags of any Comique short. A cheap rental car falls to pieces in an instant; cars and men spin dry on enormous turntables; the boys' room is rigged with time-saving mechanical gadgets in the spirit of Ed Gray. (Clearly Buster's touch, the devices prefigure the elaborate domestic appliances he invented for movies such as *The Scarecrow* and *The Navigator*.) Buster also performs an upside-down ascent of a firehouse pole and other such seemingly effortless feats of strength and agility. After two-and-a-half years and fourteen films, he was coming into his prime. Keaton often is remembered—incorrectly—as a custard-pie comedian (that was more Arbuckle's thing), though it is interesting (and a little ironic) to note that in his last Comique short—as in his first—Buster throws a pie.

The final year of the decade had turned into a glorious one for Buster and Roscoe; the boys were inseparable clown princes of Hollywood, good-time guys gone manic with creativity. Buster labeled those days "when the world was ours," and it was—socially, financially, artistically.[15] They could do what they wanted; they were part of a movement, a comic vanguard unwavering in its dedication to the pursuit of the Laugh, a band of radicals fueled by a twenty-four-hour, all-consuming intimacy with the Joke. The fastidious and practical kept their distance; comedy was best left to its own mysterious ways. If Arbuckle felt the gags weren't popping, he and Buster might hop a ferry to San Francisco, say, and disappear for a few days. The crew would simply sit around the quiet set, playing cards and awaiting their return. Joe Schenck never begrudged his stars their quirks; he knew they would get it done in the end.[16] The only thing predictable about this job was the profits.

Somewhere between the rigors of work and the unavoidable demands of sleep, Arbuckle and Keaton found time to continue to practice what Buster called a misunderstood, "earthy art"—that of the practical joke.[17] The boys were merry, dedicated pranksters; they burned with jokes, gags, and setups—comedy was something hardwired in them, a font that could not be capped. And so their friends, neighbors, and acquaintances suffered a devilish range of mischief. These were Comique professionals—no setup was too elaborate, not a soul was safe.

Adolph Zukor, the mogul who headed Famous Players-Lasky, was on his annual pilgrimage to Hollywood to inspect his operations. Arbuckle sent a telegram inviting him to a small dinner party in his honor. Zukor was delighted to accept. The guest list included Sid

Grauman (owner of the renowned Chinese Theater), an exhibitor from Kansas City, and a handful of Hollywood beauties: Viola Dana, Alice Lake, Anna Q. Nilsson, Bebe Daniels—gals who could keep a straight face. Zukor had never met Buster, who was assigned the role of the butler. Lest Zukor recognize him, all of the downstairs lights were dimmed. After the guests had tossed back a few drinks, the butler entered with a plate of jumbo shrimp. With impeccable composure, he went out of his way to offer the shrimp to each of the men first, presenting them with an awkward social dilemma. When Arbuckle saw what was happening, he apologized to his party and stalked Buster into the pantry, where he loudly scolded him for his incompetence. The butler quickly remedied his mistake by taking the plates of half-eaten shrimp from the men and depositing them before the ladies. Arbuckle fumed. With the appetizers ruined, it came time for the soup. Buster appeared with a stack of fine bowls. He then went into the kitchen and began rattling utensils about, creating a ruckus that culminated in a loud, decisive crash. In an uncomfortable silence, Buster—drenched head to toe with what must have been the soup course—cleared the unused bowls. Red-faced, Arbuckle began to rant about the difficulties of finding good help. The bumbling manservant underscored the point by spilling ice water down his master's shirt. He managed to escape to the kitchen, and in a few minutes returned with a gorgeous twenty-four-pound turkey, roasted to perfection and served on a silver platter with all the trimmings—potatoes, parsley, and a cranberry sauce sculpture.

It was like a two-reeler. Buster presents the bird to Arbuckle who, nodding his approval, sends him into the kitchen to carve. As Buster walks out, he drops his napkin. He sets the platter down and bends to pick it up when the pantry door swings open—sending him headfirst into the turkey. Arbuckle springs to his feet, collars Keaton, and drags him and the platter into the pantry. A terrible noise arises, and as the door swings to and fro, the seated guests are privy to various scenes of homicidal violence: Roscoe throttling Keaton, smashing his head with a (breakaway) bottle, chasing him about the kitchen. The guests rush to restrain the host, allowing the troublemaker to flee the house.

Visibly shaken by the tantrum he has just witnessed, Zukor tries to calm Arbuckle. Buster sneaks in the front door, unnoticed.

After Roscoe's "chef" (the real butler) announces that he had cooked an extra turkey—as a precaution—the phone rings. It is Buster calling (from upstairs); Arbuckle invites him over, saying he is holding a dinner party. Buster slips outside and rings the doorbell. Dressed for dinner, he takes a seat at the table. Over slices of backup turkey, one of the guests begins to recount the story of the dreadful waiter, trying to ease the tension still in the room. Buster simply nods his head. It wasn't until the Kansas City exhibitor innocently noted that Buster looked a lot like the dismissed manservant that Zukor got the joke.

Zukor returned east and told everyone about the reception the Comique bunch had given him. Fellow mogul Marcus Loew marveled at his friend's gullibility. Why hadn't Zukor been on his guard in such notorious company? He should have known better. Reports of Loew's incredulity got back to Arbuckle and Buster. The man was simply asking for it. In time, he too would have to come west.

On the day Loew was in town visiting his Metro Studio, he ran into Arbuckle. By a happy coincidence, both men were heading to the Alexandria Hotel. Arbuckle nodded towards his chauffeur—a silent gent in a moustache, goggles, and cap—and offered Loew a ride. Not recognizing Buster, Loew got in. A love of cars and years with Comique had made Buster an accomplished stunt driver; the vehicle shot off, roaring up hills in low gear (to give the illusion of greater speed), and taking slaloming short cuts through orange groves. Suddenly, as they were crossing a cluster of trolley tracks, the car stalled, leaving them astride the middle set of six tracks. Per usual, Buster and Roscoe had scouted their location thoroughly: they not only knew the trolley schedule, but they knew which tracks were express, which were local, and which were kept clear for emergencies. They were safe on the middle set—they had measured the car and found it wouldn't overlap onto the other tracks. Buster lifted the hood and started pounding on the engine as express trains began to zip by—at sixty-five miles per hour—inches from the ends of the car. Occasionally, local trolleys trundled past on the outermost tracks. Loew cowered in the back seat, waiting for the inevitable collision. Miraculously, it didn't come; the chauffeur's efforts started the engine, and suddenly they were off again, fish-tailing down wet streets and taking turns on two wheels. When they crashed to a stop outside the Alexandria—half the car on the sidewalk—Loew was out like a flash and up in his suite before Arbuckle or Keaton could say anything. The boys knocked on his door; inside they found the industry titan swigging whiskey. With exaggerated care, Buster removed his disguise. And so Marcus Loew got his.

You didn't have to be an out-of-towner to get burned by Buster and Roscoe; the boys most often struck close to home, and even a common Hollywood peccadillo, such as vanity or greed, could make you their next target. Pauline Frederick was a Broadway bombshell who had made the transition to movie star. She had rewarded herself with a Sunset Boulevard manse with a sweeping 150-foot front lawn, which a platoon of landscapers (and thousands of dollars) kept impeccably manicured. Every time the boys drove by, they saw men working on the lawn. Early one Sunday, Roscoe, Buster, and their actor pal Lew Cody went to the studio. They emerged from the wardrobe department in matching hats, bandannas, and dirty overalls. They picked up some shovels and picks, borrowed a batch of surveyor's tools, and took off in a beat-up old Model-T. The crew pulled up in front of the Frederick estate and immediately went to work surveying the lawn. A distressed butler appeared. They informed him they were from the Beverly Hills Gas and Electricity Department. There was a leaking main; they would need to dig up the yard—otherwise, the whole block could blow. The butler's protestations grew louder and louder; as the men lifted their shovels and picks, out rushed a frantic Polly Frederick, begging them to spare her lawn. When she took a second look at the dutiful workmen, she invited them in for breakfast.[18]

And so the comedy continued to flow every which way. As the boys' legend grew, pranks became harder to play, requiring evergreater measures of comic daring. Then Arbuckle pulled off the bravest stunt of all: he agreed to leave Comique and his tried-and-true two-reel formula to undertake a grand experiment—he would go into features. While *Tillie's Punctured Romance* had proven a hit in 1914, the feature-length comedy was largely uncharted territory. Could an audience stand five reels of gags? Adolph Zukor thought so. He bought up the remainder of Roscoe's contract with Schenck, signing him for twenty-two pictures—all features—at a salary of $3 million over three years.[19]

Arbuckle threw a stag soiree for his old boss, Joe Schenck. Everyone knew that Roscoe was going abroad on vacation; what they didn't know was that he would return to begin the next chapter of his career without them. After dinner, Schenck took Buster out onto Arbuckle's front porch and—after a few pleasantries, mainly inquiries about Buster's love life—told him of Arbuckle's decision. Buster's mind raced: he wanted to dash off and toast his friend; he wanted to know what would happen to the rest of them—a studio without a star wasn't a studio. Was the delirious Comique dream finally over? It was then that Schenck reached out and—with nothing more than a handshake—handed over the studio to Arbuckle's bewildered successor.

Buster signed the contract two days before Christmas 1919. He would make Schenck eight two-reelers a year, costing no more than $30,000 each. The films would be released by Metro Pictures, whose owner, Marcus Loew, ran more movie theaters than anyone in the country. Metro paid Comique 70 percent of the box office; Comique paid Buster $1,000 a week plus 35 percent of its yearly take. It was the same deal Arbuckle had enjoyed. Buster wasted no time moving into a modest bungalow on Ingraham Street. He placed an elated call to his parents, who bought a Cadillac and rang in the New Year with a long drive to Los Angeles—with fifteen-year-old Jingles at the wheel. The family settled in together on Ingraham Street.[20]

As it would turn out, the Arbuckle/Keaton split signaled the end of the boys' parallel success. Roscoe's experiment was a failure. His enormous salary ate up most of his film budgets, so the studio tried to save money by putting him in ill-conceived remakes of earlier movies; they also saddled him with more than one film at a time. Then Arbuckle fell victim to scandal and—unjustly convicted in the sensational court of public opinion—his career was over.[21] Buster's star would eclipse his mentor's; he finally had been given the means to manufacture his meteoric rise—a studio of his very own—and as the new decade dawned before him, he eagerly went to work dreaming up some of the most ingenious and enduring comedies ever to play on the silver screen.

CHAPTER SEVEN

The Clown to Do the Job

But the golden age of comedy was just beginning. The whole world wanted
to laugh as never before, and Hollywood had the clowns to do the job.[1]

Buster Keaton

Not far from the house on Ingraham stood 1025 Lillian Way. Bor-
dered by Romaine Street, Cahuenga Boulevard, and Eleanor Avenue,
the compound took up a square Hollywood block. The address had
passed through various hands, including those of Charlie Chaplin,
when it was called the Lone Star Studio. Its walls housed an enormous
open-air shooting stage, a developing lab, a screening room, offices,
workshops, twenty dressing rooms; inside could be found the sundry
clutter of comedy-making: cameras, ropes, pulleys, lights, props,
costumes, likely more than a pinch of gunpowder and a box or two of
blanks. In January of 1920, 1025 Lillian Way was a ready-made film
factory anxious for the arrival of its foreman, the man who would
whip it all into glorious commotion. Above the studio there hung a
sign: "BUSTER" KEATON COMEDIES.[2]

That it took less than three years for Buster to go from a cinematic
nobody to head of his own shop is the kind of breathless narrative that
drives the Hollywood imagination. The film industry had begun as a
kind of craftsmen's democracy; shunned by proper Los Angeles society,
movie folk banded together on the outskirts of a city entirely foreign to
them, where stars and set carpenters alike—bound by their peculiar,
relentless business—drank at the same bars, lived in the same areas (for
even the newly rich were shut out of the Old LA apartment buildings),
and welcomed every bright-eyed newcomer with an exile's appetite for
company. But the industry grew up, and seemingly overnight it became
an aristocracy, with its own rules and customs, lords and ladies, the
social order firmly pegged to the flux of the mighty dollar. Big business

69

ruled the game, and leading the Hollywood combine was United Artists—the company founded in 1919 by D. W. Griffith, Charlie Chaplin, Douglas Fairbanks, and Mary Pickford to be the sole distributor of the films each of them independently made.[3] Accordingly, the Buster Keaton Studio needed its own set of deep pockets. Comique's board included Joe Schenck, his brother Nicholas (who would later control MGM), David Bernstein (the secretary-treasurer of Loew's, Incorporated), Marcus Loew, A. P. Giannini (president of the Bank of Italy, which would become the Bank of America), and Irving Berlin.[4]

Buster told Joe Schenck that he wanted to make features, not shorts, but Schenck said no—he insisted Buster stick to the tried-and-true two-reeler. In 1920 shorts were the safer bet, but Buster was right—comedy features were the future—and had he been listened to, he would have had a jump on both Chaplin and Harold Lloyd, neither of whom had yet dedicated himself to making feature-length films.[5] Form notwithstanding, Schenck allowed Buster a great deal of artistic freedom. Buster was left to assemble a crack team; taking his pick of the old Arbuckle gang, he hired Lou Anger, the man who started it all, to be his studio manager. He also retained Roscoe's cameraman, Elgin Lessley, an exacting and imaginative technician whose attention to focus and exposure was matched only by his precision cranking—Buster called him a "human metronome."[6] As there was no incumbent co-director (since Buster himself had occupied the position), Keaton brought in a Keystone vet named Eddie Cline to serve as his second set of eyes and comic collaborator.[7]

With his side chosen, Buster wasted no time. No sooner had the sign gone up at the Buster Keaton shop than the boys across the street at the Metro Studio heard the clamor of industrious fun-making. It was still only January—the Christmas contract hardly dry—but at 1025 Lillian Way shooting was underway on *The High Sign*, the very first Keaton two-reeler.[8]

What was meant to be the first entrance of Buster's solo career had him being thrown from a train—a happy omen of the inventive locomotion to come. *The High Sign* begins in motion; in a close shot, a freight train—a great blur of wheels and pistons—roars by on the horizontal. Out of nowhere, Buster comes flying into the frame, landing feet-first in the foreground. Our hero gets up, dusts himself off, dons his porkpie and is off—from one adventure to the next, it seems. It is a fitting start—*in medias res*—to a lifetime of restless beginnings.

Despite having a new studio (and an entire city block) at his disposal, Buster took his crew to Venice Beach to film the opening of *The High Sign*—Arbuckle had impressed upon him the unique merits of shooting on location. Another remembrance of films past is the brief, early appearance of Al St. John, but the similarities essentially end there—this is a Keaton story. And so in the first gag Buster takes a seat in an empty row of benches along a deserted stretch of boardwalk. He crosses his legs and opens his newspaper. He unfolds the paper by half, then by another half, then by yet another—in a surprising twist, he keeps unfolding halves until the paper is twice his own size and he falls backwards, swaddled in newsprint. As opening gags go, it's a calm one, with a slow build—perhaps insistently so. It is a Keaton—not an Arbuckle—bit: tidy, somewhat strange, with nary a pie or flour sack within arm's reach.[9]

The High Sign highlights Buster's love of the mechanical joke. He interviews for a job in a shooting gallery (a position for which he is wholly unqualified), and when pressed to demonstrate his marksmanship, Buster ingeniously rigs a contraption whereby with a push of a pedal, a hyperactive dog—tied up out back—pulls on a string attached to the clanger. Buster's every shot rings the bell. The film also features a house outfitted with a comprehensive security system: trapdoors, revolving planks, breakaway beds, and the like. As Buster battles the Blinking Buzzards—a notorious gang of which he is an unwilling recruit—he embarks on a wonderful multi-floor chase, scampering through walls, out windows, up floors. At one point, he dives through a painting (which was hiding an escape route). The action in every room is seen simultaneously by means of a cutaway set; shot in a long take, it is a wonderful bit of comedy choreography.

Despite such moments, the film suffered—in Buster's eyes—from an excess of pun-y titles and reality-defying gags (at one point Buster paints a "hook" on which to hang his hat). *The High Sign* wasn't up to the exacting standards he set for his first release, and so he insisted that it be shelved. Schenck complied with Buster's wish, which is remarkable, given not only that the film was good but that they were obligated to hand Metro eight shorts. When Buster screened *The High Sign* for his mentor, Arbuckle laughed the whole way through—which Buster took to be a bad sign: indication that it was only more of the same old comedy.[10] Buster wanted something new.

Disheartened, Keaton lit out for the Sierra Nevadas, where Roscoe had gone on location for the first of his new features, *The Round Up*. Buster needed to plot a better solo debut, and hunting and fishing always seemed to generate good ideas. But before he could come up with anything definite, he found himself back at work shooting a movie—this time one not of his own making. Metro wanted to add luster to its lineup by making a few "quality" pictures, and so the studio decided to adapt *The New Henrietta*, a successful Broadway chestnut that—in one incarnation—had starred Douglas Fairbanks and that already had been translated to the screen before, in 1915. Fairbanks turned down the remake, but while doing so—according to Buster—he suggested Keaton be the one to fill his former shoes. When the offer came from Metro, Schenck realized the dramatic feature—which would run an epic seven reels—would generate publicity for Keaton's shorter work. Schenck lent out his star, the project was retitled *The Saphead*, and thus Buster took his first feature-length role as Bertie Van Alstyne, the eponymous saphead.[11]

Featuring *Brady Bunch*-style moving-human-crossword opening credits and elaborate costumes and sets, the film boasted high production values—as Metro wished. But it was hardly a comedy; through artfully illustrated titles, *The Saphead* unravels as an affected, convoluted melodrama—complete with a gold mine, a broken woman, star-crossed love, reversals of fortune, death, marriage, and twins. However, as Bertie, Buster cut a dashing figure in top hat and tails; the character would become a staple of his comic repertoire: the hapless but good-hearted swell, who—though laughably spoiled—would conquer his adversaries and make good in the end. For the most part, Buster plays it straight. The film's few pratfalls are confined to a late sequence in which Buster flops about the floor of the New York Stock Exchange. His slightly dazed look and torpid bearing— variations on the still-evolving Stone Face—serve him well in a sea of overacting. The critics agreed. *Variety* gushed, "As for Buster, a cyclone when called upon, his quiet work in this picture is a revelation."[12] In New York, the *Times* echoed, calling Buster "an accomplished and peculiar clown" whose "gravity is a bubbling source of merriment." Without Buster, moviegoers would be left with just "the stupid old plot."[13] The peculiar clown was a full-length film star.

With his feature stint over, it was back to work on what mattered— Keaton comedy of the two-reel variety. While shooting *The Saphead*, Buster mulled over the germ for his next comic try: a 1919 Ford Motor Company documentary about prefabricated housing called *Home Made*—an unusual source, if ever there was.[14] Naturally, Buster's version would be a spoof. It was called *One Week*.

An iris opens to reveal a calendar: today is Monday the 9th. Without further ado, the iris closes. A just-married couple descends the steps of a church; some of the guests throw rice, others throw shoes, at which point the groom—Buster—pauses long enough to pocket a pair in his size. The newlyweds climb into the back of an idling car, where they're handed a note: Uncle Mike has given them a smashing wedding present—their very own house. They speed off to their new address, oblivious to the matrimonial benediction tacked to the front of their jalopy: "Good Luck—You'll need it."

Simply getting to the lot is a wonderful caper. The chauffeur happens to be a jilted lover, and when a car pulls alongside them, Buster decides to ditch him *tout de suite*. The groom shoves his bride from one moving car into the other, but then—as he himself is straddling the gap—he gets scooped up by an (unseen) oncoming motorcycle. Without missing a beat, Buster turns the motorcycle around, speeds past the car, dismounts, embroils his rival in a dispute with a traffic cop, and swings his girl into their original still-moving (driverless) vehicle. The entire sequence lasts less than a minute and flows like automotive ballet, an example of the motorized choreography—elegant and concise—that would make Keaton famous.

At their new address, the newlyweds are in for a surprise: no house. Rather, a house-in-a-box, complete with by-the-number directions for assembly. Unfortunately for our industrious couple, the rival reappears to switch the numbers around, and thus Buster precedes to build a great surreal mess of a house—with crooked windows, skewed gables, exterior bathroom fixtures, and doors that open into thin air. The pre-fab home serves as a giant mechanical gag, one Keaton inventively milks for all it's worth. The porch rail doubles as a ladder on which Buster monkeys about while trying to install the chimney; he swings his piano to and fro on a pulley before it crashes through the living-room floor. When one of the exterior walls topples onto him, Buster reprises the left-standing-in-the-window bit from *Back Stage*—only with significantly more peril. (The gag will grow with each reincarnation, culminating in a famous jaw-dropper in his 1928 feature *Steamboat Bill, Jr.*) Keaton was the tough sort who threw himself into his work without reservation; two hours after completing a breathtaking fall—a no-look flip out of a second-floor door into a sod-covered pile of straw—Buster noticed his elbow was twice its normal size, with the rest of his upper body quickly growing to match. To remedy the swelling: fifteen minutes in a scalding hot shower, fifteen minutes in an icy shower, an olive-oil rub-down, followed by the application of horse liniment. A night's rest and Keaton was back in business.

As the house goes up, the calendar motif continues, ticking off the days of the week with no explanation for the specificity until—a-ha!—it reaches the day of the housewarming dinner party, Friday—the 13th. We should never have doubted the calendar's function; the economic razor of a Keaton plot takes no unnecessary detour. On the unlucky night in question, there is a great storm; spun about by the wind and rain, the house becomes a whirling dervish, unceremoniously spewing out guests and hosts alike. The entire structure is mounted on a turntable, allowing it to rotate freely—another mechanical Keaton contraption. Inside, the camera follows the mayhem a full 360 degrees; the photography is fluid, slightly shaky, allowing Buster to romp in and out of frame as the room spins round and round. It is a striking sequence, blending a *cinéma vérité* look with a subjective, absurdist feel—all perfectly pitched to the comic moment.

The film also has some quieter charms, such as the manner in which Buster's nervous husband seems slightly scared of his doting new wife (the sweet and skilled Sybil Seely). They are a dear, modest pair. As the girl takes a bath, she drops the soap outside the tub, just beyond her reach. She begins to rise, then spots the camera. Suddenly a giant hand—the cameraman's!—reaches around and obscures the lens. It is a surprising moment, reminiscent of Arbuckle in the bathhouse, and one of the very few times Keaton ever breaks the filmic illusion. (And that rarity is precisely what makes his joke more successful than Arbuckle's.)

One Week was the perfect two-reel debut, a brilliant introduction to many of Keaton's favorite themes. It is a hilarious riff on the Ford Motor Company's modernist faith, with its prefabricated happiness and cheery industrial optimism. Buster loved to skewer the good times, which is best demonstrated by the film's finale—a true Keaton spectacle. *Put yourself in his shoes . . .*

Title card:

{ *"You're on the wrong lot.*
Yours is across the railroad track." }

That's what the man tells you—and you're not overly surprised. You've fought for your girl, fought for your house, tried to lay the foundations of domestic bliss, but in this modern game the dames are dizzy, your rivals many, and while the houses come with instructions for the construction they say nothing about how you're to handle the cohabitation part of this whole deal.

You're a handy, upbeat kind of guy; even as things went terribly wrong—your home wrecked by a storm, your dinner party ruined—you never lost hope: if you only thought hard and fast enough it seemed you could outwit the chaos. With this lovable, mysterious creature who is your wife beside you, you could do anything. And so, with your house a scandalous, cock-eyed mess, you've managed to jack it

75

up on barrels and tie the whole thing to your car—so you and your wife can tow it across the tracks to your proper lot.

Your plan is going great, too, until the barrels catch on the railroad ties and your car breaks down and suddenly there's a train approaching! You take cover and . . . it misses—it's on the wrong tracks! You both breathe a sigh of relief, and start to hug and tell each other that maybe the house really will look good over there on the new lot when—BAM! Another train, speeding from the other direction and definitely on your tracks. You never saw it coming. With the splinters still raining down, you dust yourselves off. It's no use. You pick up a sign and stick it in front of the pile of rubble—FOR SALE. You turn back only once—to leave the instructions behind—as you and your wife walk off, holding hands.

CHAPTER EIGHT

Hit Parade

When we made pictures, we ate, slept, and dreamed them.[1]

Buster Keaton

One Week was cited by the National Board of Review as a summer film with "unusual merit for family entertainments."[2] The trade papers were less reserved, proclaiming it the "comedy sensation of the year," a film "likely to produce the laugh heard round the world."[3] At very least the laughing reached Broadway and 49th Street in New York where, at the Rivoli Theater, *One Week* was paired with a dismal prison-conversion melodrama called *The Great Redeemer*, in which a drawing of Jesus comes to life.[4] Buster's was the better—and more deliberate—comedy. His independent debut was a sensational success.

Next up was *Convict 13*, which begins with an inept golfer and his attempts to woo a girl more at home on the links than he is (again, Sybil Seely). Buster's unorthodox technique sends him off course, first into a water hazard, where a fish swallows his ball, and then into the rough, where he hits a shot off a wall and knocks himself out. The latter bit—deft, simple, and ridiculous—is a feat of golfing brilliance. Buster hits a ball at a barn with the right speed, spin, and angle to make it ricochet off the side and smack him on the head—whereupon he executes a double-leg backwards pratfall. The shot could have been faked with an easy edit, but, whenever possible, Buster preferred to do things straight. And so with great patience (and dexterity), he presumably hit a ball at a wall until he got the take he wanted.

Naturally, an escaped convict (prisoner number 13) comes upon the downed golfer and, finding him unconscious, takes the opportunity to switch clothes. It isn't long before Buster—a fugitive in the con's prison togs—is spotted by a pair of jail guards. Walking briskly, Buster looks back and sees he is being followed; as guard after guard falls in step

77

behind him, Buster nonchalantly—one might say impossibly—marches the pursuing formation through a set of military maneuvers. It's a wonderful gag sold strictly on the magnetism of Buster's personality. With an abrupt about-face, he escapes his pursuers and eventually ducks through a gate and locks himself safe and sound in . . . a prison. Along comes a guard and takes away the key; Buster wipes his feet and enters the yard, where he learns that today he—unlucky convict 13—is to be hanged.

Buster takes the news better than the girl—who happens to be the warden's daughter—and suffers the indignities of the execution preliminaries with his typical aplomb. *Convict 13* has at its heart a wonderful strain of gallows humor—literally in that a bleacherful of inmates gathers to watch the hanging (hooting and buying concessions), and figuratively in that the film's brusque, dark mood plays rough with our softer emotions. After Buster escapes the gallows (thanks to the girl) there is a prison riot, with high kicks and bullets, in which a few guys die brutally and comically, feet twitching. And so, while not the best of Keaton's short work, *Convict 13* does anticipate *Cops*, perhaps *the* darkly funny Keaton masterpiece.

During the riot, Buster faces off against a man who would become his most frequent two-reel sparring partner: Big Joe Roberts, the comic heavy. Roberts, a Muskegon neighbor and longtime friend of the Keatons', was an enormous brooding hulk of a man—the perfect foil to Buster's strong-but-not-quite-tall-enough build. Roberts was a compelling Goliath with intense, fuming eyes and a bulky quickness that made him seem ever on the verge of smashing Keaton to smithereens. The scenes of him taking out the entire corps of guards save one—Buster, again dressed in borrowed robes—are some of the most memorable in the film.

Roberts wasn't the only familiar face in *Convict 13*. With his girl in jeopardy, Buster springs into action, tying a punching bag to the end of a very long rope. With vicious precision, he swings the bag and begins to systematically flatten the swarming convicts, one at a time. The scene is a variation on the old Three Keatons vaudeville bit in which Buster swung at Joe with a basketball on a rope. Buster's skill with the makeshift weapon is effortless and striking—more than once he knocks off a man's hat before catching him in the head the next time around. For years he had walloped his dad like that, three shows daily, so it comes as no surprise that in the film the first con to catch the business end of the rope is old Joe Keaton.[5]

Buster defeats Roberts and wins his girl, only to knock himself out with a hammer in his very moment of triumph. As the girl bends over him, the scene dissolves to reveal them in the same position on the golf course. Surprise! It was all a dream, a result of the golfing accident. While the skillful dissolve creates a nice compositional match, the ending feels like a cheat—it plays flat, without enough of a kicker, especially when compared with Keaton's later flights of dream and fancy. In many ways the ending serves to lighten (in retrospect) the gloomy cheer of the prison sequence—a compulsion Buster will soon outgrow.

Buster's December offering, *The Scarecrow*, is a more disjointed film, essentially consisting of three set pieces—an extended prop gag and two chases (one canine, one human). The prop is a single-room house Buster shares with his looming roommate and rival, Joe Roberts. The bachelors' pad is furnished with a host of ingenious appliances and space-saving conveniences, à la Ed Gray; it is a mechanical funfair in which every object—great or small—lives a double life. The phonograph turns into a stove, the bookshelf into a cupboard, the tub into a couch, the tabletop into wall art, Joe's shoelace into a necktie, Buster's bed into a piano—and so forth. At the breakfast table, a small wagon on a track functions as a lazy Susan. (The device is a precursor to the table train in *The Electric House*, which is a precursor to a poolside serving trolley Buster built in his retirement house in Woodland Hills.) Condiments—salt, pepper, sugar—are lowered by strings, on which they dangle at the ready, suspended by counterweights. Casually going about their meal, Buster and Joe fling the condiments back and forth, the shakers winging about like tiny nervous aerialists.

Eventually the one-bedroom farce comes to an end and the boys leave their house to do battle for the heart of a pert country lass (Sybil Seely once more). Buster is set upon by what he thinks is a mad dog—

79

his old friend Luke—who climbs up (and down) a steep fourteen-rung ladder in a shrewdly staged chase atop the walls of a crumbling building. After making peace with the canine, Buster falls foul of Roberts and the girl's father (Joe Keaton); on the run again, Buster impersonates a scarecrow and fords a stream by walking on his hands (so as not to ruin his shoes!). Those same shoes get him in trouble. Bending to tie a lace, Buster startles his girl, who turns around and is flattered to find him down on one knee. Blushing, she tells him it is all so sudden. Eventually the two elope by motorcycle; hijacking a preacher, they end up crashing into a river the moment they're pronounced man and wife. The film's unintentional proposal will have a funny resonance in a few months' time, when—in real life—Buster finds himself similarly engaging the expectations of a girl.

Every morning Buster woke at six and drove to his studio, arriving well before the daily story conference, which was a loose, unregimented affair scheduled for the hours between ten and six o'clock. The meeting would be attended by co-director Cline and a clutch of anarchic gagmen, eager to hammer out the latest caper; also in the room might be the prop man, the unit manager, an electrician, a pair of cameramen. Significantly, everyone talked—the relentless comic improv was open to all—and everyone kept on the same page. At Comique you knew your neighbor's business, and while each man at the table was a master in his particular craft, you were all tied to the one big thing: the picture. Cross-pollination was the rule; you pulled any weight that came your way. (Incidentally, a screen credit was worth what you paid for it—nothing.) Responsibilities even crossed the boundary of the lens; the co-director might leave his chair to take a quick turn at acting and find himself playing opposite a gagman, also making a bit appearance. The casting was pragmatic, never vain—a body was needed, and who else was around to do it? From a handful of wry, dedicated craftsmen Buster formed a cohesive, efficient unit. They spent their days showboating, ad-libbing, outdoing each other, being outdone—all part of cooking up this new comic language that was being written in celluloid. The business of their meetings was elementary: to imagine a beginning—the perfect setup, crackling with yuk potential—and determine an ending, something fitting, not too sweet or sour. That was it—the middle was left alone to fill itself in as they went. Nothing from the meeting was ever set on paper—no scripts, no outlines, no inserts, no rewrites. The funny business was approached warily, as the fluid, madcap, untamed thing that it is. At six o'clock the group disbanded, leaving the day's work to simmer in the collective Comique subconscious. Buster would dine at home, then go out for a night's entertainment, most often a game of cards lasting past midnight. Then it was a few quick, stiff, illegal drinks before bed—usually around one or two in the morning. A few hours later, the alarm went off again. And so they worked, six days a week.[6]

Buster's manic, athletic schedule was an extension of the free-wheeling Comique style Arbuckle had established. And if a Keaton story development was an all-consuming, democratic free-for-all, then the same went double for a Keaton movie shoot. Buster rehearsed his scenes only lightly, if at all; he simply discussed the relevant action with the cameraman and the other actors, then rolled film. If a sequence was difficult enough to warrant multiple rehearsals, he would look for a way to somehow "unrehearse" it. Unlike many of his contemporaries (most notably Chaplin), Keaton would shoot only a handful of takes, and in the editing room, he usually went with the first, essentially spontaneous performance. Accidents, bloopers, and gaffes all might make their way into a finished print. The camera-men—two of them side by side, one filming the negative used for domestic distribution, the other filming the one for overseas—had their standing orders: no matter what, keep filming.[7]

While undeniably the man in charge—never forget he was respon-sible for the writing (such as it was), the acting, the editing, and the directing (a level of auteurism unimaginable today)—Buster trusted his crew to gauge his performance. When the call "Cut!" eventually came, anyone from the co-director to the prop man might chime in if he thought the scene lacked punch.[8] And if the gags continued to fizzle, with no laughs on the horizon, the unit would simply drop everything in favor of the studio's number two love and backup pastime—baseball. Bats, balls, and bases would be trundled out by Buster's sister Louise—in keeping with Comique's utilitarian spirit, the script girl doubled as the batgirl—and production would cease for as long as it took for inspiration to strike, usually a few innings or so.[9]

Back in September, after *The Scarecrow* had wrapped, Lou Anger decided to add an ingénue to Comique's stable of contract players: Virginia Fox, an eighty-nine-pound former Sennett Bathing Beauty with dark hair and a size $1\frac{1}{2}$ foot. Standing an even five feet tall, the petite Fox was a nice onscreen compliment to Buster's 5'6" frame. Buster preferred a diminutive love interest, and Fox went on to appear in ten of his short films; in 1923, she married mogul-to-be Darryl F. Zanuck and gave up pictures.[10]

Fox's first Comique appearance was in *Neighbors*, a relatively humdrum short in which Buster and she play a modern-day Pyramus and Thisbe whose budding romance is made difficult by their fathers (Joe Keaton and Joe Roberts, respectively). The film opens with Buster's typical economy. The first shot says it all: there is a tenement courtyard, complete with hanging laundry and a boy and a girl separated by a wall, passing notes. As the lovers woo, fathers, mothers, even cops become embroiled in the slapstick mayhem. Joe Keaton, as Buster's halfheartedly abusive father, reprises a few old vaudeville bits with his boy, but the film's best moments come when Buster is on the go. *Neighbors* showcases Buster's amazing acrobatic skill—he flops through third-story windows, zips between buildings on laundry lines, seesaws on a plank on a fence, and balances atop a telegraph pole. The film also marks the development of Keaton's comic math. Things occur in threes, his life seems divided in two, and his world is full of lines, bisectors, even trisectors—all to humorous effect. A kind of athletic geometry builds to its logical climax with Buster's final attempt to rescue his girl from her third-story captivity. From his own third-story window, Buster calls to his friends—they happen to be his old vaudeville cohorts the Flying Escalantes—whose heads pop out of the windows below.[11] Each steps out his window, and—standing on each other's shoulders—the three-man ladder teeters its way across the courtyard. Crashing against the girl's house, the ladder splinters as each man disappears through the window on his level. Soon Buster emerges from the third story—now hoisting a trunk—and the rescue team regroups to ferry across the girl's luggage. They make another quick trip for the girl, only to be chased out of the yard—with the girl slung across Buster's shoulders! The four-person beast rushes down the street (briefly breaking formation to run along a multi-tiered scaffold), and as they dash to freedom, the ladder is eliminated one man at a time. When the middle man is taken out by a clothesline, Buster and the girl fall to the bottom man's shoulders, the momentum unbroken; then he drops through a hole in the sidewalk, and Buster and the girl continue on street level (only to eventually slide down a coal chute, where they are married by a judge). Watching the troupe meet its geometrically ordained end is—in the words of *Moving Picture World*—a real "corker."[12] Comedy, it seemed, could be engineered, just like anything else.

For the most part Buster's next effort, *The Haunted House*, favored funny mechanics over acrobatics; however, like *Neighbors*, it wasn't shy about borrowing a joke or two from Keaton's past. Early in the film, Buster, in his position as bank teller, spills a pot of glue on a pile of cash, and the ensuing (hopeless) extrication recalls his molasses-mired debut in *The Butcher Boy*.[13] (Co-director Eddie Cline even steps in to take a turn at the sticky clowning.) The haunted house in question is actually a counterfeiters' hideout made to appear uninviting by phony ghosts—some creepy, some goofy—exploding books, spinning floors, and a giant collapsing staircase on which the steps suddenly go flat. The film has very few titles, which is remarkable given that *The Haunted House* reveals a growing sophistication in Keaton's use of flashback.[14] The movie's highlights include the plentiful mechanical gags, a Keaton pratfall or two (particularly one indescribable head-over-heels shudder upon seeing a ghost), and a fiendish finale. After saving the day, Buster once again is knocked on the noggin; he dreams he ascends a ladder to the gates of Heaven, only to have St. Peter (in a reprise of the collapsing stair gag) pull a lever and send him down to Hell, where he's prodded with a hot poker. Luckily, Buster awakes merely to learn his clothes are on fire.

And so 1920 came to a close. Keaton found himself on the Christmas cover of *Moving Picture World*, hanging in a hearth stocking alongside a handful of the year's newly risen stars.[15] As one of such, Buster gained a publicist, a sharp young New Yorker named Harry Brand who had spent time as a West Coast sportswriter, a mayoral secretary, a grifter, and a Warner Brothers publicist. Brand would eventually go on to promote the likes of Shirley Temple, Betty Grable, and Marilyn Monroe. In his hands, the Buster Keaton legend would be nurtured with a relish worthy of his father, the great Joe himself.[16]

CHAPTER NINE

Wedding Bells and Hard Luck Goats

You're fired from your job, jilted by your girl, down on your luck—all before the day even starts. You've tried suicide by trolley, by traffic, by falling safe, by poison, by hanging—no dice. Then some zoo swells say they want themselves an armadillo—to complete their menagerie—and you figure you're just the cowboy to get it for them. But you end up at a country club and before you know it you're battling "Lizard Lip Luke," the nastiest of nasties, who's spoiled your fox hunt and rattled the girls. Hope seems lost. But somehow, you beat him and rescue a girl, in a nifty piece of luck that you had no right to expect. So with a swollen heart you take a knee and proclaim to the girl whom you've won fair and square that now no one can stand in the way of your marriage. She smiles sweetly, then drops the bomb: no one . . . except her husband over there.

That's it—a fellow can only take so much. You're back where you started. So you go to the pool and climb the high, high, high dive. From below, your girl waves, but it's much too late for that. You pause, then leap from the board, swanlike, sailing high and long—too long! You arc over the pool, crashing through the deck in a shower of bricks. A crowd rushes over to witness the carnage, peering into the hole, murmuring like doves:

$$\left\{ \begin{array}{c} \textit{"He is so far away you can} \\ \textit{hardly see him . . ."} \end{array} \right\}$$

Years pass. Only the ruins of a country club remain: leaves scuttle across the swimming pool tiles, overgrown shrubs list in the wind. Slowly, a man in Asian garb emerges from the long-forgotten hole, dusts himself off, and lifts out his Chinese wife and three kids. To his adoring family, he points out the diving board, briefly pantomimes the great leap that corrected his luck and brought him to them, then slowly turns his back and leads them away . . .

$$\left\{ \textit{THE END} \right\}$$

And thus the greatest laugh Buster ever got—or so he said. The ending of *Hard Luck*, shot in the first days of 1921, was a real crowd pleaser; according to Buster, audiences roared straight through the credits of the following feature. The ill-fated swan dive was an act of daredevil abandon. The far end of the swimming pool was hidden under wax paper and made to blend in with the surrounding deck. The camouflage only worked too well; from above, Buster couldn't make out where the fake deck ended and the real deck began. As he stood at the edge of the board—frozen—contemplating the grisly price of an error, listening to the wooden scaffolding creak in the wind, an unexpected gust blew him off balance, and he was forced to jump. He hit his mark, and *Hard Luck* became Buster's favorite short.[1]

On paper, *Hard Luck* is an episodic rumination on the comedy of suicide; onscreen, it plays like a cotton-candy dream. Only Buster could have struck such a tone, crosscutting despair and whimsy with a sure, simple touch. As his attempts to kill himself fail in increasingly ingenious (and humorous) ways, Buster agrees to a variety of ridiculous pursuits: an armadillo-trapping expedition (allowing for many a gun-and-tackle gag, recalling bygone summers on Muskegon Lake), a fox hunt (on which he lassos a bear), and a country-club caper that eventually leads him up that very high dive.

Hard Luck wrapped before lunch on January 9th; that afternoon, the Comique gang began shooting sequences for another tale of a habitually unlucky stiff, *The Goat*.[2] They were on a roll.

Buster, again down but not out, plays a more insouciant rascal this time; he gloats, he has bad manners, and yet he remains an amiably credulous sort. The film opens with him being sent to the back of a breadline. The line stretches in front of a clothing store; Buster falls in behind two sidewalk mannequins, thinking they're at the end of the line. The line shuffles forward, abandoning Buster and his mannequins. Eventually doubt creeps in, and Buster surreptitiously jabs one of the dummies with a pin—no response. Then the doubt turns on himself—or specifically, his pin—so he sticks himself in the leg, just to make sure. Yep, it smarts. It isn't until a shopkeeper emerges to bring in the mannequins that he realizes what's been going on. Scampering to the front, he finds the bread window is closed.

What follows is a case of mistaken identity—a mix-up lands Buster's face on the wanted poster for an escaped con, Dead Shot Dan (Mal St. Clair, who also gets a co-directing credit). On the lam, Buster doesn't try very hard to clear his name—he happens to believe, incorrectly, that he killed a man. He leads some cops on a nicely sustained chase, which culminates in a locomotive getaway. As Buster's train pulls into the next town, there is an elegant long shot of the engine arriving head-on—with Buster nonchalantly riding atop the cowcatcher. Soon he strikes up with a girl who invites him to supper. As the family sits down to eat, Buster finds that her father (Joe Roberts) is the policeman who has been on his tail all day. The big detective stands and locks the front door. The two men square off, and just as you think Buster has nowhere to go, he springs from his chair and—stepping once on the table—launches himself onto Joe's shoulders and through the transom above the door. Keaton could slip out of anything.

Or so it seemed. Not long after finishing *The Goat*, Buster was ascending a prop escalator he had built on the set of *The Electric House*—the latest and greatest realization of the Ed Gray ethos, in which Buster mechanizes an entire mansion—when suddenly the contraption went haywire. The escalator surged forward, catching Buster's right slapshoe in its jaws; after an excruciating hesitation—while various crewmembers lunged for the plug—there was an ankle-splitting crack. The shoe ripped off; Buster dropped ten feet to the floor, rolled once, and passed out. The doctors at Good Samaritan Hospital broke the bad news: almost two months in a cast, and no rough stuff for at least twice that.[3] Apparently, hard luck had finally caught up to him.

What good was a slapstick clown with a bum ankle? For the first time in his professional life—going on now two decades—Buster couldn't work. So he got married instead.

Buster was no longer seeing Viola Dana; the bold brunette had fallen for a trick flyer named Ormer Locklear, so Buster's attention had wandered back to Alice Lake—with a fickle focus, at best.[4] Buster and Roscoe were still determined nighthawks, always up to something. An evening out could mean a trip to the Vernon Country Club—an all-night watering hole where a mix of the starry and the seamy came for their drinks and drugs—or, if it was Thursday, the gang would head to the Sunset Inn for its weekly celebrity dinner theater. For a five-buck cover, diners swished bootleg hooch and watched Hollywood's brightest—Keaton, Arbuckle, Chaplin, Fairbanks, and the rest—blow off steam, test new bits, razz each other, get a little out of control. Buster would do his "Princess Rajah" belly dance; Viola and Alice would stage a game of strip poker, only to be busted by Roscoe. The entertainment was never paid; all were guests of the carnival.[5]

Then in February a rumor began making the rounds. By the 11th *Variety* had picked up the item: BUSTER KEATON MARRYING. The bride-to-be was none other than Natalie Talmadge, who was dutifully awaiting her busy fiancé in New York. No wedding date was given. Nine days later, *The New York Times* confirmed the engagement through Beulah Livingston, Norma and Constance's publicist. The paper said the groom would be free to travel in April, with a wedding following shortly thereafter. To Natalie, April must have seemed like an eternity away. Over Christmas Constance had eloped—like her sister—leaving Natalie at home with a still-smarting Peg. Natalie was twenty-four; her screen career had fizzled, and her professional life consisted of signing photos for her famous younger sister. For two years Buster and she had been no more than pen pals; now they were engaged.[6]

How exactly that came to be is a little unclear. In his autobiography, Buster maintains Natalie sent him a letter saying she was alone and would drop everything to be his—at his say so. He claims the proposition didn't come out of the blue; they had had an arrangement of sorts for over a year. After due consideration, he bought a train ticket to New York. In another version, Buster was the lonely one, sulking about in a cast and pestering Natalie with proposals, when he heard tell—in the gossip pages no less—of competition from a Midwestern dairy magnate. Thinking it was a case of now or never, he rushed east. Still another report has it that the betrothal was brokered by Joe Schenck, who was eager to unite his comedy star and his sister-in-law. The truth likely combines parts of all three.[7]

At twenty-five, Buster was a celebrity bachelor, and a Talmadge sister wedding—even if it involved the non-Hollywood one—was a newsworthy affair. So the media settled in to track the altarward progress of the Keaton–Talmadge sweethearts, though the date for the big event remained to be determined. In March, *Variety* claimed Natalie had broken the engagement for reasons unknown.[8] Apparently there was nothing to the report, however; perhaps it was bad intelligence extrapolated from the fact that overbearing Peg—now thrice thwarted by her willful daughters—had reservations about marrying her Natalie to a mere comedian. Nonetheless, with his ankle sound enough for him to travel, Buster boarded the *Santa Fe Super Chief* in the company of Lou and Sophye Anger, and sped across the country to New York.[9]

On Friday, May 27, 1921, Buster and Natalie presented themselves at the Municipal Building and requested a marriage license. Buster walked with the assistance of a spiffy gold-capped cane his former roommate and best-man-to-be Ward Crane had picked up for him at Tiffany's. Natalie brought along Constance and Peg. On Tuesday afternoon, May 31st—Joe and Myra's wedding anniversary, though none of the Keatons (save Buster) were in attendance—a city judge married Buster and Natalie on the veranda of Joe Schenck's Bayside home. The bride wore pale gray. Blooming snowballs lined the porch. Constance, the matron of honor, presented the couple with a police puppy, which Buster dubbed Captain. A Rolls-Royce awaited them in California, compliments of Joe and Norma. The day after the ceremony, the newlyweds took the *Twentieth Century Limited* to LA. There was no honeymoon.[10]

Buster's eagerness to rush back to work might seem somewhat less than romantic; the actual tenor of his feelings for Natalie is difficult to ascertain. Buster's own accounts of the nuptials, made years later,

9 Buster and the Talmadge sisters: from left, Norma, Natalie, and Constance—at his and Natalie's wedding in Bayside, New York, May 31, 1921.

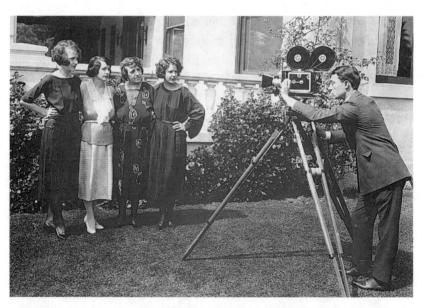

10 Keaton shoots his in-laws: from left, sister Constance, wife Natalie, mother Peg, and sister Norma with Buster outside the Keaton home on Westmoreland Place, 1922.

are colored by hindsight—it was a marriage rocked by bitterness, frigidity, and adultery. Contemporary published reports often carry a strong whiff of publicity wrangling; after all, Harry Brand reported to work every day like everyone else. When Buster spoke to the press he liked to crack wise, though his take on married life didn't extend far beyond the ball-and-chain humor typical of the day. (In fact, not long after their wedding, Buster and Natalie posed for a publicity photo in which he, shackled at the leg, stares dolefully into the distance while she brandishes a rolling pin.) Buster went on the record for *Motion Picture Magazine* in an article titled "Only Three Weeks." Married less than a month, he nonetheless had accumulated plenty of material. Through a string of tart marital maxims, Buster comes off—in the words of the interviewer—as an "old-fashioned husband." He declares he will never join what he calls the "Why, dear" club (the weak stammer of the hen-pecked husband: "Why, dear, I, I, I . . ."). The interview ends with a similar quip from the freedom-loving hubby: "Marriage—nothing can compare with it, not even the straight-jacket."[11] This kind of "Take my wife—please!" patter is a familiar Arbuckle shtick; in the majority of Roscoe's Comique films the wife is something to be eluded, a harpy ever stepping on the fun (which usually includes some extramarital dalliance). Buster would quickly pick up this bitter comic thread, scrapping notions of conjugal bliss with such two-reel barbs as *My Wife's Relations*. Still, it is a mistake to read too much into the absent honeymoon and the wife-baiting articles, to say Buster's marriage was over before it began. For four months 1025 Lillian Way had been quiet—and to Buster, that was the greatest crime of all.

On the westbound train, Buster proposed to Natalie that they buy a stretch of raw land somewhere, perhaps in the San Fernando Valley, and build it into a working ranch. A homestead was something a childhood vagabond could really sink his teeth into. Natalie wasn't so sure. Just getting her to California had taken some smooth talking; she was loath to leave New York—and her family—behind. Feeding chickens did not seem as fun as brunch at the Biltmore. The discussion was tabled, and Mr. and Mrs. Keaton quickly settled into a house in town.[12]

91

11 From left: Keaton, Keaton. *The Playhouse* (1921).

CHAPTER TEN

Welcome to the Playhouse

"This fellow Keaton seems to be the whole show."
                    A familiar-looking theatergoer in *The Playhouse* (1921)

While Buster was getting married, Comique was releasing films. When the star broke his ankle the studio had two in the can—*Hard Luck* and *The Goat*—as well as the aborted debut, *The High Sign*. That was enough to cover most of Buster's convalescence, but not quite all. That summer, with Buster's ankle out of the cast, it came time for another Keaton short. This one would have a twist—no roughhousing, doctor's orders. (Not that Buster was one to heed medical advice—he cheerfully abused his body day and night on-set—but his ankle could support him only gingerly, at best.) There was grumbling within the ranks. A static Keaton caper was like "near beer," cracked one of the gagmen, who, with the rest of the crew, was at his wits' end trying to come up with a workable scenario.[1] A stone face was one thing, but stone feet to boot? It seemed too much to ask.

At Lillian Way there was a new voice in the mix. After the escalator mishap, Lou Anger decided Buster needed a dedicated technical director—not simply someone to baby-sit the sets, effects, and gadgets, but a technician whose skill at mechanical improv could keep up with Comique's comedy on the fly. He picked one of the best in Hollywood, Fred Gabourie, an engineering wiz who could assemble anything out of nothing, a restlessly inventive sort who shared Buster's obsessive love of tinkering.[2] His first Comique film would be a technical masterpiece. Buster had struck upon an idea—let the camera do all the work.

Buster's injury had thrown off the studio's release schedule; by the time his current project would be fit for the screen, a few months would have passed without a Keaton film. So for the fans who had missed their star, Keaton decided he wouldn't just give them Buster, he would give them a multitude of Busters—up to nine onscreen at once, in fact, cavorting with each other in a vaudeville review presented by Buster Keaton, orchestrated by Buster Keaton, starring Buster Keaton, and witnessed by Buster Keaton. Fittingly, this giddy theatrical vision would be called *The Playhouse*.

We begin simply: Keaton buys a ticket to a vaudeville show and enters an opera house. As the conductor takes the stand, we realize it is Buster; he picks up the baton and launches into a furious overture. We then cut to the string section—three Busters!—on bass, cello, and violin. The maestro swivels and it's three more Busters—on clarinet, trombone, and drums. The orchestra roars on in a frenzy of activity—the bass man sawing at his strings, the drummer firing a pistol and rattling a tambourine, each man exhorting the others to keep up. Then a Buster-stagehand goes to raise the curtain. Following the logic of ascending multiples, we should be prepared for what's next, but we're not—nine Busters lined across the stage, hoofing in unison! It's none other than the Buster Keaton Minstrels.

There is, of course, a capper to the joke. After a moment it dawns on you: the audience—a dapper man and woman, a little boy with his bony grandma, and a pair of drowsy gray hairs, sitting two-by-two in the balcony—is also an all-Buster affair. Even heartily in drag, Keaton is one cool chameleon.

The audience is treated to a remarkable act. A glance at the program confirms it's a one-man show: Buster Keaton presents the Buster Keaton Minstrels, featuring Buster Keaton as everything from "Interloctor" (sic) to "Asleep In The Deep" to "Electrician" to "Vocal Instructor." The aggressively self-congratulatory program is a jab at Thomas H. Ince, an important early director-producer with a fondness for screen credits.[3] After the Keaton nine finish their bit, the backdrop changes and two Busters emerge from the wings, one from each side, holding canes. They meet in the middle, exchange some funny little pleasantries, and begin a beautiful, quirky soft-shoe, keeping perfectly in step. The audience goes wild.

Split-screen work had been done before, but never on such a scale, and never before with such technical rigor. At the time, such special effects were generated in the camera, at great difficulty. The technique Buster used to create the overflowing clown car in *Moonshine* essentially remained the industry standard: tape-off half the lens, expose, rewind, re-tape, repeat. But in his *Playhouse*, Buster didn't want the screen split but splintered—fractured into nine slivers courtesy of a custom-designed shuttered lightproof casing that fit over the camera. The device was so well crafted that his gagmen bragged they could have shot underwater.[4] To create the minstrels, the shutters simply were opened one at a time, with the film rewound in between. However, mechanical precision was not enough. It took the steady arm of cameraman Elgin Lessley—the human metronome—to crank each exposure at exactly the same speed. And then—to achieve onscreen synchronicity—Buster had to give nine flawless, identical performances. (He danced to a banjo played in time with a metronome.[5]) One slipup—by anyone, on any take—would ruin the strip of film, and with it all the previous work. And yet the end result is seamless; the exposures match perfectly. Not only do multiple Busters dance together in a single frame, but they interact: they converse, they follow orders, they drop things on each other, they wake each other up—the reactions all impeccably timed to sustain the illusion.

Buster's humility kept him from continuing the film with him in all the roles; he worried audiences would see it as a case of an ego run amok.[6] And so we fade out on the applauding audience and fade in on a lone Buster in bed, clapping in his sleep. It was just a dream. Now comes the nightmare. Big Joe Roberts is in the room, waking him up, and he means business. He kicks Keaton out of bed and summons some henchmen, who begin to haul off Buster's furniture. After some harsh words, Buster leaves the men to clean him out. They take his bed—then they remove the walls. We're still in a theater! Buster is a napping stagehand! It's the opening gag from *Back Stage*, although performed to better effect. The waking world has its tricks, too.

In fact, the remainder of *The Playhouse* is a paean to the bygone magic of vaudeville. Buster begins with his broom-through-a-knothole bit, that old Three Keatons chestnut, and the film is populated by the alluring bathing-suit acts and dark distant strongmen of Buster's youth. There is even an homage to Peter the Great, the performing chimp that so impressed Buster during the Keaton summer abroad of 1909. Buster takes the stage in monkey makeup—for he has let the real ape escape—and proves he can smoke a cigar, ride a bike, and hop about as well as any rascally monkey. The performance is an elaboration on his virtuosic transformation in *Moonshine*—a marvel of simian comportment and yet another demonstration of the plasticity of the Stone Face. Not only can Buster play men and women, old and young, but he can mimic a monkey, from his bowed limber legs to his wicked twitching face.

The structure of *The Playhouse* isn't as divided as it would appear. The film's two halves—dream and reality—are unified by whimsical echoes. In a visual pun on Buster's earlier multiplicity, twin starlets arrive, one of whom is Buster's girl. Keaton doesn't know that she has a double, and when he finds himself faced with the two of them reflected in a set of mirrors, he flees to the sanctuary of the prop room. There he pens a firm oath: "I resolve never to drink anymore." After catching his own reflection in a triptych, Buster grows suspicious, and he confronts the twins. Wise to the situation, he rushes back to the prop room with no less urgency and amends his resolution by tacking on the phrase, "but just as much." Keaton continues to confuse the girls, eventually resorting to marking his sweetie with an "X" at the nape of her neck. Interestingly, the "twins" are played by look-alikes, not actual twins. (One is Virginia Fox; the other, some speculate, could be Natalie.[7]) After the technological bravado of the split-screen beginning, it is a curious decision to have twins by way of theatrical— not cinematic—artifice. Perhaps the decision was simply practical, perhaps not. Either way, it gives the problems of the film's second reel a strange, shrewd resonance with the thrills of the first.

Having satisfied Buster's eight-picture deal with Metro, Schenck negotiated a contract with First National to distribute the next dozen, starting with *The Playhouse*.[8] The film was a hit—*The New York Times* lauded it as Keaton's best.[9] Indeed, Buster was mastering short-form comedy. His films were growing at once increasingly efficient and increasingly complex, doing more in twenty minutes than previously thought possible. Two reels of Keaton began to feel like a short story—brusque, economic glimpses rounded off with a comic flourish, which whispered of greater stakes than you were ready to admit, laughing as you were. There is a heady audacity to his short work. Buster was taking what he knew—the ingenuity, athleticism, and wit of vaudeville—and applying it to a burgeoning medium, and people loved it. His films straddled the divide between the remnants of America's Victorian Age (think of those prim ladies, those chaste kisses) and a new Mechanized Age (think how often a locomotive shows up), and he mined that gap with the giddy fervor of a boy-prankster from Muskegon. He was getting paid day in and day out to play, to tinker, to come up with larger, faster, and funnier celluloid Clown Poles. But while he loved his whizzing gadgets and gags, Buster was ever mindful of the precariousness of this modern life (its speed, its momentum)—how it all can come crashing down when you least expect it. And so it did in the late summer of 1921—not on him, but on his old pal and mentor, Roscoe Arbuckle.

With Buster reaching new heights in two reels, Roscoe was pursuing a heroic schedule to do the same in features. He had just shot three full-length films simultaneously—an ordeal, even for a willing workhorse like Arbuckle.[10] His reward to himself: a $25,000 Pierce-Arrow touring car, customized with leather interior, stocked bar, and hideaway toilet.[11] With the long Labor Day weekend approaching, he dreamt of filling the vehicle with friends and driving to San Francisco for a much-overdue vacation.

When Roscoe's invitation came, Buster was on Balboa Bay, shooting a nautical lark called *The Boat*. He declined the offer; he and Natalie would yacht to Catalina Island for the weekend.[12] It is unclear why Buster didn't want to join his friend in San Francisco, as he had so often in the past; perhaps he wasn't sure how his new wife would react to a weekend of Roscoe-palooza. The decision would be a monumental one. He would miss one of the most notorious parties in Hollywood history.

At last the much-anticipated weekend arrived. Arbuckle rode north in his lustrous vehicle with two friends, actor Lowell Sherman and director Fred Fishback, along for the ride. The men checked into the St. Francis Hotel, taking possession of three rooms on the twelfth floor. The party promptly was called to order and continued through the sweltering weekend. Word spread that the big man was in town, and by Monday thirty friends, associates, local bigwigs, and hangers-on crowded suite 1220. Over the summer Prohibition had turned two, and that weekend it was being treated like the infant that it was. The phonograph blared; good-time flunkies cut a rug while bellhops shuttled hooch like broomsticks in *Fantasia*. At some point an agent named Al Semnacher arrived with a bit-playing client of his, Virginia Rappe. Unlike most of the party-crashers, Rappe knew Arbuckle—the two had been on a few dates, but nothing serious. Around three o'clock in the afternoon, Roscoe excused himself to go clean up—the party had begun that morning with him still in pajamas. He discovered Rappe in his bedroom, drunk and vomiting. She began to convulse and wail. Arbuckle called for her friends, and when they couldn't calm her, he summoned the manager and moved her to another room to sleep it off. He then resumed the party. After a while he went downstairs for dinner, returning to his room just before midnight to kick out the remaining revelers. On Tuesday, Roscoe paid the whopping hotel bill, and the Labor Day threesome headed back to Los Angeles. That Friday, September 9th, Virginia Rappe died at a local sanitarium. On Monday Arbuckle was charged with murder.

Rappe died of a ruptured bladder, exacerbated by peritonitis. The papers called it rape, and the scandal became the media event of all time. The story of the jazz party grew sinister—there were reports of locked doors and deathbed accusations, along with intimations of impotency, deviant homespun remedies, crimes of opportunity, and unspeakable violations. Rapacious journalists seized the opportunity to put "Hollywood" on trial; to the rest of the country they bravely exposed the underbelly of a depraved town, bloated with booze, sex, and greed. Overnight, America's jolly man-child became a hopped-up pervert, a fleshy monster who dined while his victim died. There never was a legitimate case against Arbuckle; he was tried three times—for manslaughter—and after two hung decisions, he was exonerated. The jury deliberated for six minutes, then returned a verdict of not guilty in which they went as far as to imply that the defendant deserved an apology. Nonetheless, at thirty-four, Arbuckle was ruined, a victim of the yellow press and its unforgiving public. (Buster recalls William Randolph Hearst remarking that the Arbuckle affair had sold more of his papers than the sinking of the *Lusitania*.) Roscoe was stripped of his Paramount contract and—instead of his apology—got a lifetime ban from the screen from the president and moral arbiter of the nascent Motion Picture Producers and Distributors of America, Will Hays. The creation of the Hays Office—with its crusade to uphold decency in film—would be the most lasting consequence of the Arbuckle trials; the ascension of the former US Postmaster General ushered in an infamous period of censorship. Ironically, the Arbuckle scandal is often cited as the end of a certain Hollywood innocence—Buster himself would forever mourn that Labor Day as "the day the laughter stopped." Hollywood, that reputed den of iniquity, was alone in rallying behind its maligned son. While Comique would officially change its name to Buster Keaton Productions in 1922, to distance itself from Arbuckle, the studio took care of its founder until the day he died. Buster arranged for 35 percent of his films' profits to go directly to Roscoe. He also tried to get his friend back into movies, and despite the blacklist Arbuckle found sporadic directing work under his father's name, William Goodrich, going so far as to direct a Marion Davies feature in 1927. Still, the Labor Day scandal—with its public betrayal—devastated Arbuckle. He died in 1933, a broken, largely forgotten man. Buster would never get over what happened to his best friend. In the den of his Woodland Hills ranch, decades later, he would hang an enormous picture of an unmistakable grinning face.[13]

Back on the set of *The Boat*, no one imagined that the media hysteria would sink Arbuckle. Buster wanted to make a statement on behalf of his friend, even testify if necessary, but the Arbuckle defense team forbade it—public resentment raged against the movie industry; a crop of celebrities swooping to Arbuckle's aid would only make matters worse.¹⁴ And so Keaton and crew went back to work. They were having some problems of their own.

12 Buster and Sybil Seely in a publicity photo from *The Boat* (1921).

Technical man Fred Gabourie found himself particularly stymied. He was wrestling with a doozy: how to sink a boat, attractively, on cue. In the film, the boat belongs to Buster; he is taking his family—a wife and two boys, in porkpies—to live at sea in the *Damfino*, presumably a better-than-fine boat. (His reasons for forsaking the land are unknown, but he cannot go back now; extricating the boat, which he built in his basement garage, has toppled his house.) Keaton-the-director wanted the launching of his vessel to be an unparalleled poetic failure. In a long shot, audiences would watch the thirty-five-foot boat (with its captain standing majestically at the prow) slide down the ramp and, without breaking pace, continue directly to the depths of the bay. Buster asked Gabourie to build two boats: one to be sailed, the other to be sunk. But the doomed boat refused to play its part. The crew drilled it full of holes, they made the back end collapse, they saddled it with a 1,600-pound weight—all to no avail. Nothing could produce that effortless glide from triumph to tragedy that would make the bit funny. Eventually Gabourie executed the stunt by brute force; his men anchored cables to the seabed and dragged the boat down with pulleys. At last—disaster, uninterrupted. It took three days to get the sequence.[15]

The film is full of such frustrations for Buster; he's the type born to have the ship go down with him. In preparation of the ill-fated launch, he tows the *Damfino* down the ramp and into position. As he drives along the dock, his wife shouts and he turns to look—their boy is still with the boat. While Buster is facing the wrong way, the car's front tires go off the dock. Buster scrambles to safety. At one end of the towrope is his car, teetering over the dock; at the other is the boat, with his boy lying on the trailer, in peril of a good soaking. With his wife screaming at him, Buster takes an inspired moment to ponder the dilemma—save the boy or the car?—before deciding to snip the rope. He then walks over to the family jalopy and watches it sink (boy be damned).

First the house, then the car, but at least the boat—once it's afloat— is the kind of nautical marvel that only Keaton and Gabourie could build. Its best feature is its retractable stacks, mast, and rigging, which collapse at the yank of a lever. The lever is thrown (and the boat streamlined) before we even see why—to clear a low bridge, which suddenly appears in the moving frame. The sequence illustrates the endlessly inventive games of cat-and-mouse Buster plays with our expectations. He tips his hand with a mechanical gag (a convertible boat!) before showing us the need for such. It is a short but nice bit in that it is a departure from the stock A-B-A (tall boat-low bridge-collapsing stacks) setup. First we laugh at the boater's eccentricity, then at his practicality. In Buster's hands, a funny boat is no longer a punchline in itself.

The boat inevitably floats to sea, where it encounters the inevitable storm. The tempest-tossed vessel turns 360-degree cartwheels; inside, Buster struggles to keep his feet, scurrying about the spinning cabin like a drunk hamster on a wheel. (Eventually he nails his feet to the floor.) It is a lost cause; the family must escape in the lifeboat. Buster again goes down with the ship, then swims over. The waters calm, and then the lifeboat sinks. Huddled close, the family prepares for death—until they find they can stand. They walk through the shallows and onto a beach. They face us. "Where are we?" asks the wife. Buster, deadpan, shrugs and mouths, "Damfino." The End.

Buster's porkpie brood was not just a celluloid dream; during production of *The Boat*, or shortly thereafter, Natalie became pregnant. Upon notification of the impending arrival of her first grandchild, Peg moved west, taking roost in Buster and Natalie's house. That November, Constance, now divorced, followed suit. (Fortunately Natalie had insisted on a larger house than the newlyweds needed.) Then it was Joe and Norma's turn, and while they took rooms of their own at the Ambassador Hotel, they brought with them all the commotion of the Schenck–Talmadge studio, henceforth to be located in Hollywood, California.[16] Buster found himself inundated by in-laws; as he quipped in his autobiography, "There were times when I had the disquieting feeling that I had married not one girl but a whole family."[17]

And what a family it was: rich, smothering, and powerful. *Motion Picture Magazine* was quick to highlight the fact that Buster and Natalie's marriage cemented what it called "the most powerful oligarchy in pictures today," eclipsing even the renowned Pickford–Fairbanks merger.[18] And so clowns were expected to become oligarchs—or at least keep up appearances. Buster wasn't comfortable with such personal ostentation. Nonetheless in the spring of 1922, with the baby on the way, the makeshift household—Buster, Natalie, Peg, and Constance—moved into an even bigger residence on Westmoreland Place, one with the requisite twenty rooms, third-story ballroom, celebrity neighbor (Mack Sennett), and swimming pool. The scene was hardly one of hushed anticipation. Peg fussed over pregnant Natalie, while Constance set about learning to ride her bike in the ballroom. Houseguests arrived (invited or not) for indefinite visits; parties didn't as much stop and start as ebb and flow.[19] The Talmadges were social animals of the decidedly free-range sort.

The move to Westmoreland—after Buster and Natalie had been settled less than a year—marked the beginning of Mrs. Keaton's migration from bigger house to bigger house. Natalie was a buyer. At the height of her consumerism she spent $900 a week on clothes and assorted accessories, according to Buster.[20] He did little to stop her; in fact, that fall he would arrange to have the studio pay his salary directly to Natalie—hardly the act of the aggressively independent husband he played for the movie magazines.[21] Perhaps the "Why, dear" club had gained a charter member after all.

Or perhaps Buster simply couldn't be bothered with pedestrian housekeeping. His films were hits; he assumed there would be money enough for anything—for his butler, for instance, who went by the name Caruthers. Buster had met Caruthers, né Willie Riddle, in the dining car en route to his New York wedding; he shortly hired the chef away from the railroad and made him his personal manservant, cook, and bartender.[22] The two men would become steadfast friends. Buster also had another new companion, Captain the wedding present. The so-called puppy—now well on his way to a full-grown 160 pounds— had long since commandeered half of his master's bed, and woke daily in time to drive with Buster to the studio. There, the fiercely protective police dog was banned from the set after coming to Buster's aid and flattening Joe Roberts, who was only performing his duties as a heavy. Arbuckle, playing rough on one of his visits, suffered a similar fate. The overzealous dog even seemed to hold a grudge; the ban was extended to include the projection room when Captain decided to go after Big Joe onscreen, springing from his seat to shred his flickering foe.[23]

And so Buster enjoyed the full life. He had a house, a family, a career, a butler, a dog, and a burning extracurricular passion—bridge, what Buster called Hollywood's second-favorite "indoor sport."[24] On that same wedding train to New York he had played his first hand of bridge, losing badly with his overcompetitive partner, Hiram Abrams, the president of United Artists. Abrams belittled the inexperienced

Keaton to the point that Buster walked out mid-game for fear of smacking the abusive mogul. Thoroughly embarrassed, Buster dedicated himself to mastering bridge. It became a nightly pastime. Two years later, vacationing in New York, Buster got his rematch against Abrams. The stakes were a quarter a point; after two weeks, Buster left town with $3,400 of Abrams' money.[25]

13 The Great Stone Face as *The Paleface* (1922).

In November, as Peg and Constance were making themselves at home, Buster headed to the Santa Susana Mountains to shoot his next film, a dusty western epic called *The Paleface*.[26] The short starts on a straightforward expository tack, with no sign of Keaton—a daring approach, given Buster only had two reels to pack with gags. After a long and busy prologue—a smattering of titles, cuts, and flashbacks in which an Indian tribe's land is stolen by wildcatters—we have a declaration from the Big Chief: kill the next white man that enters the village. The commotion comes to a halt. Silence. Then the gate slowly swings open—enter Buster, the wayward lepidopterist, carrying his trusty butterfly net, hot on the fluttering trail of his next trophy. Buster brilliantly milks the setup; we're pitched between delight and anxiety as he struggles (at length) to net insects before a murderous crowd. The interaction between the dogged collector and his bemused aggressors is a priceless do-si-do of misunderstanding, full of simple sardonic steps (Buster gamely joins the war dance meant to seal his fate). After much ado, Buster becomes a member of the tribe.

Again Keaton makes the most of his location. The photography is beautiful, natural, unadorned, taking in the sweep of the grassy plains, the grit of the mining trail, the desolation of the oil fields with the austere eye of a documentarian. Of course the action is anything but sober. Buster parachutes off cliffs, flops down gravel inclines, and drops into treetops. The climactic stunt involves a fall from an impossibly high rope bridge into a river. (The span is revealed in a vertigo-inducing extreme long shot.) The sequence was to be a composite of shots—after some high-wire clowning Buster falls eighty-five feet into a net (hung just out of frame), then he plunges into the river. The first half was the more dangerous. One of the crew tested the drop and broke both his shoulder and his leg. The next day, Buster made the jump anyway and landed without a scratch.[27]

Thanks to Buster, the Indians defeat the oil barons, and the drama ends with our hero giving his squaw a magnificent smooch on the lips. Then there's a title: "Two Years Later." The couple hasn't moved. Buster comes up for air, sighs, then dives right back in. Fade out.

The exuberantly happy ending fits *The Paleface*'s lightly satirical tone. Still, Buster's great western parody was yet to come. And while the film anticipates a number of outdoor Keaton spectacles, its frequent long shots and comedic use of deep space—the ingenious ways Buster travels in a crowd that's looking for him—most strongly call to mind Buster's next short, his magnum opus of the two-reel chase: *Cops*. For one reason or another, Buster was becoming particularly interested in the art of escape.

14 Publicity photo from the greatest chase in two reels, *Cops* (1922).

CHAPTER ELEVEN

Love On the Go

You—smartly dressed in a vest, porkpie, and tie—are being hounded by a herd of rabid cops for disrupting a parade you didn't mean to join (by throwing a bomb you didn't mean to throw), and the only reason you're even out on the street is because this morning your girl informs you—out of the blue—she won't marry you until you become a big business man. Things clearly are slipping downhill; you still have those cops on your tail and that girl you want to win, and so you sprint down an alley, reach a street and turn to face your pursuers. You plant your feet: you're suddenly still, not even out of breath. It seems the jig is up. Then a car whizzes in from the left side of the screen. With Zen-like purpose, you put out your arm and grab on to the roof of the passing auto—which yanks you completely horizontal as you fly off screen right. You're in the clear! You pulled a fast one! But when you let go of the car, you've landed between two more cops—with their batons raised. And so it goes; it is turning into a very bad day . . .

Cops, which Buster began shooting during the Christmas season of 1921, is just about a funny chase in the way that *The Playhouse* is just about a vaudeville show.[1] The film—arguably *the* iconic comedy chase—tests whether the merits of multiplication ever plateau. (If one cop chasing Buster is funny, then two cops would be funnier . . .) By the end of the film, hundreds upon hundreds of cops are after our hapless hero—a spectacle of breathless flight, of a plucky one against a relentless many. In Buster's signature fashion, the spontaneous, explosive chase has at its heart a scrupulous geometry. *Cops* achieves an effortless union of disparities—of controlled folly, of dark humor, of madcap logic. It is a quintessential example of the whirling kinetics that drive a Keaton film, in which not just the medium but the human body—the permutations of the sinews, the shock of the limbs—seems infinitely elastic, an unruly instrument to be wielded with a cheeky kind of grace.

The film starts small, with a seemingly familiar scene of prison drama. We open on Buster behind bars, dejected, talking to his girl on the outside. As she makes to leave, she offers him a disheartening handshake; he doffs his hat and sags once again against the bars that separate them. Then we get a wider shot: Buster's not in jail—he simply is leaning against the massive front gate to her house. She turns in the driveway and delivers her ultimatum: "I won't marry you until you become a big business man." At that, Buster walks off, agitated. The girl's line has the dramatic density of a Shakespearean opening, singling out the simple sticking point that will expand to disastrous ends.

As Buster ponders this latest setback, he notices a giant man drop his wallet. Buster tries to return the property, but instead of thanks he gets a shove in the chest. The man hails a cab and trips over the running board. Again Buster assists the stranger but receives nothing but rudeness in return, so he pickpockets the wallet and steals the cab. As the man stands fuming on the sidewalk, his jacket opens to reveal a badge. Thus we get our first irate cop, big bad Joe Roberts.

Buster, now a man of some means thanks to the contents of the wallet, embarks on his journey to financial accomplishment. Unfortunately, our venture capitalist is soon grifted by an operatic con, who sells Buster a sidewalk's worth of household goods with a sob story about eviction, poverty, and hungry mouths to feed. (They in fact belong to another man, who is in the process of moving and has piled his possessions outside to await the moving man.) Buster buys the junk to prove himself a "good" businessman, conflating the moral and the economic sense of the word. To haul off his new load, Buster engages in another equally confused transaction in which he purchases an old horse and cart for $5. The family, seeing Buster's new rig, assumes he is the moving man, and does the job of loading the cart for him. Perplexed—but grateful— Buster settles down to watch. Things seem to be looking up.

Thus Buster sets off, his possessions teetering over his head, his progress at the discretion of a mulish old nag with false teeth (with whom Buster shares a touching amount of empathy). Keaton quickly outfits his buggy with some customized touches, ranging from the practical (a boxing glove attached to the accordion arm of a tie-rack, to better signal his turns) to the ludicrous (a pair of headphones for the nag, so that Buster can phone in his instructions). Buster manages to flatten a traffic cop (twice) with his turn signal, but the real problems come when Buster and his joke of a cart unwittingly fall in with a police parade. Incongruous as they are, they almost pull it off—Buster acknowledging the crowd with regal composure—until a wooly anarchist lobs a bomb from a rooftop. Below, Buster is searching for a match for his cigarette. When the sizzling bomb plops at his side, he simply picks it up, lights his smoke off the fuse, discards the bomb over his shoulder, and—blam!— all hell breaks loose. The ranks topple like dominos; Buster's horse sprints off, overturning the cart and dumping his master at the mercy of the cops, who swarm the wreckage like fire ants.

Buster's girl and her father (who happens to be the mayor) are in the reviewing stand and witness the deed. In the pandemonium— galloping cops, geysering fire hydrants—the platform empties. There has been no sign of Buster. The stampeding crowd clears the foreground. Inexplicably, the shot stays on the still, soggy stand; deep in the background, an abandoned umbrella stirs, then rises to reveal— Buster. The horde rushes back onto the platform, but our man eludes them. The mayor barks an order, "Get some cops to protect our policemen!" And so the game is afoot.

The mayor's words are the second to last in the film.[2] What follows is essentially five minutes of pure visual ballet, as Keaton manages— by exacting, nerve-racking turns—to stay one step ahead of the pack. Buster bobs and weaves at full tilt, diving through legs and dodging open-field tackles. He runs at the camera and away from the camera and darts into frame from a variety of offscreen angles—always trailing a complement of cops, like the pied piper of law enforcement. But while the sequence rides on the visceral thrill of movement—thundering cops, churning legs, speeding Buster—not everything is bluff and bluster. The chase is perfectly punctuated with quiet moments: Buster walks, he stops, he hides (in trash barrels, in parked cars, in luggage trunks)—often he is the calm in the storm. At one point he seesaws on a ladder straddling a fence, before being launched, catapult-style. (He lands on Joe Roberts, of all people.)

Not only is the chase brilliantly syncopated, but it is deftly framed—in easy, geometrical compositions that often themselves serve as punchlines. His back to the camera, Buster rushes at a wedge-shaped building, which comes to a point in a door. He peers down each sidewalk; cops are converging from both sides—he's trapped in a vice. Just as the police are upon him, Buster saunters through the door. The men crisscross, racing down opposite walks. With the coast momentarily clear, Buster exits the building. Of course Buster won't always seek shelter in the foreground; *Cops* reveals Keaton's developing interest in the use of deep space, often mining the comic potential of an overlooked background (think of Buster under the umbrella). The long shot—fast becoming one of Buster's favorite vantage points—also adds to the fun. A wide view suits a big chase—exhibiting the cast of thousands in all its numeric glory—but Buster doesn't just milk the sight gag. He positions the camera to multiple revelatory effects. In a kind of god's-eye view, Buster scurries down a wide boulevard towards the camera. A lone patrolman waits for him in the foreground; a marvelous flood of cops is on Buster's heels. Buster ducks the loner and races under the camera. Waves of blue run off towards our right. Beat. The street is empty. Then, inexplicably, Buster veers in from the left, heading under us and back the way he came (with the same unwieldy mob in tow).

The film's fourth-quarter scamper is a sight to behold—a treasure in its own right—but the excellence of the chase is outshone by its astonishing finale. Fresh off his unpredictable U-turn, Buster ducks into a wide doorway. A hundred cops pour in behind him. A wider shot reveals it to be the door of the police station. The force descends en masse; in successively distant shots, streams of cops plug the entrance. The crowd crams itself in. As the door finally swings shut on the empty plaza, one cop slips out and locks everyone inside. It's Buster—in uniform! He tosses the key into a trashcan, then dusts his hands of the whole operation. Suddenly, he spies his girl walking down the street. Hopeful, he lifts his hat. She snubs him, passing with her nose in the air. Without a moment's hesitation, Buster retrieves the key. He opens the door and—as he turns to face the camera—lets himself be hoisted over the cops' heads and dragged inside. Then come the words THE END—with an illustration of a porkpie *resting on a tombstone.*

The ending—with its strangely moving twist—is sad, dark, and funny. By highlighting the absurdity of the escalation (How has it come to this?), Buster gives his chase the perfect comic kicker. The race ends—permanently—and we in the seats are left with unsettling closure, a final, unexpected laugh against folly.

In real life that final laugh was somewhat pointed. Less than eighteen months earlier—at noon on Thursday, September 16, 1920—an explosion had ripped through New York's financial district, spewing two-inch iron slugs, killing thirty people and wounding 300. The TNT bomb had been concealed in a one-horse cart abandoned at the intersection of Broad and Wall Streets, the fiscal crossroads formed by the US Assay Office, the Sub-Treasury, and the J. P. Morgan building. The scene was grisly—strewn bodies, eviscerated horses, smoking metal and glass—and the panic immediate: the Stock Exchange, only 200 or so feet away, closed immediately, and detectives were dispatched to guard the homes of prominent capitalists. The ensuing unrest fueled the country's growing Red Scare; the bombing was assumed to have been a communist or an anarchist plot.[3] In a nation flushed with low-grade hysteria, with a nervous public struggling against the daily corrosions of a dim paranoia, it seems bold of Keaton to riff on tragedy, to let a bomb-thrower loose in his comedy—even worse to make it funny. But Buster was whistling in the graveyard—brightly, brilliantly so, insisting that laughter is the stubborn reward of grim times.

While perhaps few comedians would have taken such a risk, Buster enjoyed his audience's utmost confidence. The new year began with an article in *The New York Times* listing no fewer than five Keaton films among the best of 1921.[4] (Crowds—and critics—would continue the applause at New York's Rivoli Theater, where *Cops* stole the show from a maudlin stinker called *While Satan Sleeps.*[5]) However, on the set of the film, not everyone was bowing to Keaton's directorial will. His four-legged cohort, bought by the studio to play the pathetic part in front of the cart, was giving the crew more trouble than expected. Buster wanted to have a scene in which he and the horse switched roles—Buster tugging at the bit, the horse lounging in the wagon—but the animal refused to be led up a ramp and into the cart. A crane was brought in, but the horse resisted so violently that all attempts to lift her off the ground failed. Over the weekend, Buster contemplated the ridiculous—finding an equine double. When the director arrived at the studio on Monday, the headstrong horse had another surprise waiting for him: a newborn colt. The nag's name was Onyx; Buster christened her foal on sight—and Onyxpected became the new studio pet.[6] Subsequently Keaton and his co-star got along fine.

Meanwhile, at home, Buster had another willful expectant mother to contend with—as well as his intractable mother-in-law, two hyper-social sisters-in-law, and a formidable brother-in-law (who was also his boss). Keaton's next film would be a smaller, quieter, indoor comedy, a poison-pen ode to familial suffocation. It was called *My Wife's Relations*.

Buster is a poor taffy-puller who one day—in a swift series of mix-ups—finds himself unwittingly wed to a grouchy bear of a woman (played by the excellent Kate Price). The scene in which the two strangers are married by a judge—who only speaks Polish—is made priceless by Buster's unmotivated, uncomprehending nod (*why not?*) when asked if he takes this woman to be his wife. (The wheels of fate turn on our silliest whims.) Dissatisfied with her catch, the angry bride drags her undersized husband home to the in-laws, her father and four oak-hewn brothers of menacing health (a cop, a man with a pickaxe, Big Joe Roberts, and a stout bruiser in a bowler). The inspection of the groom—a hands-on, head-to-toe once-over in which Buster is found sorely lacking—seems to poke at Talmadge snobbery. In the film, the family runs roughshod over Buster until they mistakenly "discover" that he is worth a great deal of money. The clan scraps their tenement for a swankier pad (with butler), occasioning a slew of fish-out-of-social-class jokes. When the in-laws learn Buster isn't the cash cow they thought he was, the family frost turns murderous. Keaton barely manages to escape the house; the parting shot is of him sitting on the caboose of the *Reno Limited*, headed for a quick divorce.

While not a great film, *My Wife's Relations* is a cheerful deviation from standard comedy casting (the star, his rival, a cutie caught in the middle). There is no sweet, slight girl in the picture; the love interest, such as she is, is a hefty, imposing gal with a tattoo. Kate Price was a personable character with a quick sailor's tongue. On set she enjoyed a salty ad-lib—coming home to a family clamoring for food, she bellows, "Dinner my ass! Look what I married!"[7] (She goes unquoted in the titles.) The scene in which she and Buster spend their first night in matrimonial twin beds is also quite funny. Fed up with the abuse, Buster—in a stirring, feeble moment of acting out—smacks Price's sleeping rump, then pretends to be dozing himself. He strikes repeatedly, each time growing bolder, until she shatters a pitcher on his head, knocking him cold.

Perhaps an exercise in wish fulfillment, the film clearly picks at threads from Buster's personal life: overwhelming in-laws, class and social discomfort, the lunacies of ostentation (particularly in housing). Fittingly, the Keaton-Talmadge clan would make the move to Westmoreland Place just before *My Wife's Relations* debuted in May.[8]

Buster's next film was less social satire and more straightforward gag-and-prop clowning—it too is something of a disappointment. Titled *The Blacksmith*, the film reuses bits from such Arbuckle collaborations as *The Garage* and *Back Stage*, and the jokes feel more recycled than refined. Full of impossible gags, the episodic, cartoonish short is often cited as a ham-handed throwback to the earlier Arbuckle and Sennett styles.[9] Buster plays the beloved village smithy, though of a less stalwart breed than the one in the famous Longfellow poem (which opens the movie). Joe Roberts is on hand to cause trouble, as is Onyxpected's mother from *Cops*.[10] Buster shoes the horse with all the savior faire of a department-store clerk, much to his customer's delight; the well-trained equine preens magnificently in horseshoes of her choosing. In general, Buster's customers tend to be prissy neatniks, and in the course of two reels he manages to dirty the white horse and wreck a white Rolls-Royce (the latter destruction beautifully wrought by fire, oil, sledgehammer, and swinging engine block). Surprisingly, audiences didn't enjoy the demolition of the car; they resented the wasteful destruction of something so expensive, something they themselves could never afford. The saving grace of *The Blacksmith* is its conclusion. Buster and his girl have bested their adversaries and hopped a train; victorious, they recede into the distance, waving. An illustrated postscript announces, "Many a honeymoon express has ended thusly," and an iris opens to show a distant train toppling off a high track, plunging to its doom. A dour surprise! Then Buster steps into the frame and picks up the wreckage. A full shot reveals Keaton at home—with pipe and smoking jacket—demonstrating his model train to his happy wife and baby. He yawns and reaches to pull down a shade that reads, THE END.

The bitter feint of the finale—a stab, then smile at domesticity—nicely caps the film's comic build-up. While the jokes may be lackluster, they at least get bigger and faster as the film wears on, establishing a visual and comedic rhythm that is rarely interrupted by titles. But for all the film's skillful pacing and amusing motifs (white horse, white car), Buster appeared to be in a bit of a slump.

It seemed a good time to get out of town. Buster went north, trading soft, sunny LA for the cold austerities of Truckee, California. He was seeking snow for his next film, *The Frozen North*, and he wasn't disappointed—he found little in the High Sierras that wasn't frozen (after all, it was Donner Party country).[11] Inspired by his stark surroundings, Buster turned out one of his most antic parodies. His target: William S. Hart, a popular celluloid cowboy who had condemned Arbuckle publicly during the scandal.[12] Hart was known for making histrionic westerns in which he—the tough, tortured hero—shot, kissed, and sobbed with deadly severity. The farce begins with Buster emerging from the subway into the middle of a frozen lake (the end of the line). Wearing a ridiculous double-holstered manly getup, this cowboy, we quickly learn, is fabulously amoral—equal parts a thief, murderer, cry-baby, wife-beater, and sleaze. He returns home to find his spouse canoodling with another man. Buster clutches his heart while a plump glycerin tear rolls down his cheek; he promptly shoots them both, then realizes he had the wrong house (*c'est la vie*). The hyperactive narrative takes off from there, involving bears, sleds, fishing, girls, and Big Joe

Roberts on skis—all the while making the most of the film's photogenic environs and satirical license. Buster performs some snowy pratfalls—some of which were picked up by Chaplin in *The Gold Rush*, also filmed in Truckee—and manages to lampoon Theda Bara and Erich von Stroheim along the way.[13] (The only one who didn't take the ribbing well was Hart; after seeing *The Frozen North*, he didn't speak to Keaton for two years.[14]) The film ends with Buster lying dying, shot in the back by his wife. As he takes final aim with his revolver at either the woman he captured or the Mountie who saved her—it's not clear—the scene dissolves to show Buster sitting in an empty movie theater, mowing them down in his dreams, before he's woken by an usher.

Keaton had a hit. *The New York Times* went so far as to praise the burlesque in two separate reviews.[15] (Interestingly, in one, the reviewer pauses to take cheap shots at Arbuckle, labeling him a best-forgotten clown and gleefully predicting his career would be eclipsed by a chubby comedian named Walter Hiers, whose film that week happened to share the bill with Buster's. Would-be soothsayers beware the longevity of print.)

Returning to Los Angeles, Buster found the new Westmoreland house fully prepared to receive another occupant. Natalie had finished decorating the nursery with help from her mother and sisters. The room was stuffed with orchids, sweet peas, blankets, and hand-sewn baby clothes; there was a pink wicker crib with a satin bed festooned with pink ribbons. Natalie had decided on a girl. But on the evening of June 2, 1922, she and Buster got a boy, and while it is quite unfair to say she was disappointed, she did refuse to switch the ribbons on his baby clothes from pink to blue. That was fine with Buster—he was the proud father of Joseph Talmadge Keaton, named for the six generations of firstborn Keaton boys before him. Captain dutifully stood watch over the crib, forgoing his daily trips to the studio; Grandpa Keaton paraded streams of visitors through the nursery, pleased to introduce them to Joe Keaton VII. Little did he know the baby would never be a "Joe." Natalie had taken to calling her son Jimmy, and eventually had him christened as James, a name she preferred. Buster was deeply hurt.[16]

15 Publicity photo from Keaton's last silent short, *The Love Nest* (1923).

CHAPTER TWELVE

Six-Reel Star

Love is the unchanging axis on which the World revolves.

The Three Ages (1923)

In the summer of 1922, Jimmy wasn't the only youngster to be named after his father. In the Mexican border town of Tijuana, a few miles south of San Diego, there was a Buster Keaton Jr. running free. The chestnut colt was beginning what would become a storied race-track career; in the next four years he would rack up more victories than any of his competitors. That was also the summer the Hollywood smart set spent crossing the border to Tijuana; the sunlit Baja pueblo had blossomed into an adult amusement park, with all the cocktails, gambling, bull fights, and recreational irresponsibilities a vacationing American could ask for. Prohibition-weary Californians flocked south, Buster and Natalie included. They—along with the Angers— would be on hand to watch Buster's two-year-old namesake break the track record at the Debutante Stakes. Joe Schenck eventually would own an interest in that Keaton, too, whose winning days were cut short when he went lame mid-race. (Myra would claim he was pushed too hard.) When the horse died, in 1929, part-owner Norma Tal-madge sent a telegram.[1]

Not even fatherhood could slow the two-legged Buster down. When Jimmy was born, he had already begun work on *Daydreams*, one of the four films he would crank out in almost as many months.[2] In the movie, Buster is a country boy who goes to the city to make good and win the hand of his hometown girl—else he promises he will shoot himself (to the satisfaction of her father, Joe Keaton). The ludicrous premise is established with matter-of-fact haste, and the rest of the film unfolds through Buster's vaguely upbeat letters home. Reading them, the girl envisions his great success, while we are privy to the mean reality. While she thinks he has become by turns a surgeon, a financier, a Shakespearean actor, and a police chief, we see him working in a pet hospital, sweeping up Wall Street, dancing (clumsily) in a third-rate chorus, and going on the lam from the cops. The police chase begins with a brilliantly extended tracking shot of Buster (in his chorus getup) slowly accelerating from a nonchalant stroll to an arm-pumping sprint, with a cop behind him, step for step. Naturally Buster ends up all wet, and so, beaten by the city, he mails himself home to his girl. She, recognizing a failure by his black eye, drops her gaze. Her father pointedly sets out his pistol before leading his daughter into the next room. They wait. Blam! Smoke curls into the parlor. The girl buries her head in her father's shoulder. Then Buster steps in to return the gun, confiding, "I missed." Another letdown? The father sends him through the window.

There is a moment in *Daydreams* in which Buster seeks refuge inside a giant paddlewheel. He is safely hidden from his pursuers—until the boat starts up. He tries to run in place, but the treadmill quickly outpaces him; Buster winds up latching on to a spoke and riding the wheel. The picture of frothy futility, he spins round and round, receiving his periodic dunking. That was how Keaton began to see his career. He was bucking up against the narrative limitations of two-reels. Bored with the format, he could churn out a gut-buster in record time, but it was only more of the same. He felt penned in, forced to go in for his monthly soaking. He could be funnier than that. In his words, he wanted "room to develop the thing. To wring it out. To really say it."[3] He resumed pestering Joe Schenck—it was time to make features.

Again Schenck said no. The contract with First National wasn't fulfilled; Keaton still owed them four more shorts. And so it was once more unto *The Electric House*—Buster wanted to go another round against that ankle-breaking escalator. Not a piece of the old bad-luck set remained—it had been completely destroyed—so he went back to the drawing board. This time, with the help of Fred Gabourie, he constructed the perfect prop house, fully mechanized with all the creature comforts of modernity. The film's plot, such as it is, is mere pretext: Buster is a botanist mistakenly hired to electrify a mansion. There's a girl to win, a father to impress, and a genuine electrician to battle, but the real co-star is the house itself. (The exterior shots of which are of Keaton's Westmoreland home.[4]) Buster, the kind of guy more interested in the flower in a girl's hair than the hair (or the girl), somehow manages to electrify the stairs, library, bathtub, bed, pool, pool table, dinner table, dishwasher, a handful of chairs, and a sliding door. Hilarity and complications ensue, however, when Buster's home improvements turn against him—most notably that malevolent escalator. But the slapstick gadgetry, while clever, can't sustain the film. *The Electric House* is a one-note song. At least it's consistent: Buster never woos his sweetheart; after being flushed through a drainpipe, he ends up on a bank with the engineer. Even then gadgets trump girls.

The paddlewheel turned once more and Buster dispatched another short subject—on the dangers of ballooning without a license. *The Balloonatic* (rhymes with lunatic) was a rote Keaton effort involving another massive prop, a hot-air balloon, which takes off—sans pilot—with Buster riding on top. (He had climbed up to fasten on a "Good Luck" pennant.) After crash-landing in the wilderness, our hero demonstrates himself to be a sweetly inept woodsman. There are many hunting and fishing routines, the best of which involves Buster shooing fish into a rivulet, then building a dam to trap them. (The outdoorsy bits are all the more amusing given that Keaton was a crack shot and a skilled and dedicated angler.) The girl he encounters fares much better in the wild. She is amusingly competent under duress; at one point, impatient with her hopeless would-be savior, she wrestles a steer to the ground. After Buster defeats a pair of bears the girl comes around, and the two lovers drift off into the sunset in a canopied canoe, Buster strumming a ukulele and positioning himself for smooches. However, they are not out of the woods yet. In a film oversaturated with sight gags, Buster has saved the best for last. Blithely unaware, the couple is on a death course, poised to slip over a lofty waterfall. But as we watch their progress in a long shot (a handy piece of miniature model-work), the canoe sails straight past the drop. Buster points to the balloon attached to the canopy as they float into the skies.

Buster continued floating in *The Love Nest*, the next delivery from the Keaton Studio. Spurned by a woman, he goes to sea in a one-man covered boat. After several days, he is taken aboard a whaling ship run by maniacal Captain Joe Roberts, a man in the habit of killing his stewards. In this watery farce, Buster—the new steward—swabs the deck, shoots a fish, and hauls in a harpooned whale. After leading an unintentional, short-lived mutiny, he is thrown overboard. (Under the cover of darkness, Keaton returns to sink the ship, presumably drowning the captain.) Having slipped away in the lifeboat, Buster happens upon a floating naval target, from which he decides to fish. Target practice commences, and the artillery blasts Keaton high into the air. As he hurtles back down towards the water, he wakes to find himself flopping on the floor of his boat—the whaling adventure was just a dream. However, waking life is no better. Hopelessly adrift, his provisions depleted, Buster expires theatrically on the prow of his boat. Then along comes a lady swimmer, in a cap, doing the sidestroke. Noticing her, Buster gets up. He peers around the cover of his boat—it is still tied to the dock, bobbing in place.

The Love Nest is the only film on which Buster alone is credited for the writing and directing.[5] Despite the black humor of the whaling sequences and the well-managed final surprise, it is a mediocre short. It would be his last.

That November, Buster and Natalie went east to meet a boat. The *Mauretania* docked in New York City on the 24th; arriving on the transatlantic steamer was Buster's brother-in-law boss, fresh off a European vacation cum royal-meet-and-greet with the Talmadges.[6] The board of Buster Keaton Productions was scheduled to meet in Manhattan the following week. There, the shareholders decided to grant Keaton his wish—he could go into features. The final two-reeler due to First National would never be made. Marcus Loew agreed to distribute the new batch of feature-length Keaton comedies, and Schenck immediately raised his star's salary from $1,000 to $2,000 a week, plus a quarter share of the profits. Henceforth Buster would make two features a year, one released in the spring, the other in the fall. He would have eight weeks to shoot each film, with plenty of time in between to cut, tweak, tinker, and dream.[7] Buster's persistence had paid off.

The board's decision was not particularly bold. Charlie Chaplin and Harold Lloyd already had made the switch to features, with great economic success.[8] The shareholder's change of heart was more a case of financial prudence than artistic imperative. Nonetheless, it was a tremendous vote of confidence for Keaton. The year 1922 would be remembered for many things. Americans had witnessed the publication of T. S. Eliot's *The Waste Land*, James Joyce's *Ulysses*, and Sinclair Lewis's *Babbitt*, along with the discovery of the tomb of King Tut, the formation of the Soviet Union, the first network radio broadcast (of the October World Series), and the birth of the *Reader's Digest*. Perhaps less famously, but of certain importance, at the tail end of 1922 Buster Keaton got his chance. He could finally *really say it*, whatever it was.

16 Buster and his caveboy caddy in a publicity still from *The Three Ages* (1923).

For their first feature, the boys at 1025 Lillian Way would turn to that old Keaton favorite, the burlesque. Their prey: D. W. Griffith's colossal 1916 historical spectacle, *Intolerance*. To make his point about the poverty of the human condition, Griffith had tracked prejudice through four separate ages. Buster would only need three. His film, *The Three Ages*, would remark upon the constancy of love, as seen in the Stone Age, the Roman Age, and the Modern Age. In each era Buster plays the underdog suitor in pursuit of a girl; as the narrative crosscuts between the parallel love stories, our man—by persistent virtue of his wit—emerges triumphant. The film's tripartite structure wasn't just part of the send up. Keaton was hedging his bets; should the six-reel film prove unpopular, it could be sliced neatly into three two-reelers.[9]

Bigger movies required bigger stories, bigger effects, bigger laughs—which meant a bigger crew. By the time *The Three Ages* went into development, the Keaton Studio had acquired three gifted comics; the jolly trio were the greatest gagmen Buster would ever have. Joseph Mitchell, an ex-vaudevillian, was new to the bunch, while the other two—Clyde Bruckman and Jean Havez—were sheep returning to the fold. Both had worked for Comique: Havez, who appears briefly in *The Goat*, had been lured away to work with Harold Lloyd; Bruckman, the former sportswriter, recently had written the titles for a Viola Dana film.[10] It was a top-notch, close-knit scenario department. They would congregate after hours in Keaton's kitchen, often four or five nights a week, working jokes and eating hamburgers until three in the morning.[11] With cameraman Elgin Lessley at the crank, and technician Fred Gabourie in the workshop, Buster's dream team was now in place.

Keaton's new feature was meant to gain from a bit of stunt casting, though in reality the effort backfired. In the late fall of 1922, Margaret Leahy, a blond British shop girl, had won a beauty contest sponsored by the London *Daily Sketch*. Thousands had entered. The judging took weeks. The prize: a leading role in Norma Talmadge's next film, *Within the Law*. Vacationing in Europe, Norma was on hand to pick the winner; she declared Leahy to have the perfect movie face.

Then, after it was shipped to Hollywood, Schenck and others found the face couldn't act. The director of *Within the Law* threatened to walk after only three days. Schenck was in a pickle. That January it was discovered that Leahy possessed "unusual comedy ability." She would now star in the new Buster Keaton feature.[12]

Buster had wanted Constance for the role; after all, she had been in *Intolerance.* But Schenck balked at putting two stars in a single film; it seemed excessive.[13] He was also nervous about a lawsuit—the British woman had to be in something. Thus Buster picked up a beauty queen.

Playing opposite the handsome but dismal actress (whose scenes had to be re-shot ad infinitum) was Wallace Beery, a popular character actor of the day.[14] A more bankable rival for Buster than Joe Roberts, Beery was further protection at the box office (Roberts was relegated to playing the girl's father).[15] Rounding out the notables in the cast—conspicuous more for her stature than her stagecraft—was the 6'3" Blanche Payson. New York's first policewoman, Payson plays a robust cavegirl who successfully repels Buster's attempt to drag her off by her hair.[16]

The Three Ages benefited from rich production values; the spoof had to make at least a passable attempt to match the opulence of its blockbuster predecessor. We begin with the Stone Age, and after the manly, bearded Beery is introduced riding astride an elephant, we see Buster, reclining on some sort of moving rock. With his smooth cheeks and foppish locks, he's clearly a caveman of the more romantic sort—though it turns out he enjoys similarly impressive transportation, a rather friendly looking brontosaurus, which lets Buster ride on its head. Cartoonist Max Fleischer was brought in to create the dinosaur effects, which were achieved by using miniature models and stop-action animation. The film also employs sophisticated "glass shots" to recreate the many splendors of Rome. For a chariot race around the Colosseum floor, Gabourie blended a few tiers of real amphitheater with carefully placed panes of glass on which the rest of the background was detailed.[17] The result is a convincingly overwhelming Roman vision.

The grandeur of his production notwithstanding, Keaton remained the same delicate director, with the same tireless compulsions and consuming aesthetic ethic. He firmly believed in the fidelity of the long shot. At one point during a prehistoric rock fight, Buster scurries into frame and is confronted by an attacker. The thug heaves a stone at him, which Buster bats back with his club—sending a line drive into the man's gut. Buster races past his downed enemy. The altercation is viewed in a continuous overhead shot. Like the improbable golfing accident in *Convict 13*, Buster refused to cut around the issue (rock thrown, cut, rock batted, cut, rock hits stomach)—the bit had to be authentic. It took seventy-six takes and hours of shooting to get it right; the sequence lasts about five seconds.[18]

Equally real—painfully so, Keaton would say—was the shot of the modern-day Buster misjudging a daring rooftop-to-rooftop leap. Springing from a plank he had laid over the edge, Keaton meant to land on the other building; instead, he fell short, his fingers barely grasping the cornice of the building as his body slapped into a wall of brick—before dropping thirty-five feet into a net. He was in bed for three days. As usual, the cameras hadn't shied away from the accident; they simply kept cranking, and the resultant footage was so good the scene was written into the movie. When Buster recovered, he filmed an aftermath to the fall in which he plunges through two awnings before grabbing onto a drainpipe, which pulls away from the building, swinging Buster through an open window and down a pole into a firehouse. Buster claimed the unintended stunt got the biggest laugh of the picture.[19] The episode reinforced Keaton's faith in shooting with a disciplined crew—and no script.

In another sequence culled from reality, Buster sits slumped at a table in a nightclub, passed-out drunk. He has unwittingly polished off a pitcher of booze; he hadn't seen the man next to him dump the contents of his hip flask into it—Buster thought it was water. Spotting an opportunity, Beery has a waiter deliver an anonymous note to a girl sitting at another table. The note is intercepted by her quick-tempered companion; it tells the girl to ditch her fellow and meet the author outside—he's the one sitting right behind them, pretending to be asleep. Poor Buster gets belted in the face for that one. In real life, the victim of the gag was Slim Summervile, a lanky Keystone Kop. The scene: the Vernon Country Club. Bobby Dunn, who had paid the bartender to spike Slim's highballs with double shots of whiskey, wrote the note. The jealous boyfriend was a real brute; when Slim awoke on the sidewalk, Dunn told him there had been an earthquake.[20]

The Three Ages is filled with such sharp interactions. In a curious scene of Latin love, Buster and a Roman girl drop from a spicy carnal embrace right into the neutral wrestling position, from which they grapple Greco-Roman style. With a handy flip, she pins him. Sadly, Buster fares no better with his true love's parents. Judging him by the standard of each age—strength, rank, wealth—they find him unsatisfactory. Nevertheless, Buster rises to the occasion, besting his rival in successive showdowns—a Paleolithic duel, a snowy chariot race, and a big-time football game. The rival then takes revenge and abducts the girl, necessitating a last-minute rescue from Buster. In the Stone Age, the liberation is capped by a close-up shot of the rapturous girl being dragged off by her hair. Interestingly, it is one of the very few scenes for which Buster required a double. Conscious of his missing fingertip, he had a stand-in pull Leahy (who rolled on a hidden dolly).[21]

Taken as a whole, the film suffers from the timidity of its structure—a clear case of first time jitters. The three ages play like the two-reelers they might have become, and while there are some bright flashes, the film relies too heavily on wacky anachronisms that lose punch with repetition (prehistoric golf outings, stone tablet calling cards, Roman No Parking signs, sundial wristwatches, taxi meters on litters, chariot anti-theft devices, and so on and so on). However, like other lesser Keaton films, *The Three Ages* manages to go out with a bang. In an epilogue meant to show love triumphant across time, we get three domestic views. First, caveman Buster emerges from his den, trailed by his wife and a bear-skinned litter of ten or so kids. Together the couple herds off their family. Next, Buster exits his Roman villa; he calls to his wife, who escorts out a string of five well-scrubbed youth of descending size in robes and headbands. Last we open on a groomed suburban stretch, all matching houses and lawns. Out comes Buster with a cane. His well-heeled, thoroughly modern wife appears behind him, leading their beloved . . . Pekingese.

And so the unfettered modern life. *The Three Ages* was a big draw at the box-office, reportedly grossing $448,606 domestically, though given the creative bookkeeping in Hollywood, truly accurate figures are hard to come by.[22] Subjective returns were up, too. Influential critic Robert Sherwood praised Buster with gusto in his weekly column in *Life*, thanking him for distracting the world from Mussolini and banana shortages.[23] Buster had worked hard to fine-tune his achievement. Before the film was released he held eight previews, after each of which he tweaked the print based on the audience's reaction. Test-screenings were an old Arbuckle stand-by; as long as you showed the rough cut outside of Hollywood (in Long Beach, say), your gags wouldn't be stolen and you could shoot new ones as necessary.[24] While in this instance the high number of previews was due to Leahy's inexperience, post-production tampering was par for the course—nothing was static about a Keaton film. Buster claimed never to know what was funny; it was whatever made the people in the seats laugh.[25]

Keaton would next undertake a period piece. Given the mildly acidic ending of *The Three Ages*, perhaps he was temporarily uninterested in the present time of—as the film put it—"speed, need, and greed." As a coda, it is worth noting that *The Three Ages* was the last moviegoers ever saw of Margaret Leahy on the screen. Not all Cinderella stories come true; the contest winner made one film and one film only, and while the decision to give up movies was her own, the years seemed to play out a narrative of broken promise. Decades later, after torching her Hollywood scrapbooks, Leahy would kill herself with drain cleaner.[26]

17 Keaton clowning on the set of *Our Hospitality* (1923).

CHAPTER THIRTEEN

Southern Discomfort, or A Family Affair

Title card:

$\left\{\begin{array}{c}\text{"Well, my boy, you must come and}\\\text{see us again sometime."}\end{array}\right\}$

And with that, the plump, antebellum Southern gentleman seals your fate. Supper is over. It's time to go home. But the polite man in front of you happens to be the father of your girl, and he happens to be cheerfully homicidal. He wants you dead—not for anything you did (you, a stranger to these parts, hardly know the man), but simply to settle the score between your family and his, a blood feud stretching through the generations, a grudge that was never your own, one that you only recently heard about. However—and you're a bit vague on the details—it seems that while under his roof you're safe: a gentleman simply does not kill his own guests. But step outside and he—and his two sons—gleefully will shoot you. Did you happen to notice that they're armed to the teeth?

Meanwhile, the other dinner guest, the kindly parson, is making to go. Providence seems particularly cruel in the peculiar South. Dazed, you shake hands with the father, then with your girl, then with the parson, then with the brother, then the other brother, now back to the girl, then with her father again. You turn to go, but when no one's looking you toss your hat under the sofa. Has anyone seen your hat? They all begin to look. But your dog, your own best friend, is more than happy to retrieve it for you. Again you flick it under the couch. Again you are betrayed—and this time they see it happen! You demonstrate it was merely a trick: he's quite a smart dog; you were just showing off. So you bow, take a last look back at them, three of the five with hands in their pockets, fingering cold steel. You pause at the door. Perhaps another trick? The dog jumps through your arms and over your leg; you try to make him hop, but he won't, so you throw him over your leg again. While you're dreaming up his next feat, the dog starts to slip out the door—you lunge and grab your accomplice by the tail. But now the parson is saying goodbye. The father opens the door . . .

Rain! Buckets of it—and lightning!

$$\left\{ \begin{array}{c} \textit{"It would be the death of anyone} \\ \textit{to go outside tonight,"} \end{array} \right\}$$

observes the father in his honeyed drawl, as he bids the parson to stay. The girl leads the old man upstairs. You look at the rain—and before anyone can turn back to you, you're already halfway up the landing, carpetbag in hand. With a tip of your hat, you bid your hosts goodnight.

In July of 1923, the Keatons went on vacation. It being a working vacation, they brought with them a replica of an antique locomotive, passenger carriages, thirty exterior sets, a twenty-person crew, and a few miles of railroad track.[1] Their destination: Truckee, the alpine landscape in which Buster had set *The Frozen North*. This time, the Sierras were to double for the Blue Ridge Mountains; the warm, evergreen days in Truckee would stand in for the lazy Appalachian summer of yesteryear. Joe Roberts was on hand. So was Joe Keaton— with Myra, Jingles, and Louise. Natalie had even brought baby Jimmy. The family had driven up in Buster's new Packard.[2] They all were on location to film the new Keaton costume comedy about love and feuding in the Old South, *Our Hospitality*.

Natalie hadn't wanted to go to Truckee, originally. For her the out-doors held little charm. Then her husband began dangling carrots— there was a part in the film for little Jimmy, and what was more, Buster was looking to cast a leading lady. Would she be interested?[3] That sealed it—off they went.

The scenario was the brainchild of Jean Havez. The picture would riff on the infamous blood rivalry between the Hatfields and the McCoys, here changed to the Canfields and the McKays, lest there be any surviving feuders still carrying a grudge.[4] Buster would play the last of the male McKays, a city-dwelling Yankee raised in ignorance of the family feud. He travels south to claim his ancestral home, and on the train down he falls for a pretty girl, who (unbeknownst to him) is none other than the young daughter Canfield. Buster spends a bewildering day about town: he chivalrously intervenes in a domestic squabble only then to be socked by the ungrateful wife, and wherever he goes he's plagued by a curious buzzing in his ears—the Dixie mosquito? he seems to wonder. (It is the Canfields taking potshots.) After a visit to the McKay estate, he finds not all houses are alike in dignity—his is a dump. (In a model shot, we see his beau ideal of plantation life blown to smithereens.) The girl's home is much nicer; she has invited Buster to supper (and unwittingly into the lion's den). The feud comes out into the open, whereupon Buster—drawing on his new understanding of Southern hospitality—decides to become a permanent houseguest, for safety's sake.

18 "Well, my boy . . ." Buster takes leave of his murderous hosts, his girl, and the good parson in a publicity photo from *Our Hospitality* (1923). From left: Ralph Bushman, Monte Collins, Joe Roberts, Buster, Craig Ward, and Natalie Talmadge Keaton.

It is a typically rich setup, one worthy of a Keaton fugue, but from the start *Our Hospitality* is unlike any of Buster's previous work. It opens with a long prologue, which introduces the feud in grand, melodramatic strokes—a stormy night with heaving chests, expressionistic lighting, a rain-soaked duel, muzzle flares in the dark, a frightened wife, and a howling baby (Jimmy, who by the looks of it had a great set of lungs). A McKay and a Canfield kill each other. The baby, sent north for his protection, will grow up to be Buster. Almost eight minutes elapse without a joke.

Twenty years later, enter Willie McKay, Buster in a ridiculous top hat, whose first move is to mount a wonderful, outrageous, primitive pedal-less bicycle and propel himself effortlessly on two oversized wheels, his swinging feet just brushing the ground. We follow him as he glides down a bright dusty New York street, wobbling to a stop before a waistcoated "traffic cop." It is a dreamy, jaunty sequence, especially in comparison with the high drama of the prologue, and its understated humor speaks volumes about law and order in the North and South and the carefree life of a Yankee dandy. The prop was a reproduction of the Gentleman's Hobby-Horse, the first-ever bicycle; the copy was so precise that the Smithsonian Institution asked to have it after the film was released.[5] Buster's ride through town is amusing

19 Buster astride the Gentleman's Hobby-Horse built for *Our Hospitality* (1923).

(have you ever seen such a contraption?) and beautiful (how it flies!), but had this been a two-reeler, he would have smashed his bicycle by now—or at least fallen off. Something new was going on.

To wring out his clowning into six reels (and beyond), Buster knew he would have to make some changes. *Our Hospitality* couldn't unfold like a helter-skelter short. In two reels, the more gags the merrier, but a feature film needed pacing. Buster wanted to create a kind of comic escalation, in which small gags would build to larger catastrophes, and larger laughs. If you hit the audience too hard too early, where could you go from there? Furthermore, not all jokes were fair game. No more impossible gags—events could be fantastic, unlikely, extraordinary, but there always had to be a shred of plausibility. No more painting coat-hooks on walls, or diving down to China. Slip into a cartoon, and there is no real affection for the characters. Timing mattered more than ever—too much tomfoolery on the way to save the girl was considered bad form, if you really cared about the girl.[6] This kind of comic blueprint sounds more solemn and restrictive on paper than when adhered to onscreen—as Keaton's subsequent films will attest. Buster was after a more sophisticated effect; he might have been becoming something of an intuitive slapstick theorist, but he was never, ever a killjoy.

The Gentleman's Hobby-Horse wasn't the only historical marvel on the set. While the backdrops, costumes, and props were all true to the period, the pride of the production was the train Buster rides south, a replica of one of the earliest steam engines. Historical accuracy allowed the Keaton crew two locomotive options: the American *DeWitt Clinton* or the British *Rocket*. The *Rocket*'s goofy tall-spouted design made it the obvious choice, even if it meant the train was running a little far from home.[7] The narrow-gauge replica engine was hitched to a set of open-air four-wheeled carriages modified to run on rails. The flimsy tracks were laid over a diverse and humorous terrain—including fallen trees and rocks—making for a bumpy ride. When a stubborn donkey blocks the way, the light, moveable rails are dragged around him. The southern progress of this toy locomotive, with its fairy-tale carriages, is a simple steady joy; never going faster than a trotting dog (until the very end), the improbable, undulating caravan occasions a clever slew of gags and hints at the variegated rail humor to come in Buster's masterpiece, *The General.*

The *Rocket's* long-suffering engineer is played by the unmistakable Joe Keaton. After a switching error sends the coaches ahead of the engine—and crashing into town—Joe silences his fuming coachman with one of his stealth high kicks. He stands nose-to-nose with the coachman, a white-bearded fogey in a tall fuzzy hat; like quicksilver, there is a flash of leg, and the man's hat is on the ground. Diapered Jimmy Keaton filled his part equally well; the pretty infant got his on-camera motivation (cranky) from his parents, who simply let dinner come a little late.[8] It had been reported that the youngest Keaton might make his debut with Aunt Dutch, in her film *Dulcy,* but apparently father won out.[9] Buster thrilled at having three generations of Keaton boys onscreen.

Natalie, on the other hand, fails to stand out. Buster gives her a fair share of lingering shots—and certainly she is glamorous in her long tresses—but Mrs. Keaton displayed a regrettable taste for making eyes at the camera and appeared to confuse emotion with heavy breathing. In a less conspicuous bit of casting, Buster is supported by a very self-possessed dog, who, like Keaton, is scrawnier and somewhat mangier than his Southern counterparts. The faithful mutt follows his master's train all the way from New York.

As the first rushes reached Hollywood, the gang at the Keaton Studio grew worried. Where were all the gags? Was a funny train the best they had? Worse, the *Rocket* seemed to be upstaging their clown, who was playing it awfully straight. Buster consoled them over the phone—he knew what he was doing.[10] In truth, they had no cause for concern. Despite its (relatively) understated early reels, *Our Hospitality* distills the best of the Keaton shorts. All the components are there. A flooding waterfall inspires a depth-of-field joke, a daring stunt (Buster riding a galloping horse—blind—while dragging an open umbrella) morphs into a surprising sight gag, and innocent motifs escalate with damning precision (after Buster goes fishing, it isn't long before he himself hangs from a line). On top of it all, Elgin Lessley's photography was catching the wooded vistas in full summertime splendor.

Indeed, shooting in the Sierras was producing some remarkable results—not all of them intentionally scenic. The film's climactic sequence begins with Buster running the rapids of the Truckee River without a boat. During filming, he was prevented from being washed downstream by a sixty-foot wire; when the wire snapped, off he went into the whitewater. Fred Gabourie and two others scrambled after their boss, but the current was too fast—Buster shot far ahead of them. At a bend in the river, he managed to grab onto some waterside brush; Keaton hung in the foam as a school of water snakes slithered against him, then he dragged himself ashore. Eventually the crew caught up with their nearly drowned director, who only had two questions. First it was, "Did Nat see it?" Then, "Did you get it?" The reply was yes on both counts.[11]

The footage appears in the film. After Buster floats by, the Canfield daughter goes after him in a rowboat, but she falls overboard. Keaton— who has a rope around his waist—ties himself to a log; he and his girl wash downstream, where a giant waterfall awaits. Miraculously, Buster's log becomes stuck; the arm pivots, dangling him out over the falls. He shinnies up the rope to relative safety. Then comes the girl. As she is swept over the falls, Buster swings out and catches her by her arms; hanging upside down, he deposits her on a cliff. Father Canfield and his sons will return to the house, empty-handed, to find them wed.

The final acrobatic rescue didn't take place in Truckee; it was shot in Hollywood, over a swimming pool. Four eight-inch pipes supplied the waterfall; there was a net below. The breathtaking view from the falls was a fake; behind the set the crew placed a detailed illusionistic model, complete with a forest of mini trees and a river winding into the distance. The forgery goes unnoticed. To catch the floating girl (a dummy, of course) took flawless timing; twice Keaton missed and ended hanging inverted under the falls. He got so waterlogged a doctor had to drain his ears and nose. On the third try, Buster nailed the stunt.[12]

Waterfront accidents were not the only misfortunes to befall the troupe. While on location, Joe Roberts, the Keatons' longtime family friend, suffered a stroke; he was sent to Reno, where he recovered sufficiently to come back and finish filming, but he remained a weakened man. Nonetheless, Joe's performance in *Our Hospitality* is his scariest—with his feverish eyes, thick bristling moustache, and sinister ponderous gait, he is a true Southern parlor demon of the mint julep–sipping kind. Sadly, only a month after retakes were finished, the great Joe Roberts died.[13]

Trouble continued to dog the set. Baby Jimmy's eyes were harmed by the strong klieg lights; the damage wouldn't be permanent, but his work in the prologue was put on hold.[14] Further complicating matters, three weeks into the picture Natalie announced she was pregnant again; by the time the crew was ready for re-shoots, she was showing, and had to do her scenes shielded by shrubbery.[15]

Despite such adversity, *Our Hospitality* was finished by fall and released in November. It was a great and unique accomplishment—a fact that did not go unnoticed. *The New York Times* complimented Natalie and everything else in the film (having detected—and enjoyed—the comic crescendo). *Variety* called it Keaton's best and suggested it marked an advance in movie production—perhaps heralding the death of the plotless comedy. There were a few dissenting voices. Arthur E. Hancock, exhibitor at the Columbia Theater, offered some advice in an open report to *Moving Picture World*: "Better go back to two-reelers, Buster; you fit them."[16] Keaton didn't listen. Nationally, *Our Hospitality* would out-gross *The Three Ages* by nearly $100,000.[17] Buster was only getting started.

Buster, Natalie, and little Jimmy spent Christmas Day at home sitting around an enormous tree laden with presents shipped in from New York. The whole family came over, including Norma and Joe Schenck, whose birthday it was.[18] Two days earlier, it had been reported that Buster had been forced to replace the leading lady in his next film—to be called *The Misfit*—due to an illness. (Luckily for Buster, with Natalie pregnant there was no need to discuss the possibility of a follow-up to her star turn in *Our Hospitality*; instead he recruited Kathryn McGuire.) The casting update appeared just below an item announcing the fact that Norma Talmadge would wear seven hoop skirts in her next picture.[19] Still, Buster was quickly becoming the family headliner. That June, *Photoplay* had registered Norma's surprise at being identified as Buster Keaton's sister-in-law.[20]

Meanwhile, New York City was preparing to ring in the New Year as it had since time immemorial; even rumors of a special cadre of liquor agents en route from Washington did little to quell the festive anticipation. The mood on the West Coast was no different. Joe and Norma had decamped for Coronado Island, to throw a party. Harold Lloyd and his wife had gone south to Tijuana. And in LA, at the recently opened Los Angeles Biltmore, as the clock struck midnight on December 31st, there was Buster and Natalie and Constance and friends, raucously greeting 1924 as the banner year it had every right to be.[21]

In reality, it would be a year of professional success and domestic disappointment. After the joyous birth of her second child, Robert Talmadge Keaton, on February 3rd, Natalie informed Buster that she was finished with him—henceforth he was to sleep in the guest room. They had been married less than three years. Natalie's decision was supported by her sisters, who had many marriages and no children between them. As Keaton later joked, by siring two boys he had lost his "amateur standing." The pro took his case to Peg the matriarch only to have his plea dismissed—the family had spoken. Upset by Natalie's rebuff, Buster told Peg he didn't expect to forgo sex for the rest of his life. To her, and initially perhaps even to Natalie, that seemed reasonable—as long as he kept out of the way.[22] Both boys were to be baptized Catholic, as the Talmadges preferred—though Buster himself was not the religious type. (At the sight of the baptismal font, Jimmy raced through the church bawling, "Wanna be kept! Wanna be kept!" The big event at the house that week had been the cat giving birth; as was the practice of the day, all of the kittens were drowned—save one, which was kept.[23]) Despite the devoted comfort of his sons, Buster was becoming a misfit in his own home. His banishment was a nightly reminder of Natalie's disdain. Like a dutiful husband he began sublimating desire through work and even more obsessive bridge playing—though he retained a license of sorts for other extramarital extracurriculars, should the mood strike.

20 The sleuth at his day job. Publicity photo from *Sherlock, Jr.* (1924).

CHAPTER FOURTEEN

The Misfit

You, the Great Sherlock, Jr., the crime-crushing criminologist, are perched on the handlebars of a motorcycle, hot on the trail of the thieves. Your man Watson, named Gillette, is driving; you're speeding off to recover the pearls, to rescue the girl. You cut through traffic and shoot through a busy intersection—cars nearly collide at every turn. Eyes forward, you call back to Gillette, telling him to be careful.

You whiz by a row of industrious ditch-diggers, catching a face-full of dirt from each. You clear your eyes only to see that Thomas Murphy's stag party is playing tug-o-war; you drag the rope (and men) across a shallow stream. Next you're careening over a high-trestle bridge. In front of you there is a gap! But just as you come to it, two tall trucks cross underneath, their roofs forming for an instant—your instant!—a bridge. Still there's no time to relax because the unfinished trestle dead-ends in midair. As you speed towards the high open space, the bridge begins to collapse so that at the moment you reach the end you're level with the ground. Up ahead a sign reads "Street Closed"—a tree is lying across the road, but as you're about to hit it, a charge of dynamite splinters it in two. You smash through the road sign, and find there's a colossal farm vehicle turning right into your path! Only when it's facing you head on do you realize—with great relief—that its cab is raised on stilts. You zip under the cab and between the wheels. Looking ahead, you shout to Gillette,

$$\big\{\textit{"I never thought you'd make it!"}\big\}$$

By now you're out in the country, and field after field rolls over your shoulder. You're calm, impassive, slightly slumped—perhaps the worst is behind you. In the distance, a train approaches on the diagonal. You note, with some interest, that it seems to be on a collision course. You cover your eyes and ears—a narrow miss! Suddenly even closer—there's a car! It barrels past. This is getting entirely out of hand. You've had enough. You turn to rebuke Gillette, only to find that HE IS NOT THERE . . .

By January Buster was shooting *The Misfit*, later to be retitled *Sherlock, Jr.*[1] The film would become one of the greatest movies about movies ever made; it is perhaps the premier example of Keaton's exultant filmmaking, poetic imagination, and physical dexterity. It is also damn funny. Through the years, the film has inspired—and continues to inspire—a brilliant host of cinematic riffs (foremost among them, Woody Allen's *The Purple Rose of Cairo*).

Buster plays a moony projectionist trying to win his girl. The opening title tells us this is the story of a small town boy who—despite the proverbial advice to the contrary—tried to do two things well at the same time. That is, our hopeful theater employee is a wannabe detective. He is also poor, so he needs his day job, which doesn't pay enough to afford him a decent box of chocolates for his sweetheart. Buster manages what he can, however, but he is bested by the slick local sheik (his equally insolvent rival). While both men are visiting the girl, her father's watch is stolen. The culprit is the rival though Buster takes the fall—it's a frame job, and he walks right into it. Buster is disgraced. The girl is crushed, the guilty suitor elated. It is our budding sleuth's first—and biggest—case.

Joining Buster on the set was a cast of familiars. Joe Keaton played the girl's father; Buster's real-life best man, Ward Crane, was the rival. The love interest—last month's healthy substitute—was Kathryn McGuire, a former Keystoner and up-and-coming pretty young thing.[2] This time there was also the role of co-director to fill. Eddie Cline, Buster's two-reel partner, had stayed on to co-direct *The Three Ages*; he had been replaced on *Our Hospitality* by John G. Blystone, a longtime industry man. (Cline's career continued apace; after leaving Keaton, he directed many popular W. C. Fields films, including *My Little Chickadee*, co-starring Mae West.) While losing Cline meant losing a chum, the cinematic impact had been unnoticeable—it was Keaton who called the shots. And so for *Sherlock, Jr.*, Buster brought back an old friend, the man who had gotten him into the game in the first place: Roscoe.

In his autobiography, Buster says he offered the blameless black-listed director the job because Arbuckle was penniless and depressed.

Schenck had paid Roscoe's legal tab, but work was not forthcoming for America's least-favorite forgotten clown. Enter Buster. While it is unclear whether Arbuckle directed the whole of *Sherlock, Jr.*, or only the early sequences (Buster claims the scandal had made his friend an insecure man, impossible to work with), it must have been refreshing for a moment—however fleeting—for Buster to be back where he started, working with the rotund enthusiast, dizzy again with the idea of making a living out of light.[3] The picture brims with the excitement of going to the movies; perhaps it's some of that old Comique innocence coming through.

Framed for the theft of the watch, then banished from the girl's home, Buster doesn't know what to do. He spies his rival leaving the house and, following How To Be A Detective rule #5—*shadow your man closely*—takes off in close pursuit. Our literal-minded gumshoe falls perfectly in step, mere inches behind his suspect, and we follow their progress in a long tracking shot. Sudden stops, starts, trips—nothing throws off Buster, whose legs move like pistons in synch. When Crane tosses his cigarette over his shoulder, Buster intercepts it in the air, then takes a puff. The matchless bodily precision will be echoed later by larger, faster mechanical precision—as footraces give way to motorized escapades (a typical Keaton escalation). Unfortunately, Buster's man gives him the slip, and our dejected projectionist returns to his theater to put on tonight's feature, which, fittingly, is a melodrama about stolen pearls and lost love.

The house is full, and in his booth Buster threads the reel. Wheels turn, light flickers, and the tall alien box comes alive. As the credits roll, the audience settles in; so does Buster, and as he leans against the backup projector, he slowly drifts off. What happens next is pure magic. There is Buster, asleep on his stool; suddenly, he splits in two, as a ghostly version of himself wakes and rises to his feet. Ignoring the solid sleeping Buster, the ethereal self peers out into the darkness. The movie seems to be playing on the screen as normal: a man and a woman stand at the base of a staircase. They turn their backs to the camera, there is a slight dissolve, and when they face forward again, they look strangely, unmistakably familiar. It is

Buster's girl—and the rival! The phantom Buster tries to slap the real Buster awake, but his hand passes through him. Onscreen, the girl storms off. Realizing he's alone in this, Buster's double puts on his hat, walks into the audience, and politely takes a seat. All eyes are on the screen. The rival is grabbing at the girl! In a long shot looking down the length of the theater, we see Buster get up from his seat, walk down the aisle, climb over the organist, and *jump straight into the movie!* The rival shoves him right back out, sending Buster tumbling down into the theater. (In the booth, the sleeping Buster experiences a slight jolt.) Once again Buster jumps into the screen, but not before the scene has changed. Now he stands before a house. He knocks on the door, but no one answers, and as he walks down the front steps the film cuts to . . . a garden at night. Now Buster stands on a short pedestal; still stepping forward, he falls and crashes on his head. Puzzled, he makes to sit on the pedestal as we cut to . . . a daytime street. The pedestal gone, Buster falls backwards as people and cars engulf him. He starts to march off to the left of the frame when suddenly . . . it's a cliff. Buster teeters at the edge, waving his arms. He peers over the precipice, only to find himself . . . in the jungle, gazing into the eyes of a lion. Sandwiched between two beasts, he slowly steps away as we cut to . . . the desert. Buster stands in a shallow hole. He steps out only to leap back—as a train roars in from offscreen. After it passes, he mounts a small sandy mound, surveys the horizon . . . and discovers he's on a rock in the middle of the ocean. A wave crashes into him. He dives into the water . . . only now it's a snow bank. Buster leans against a tree . . . and topples back into that garden again. What hellish film editor is this? And why does the organist—unhelpful wretch—continue to play? Mercifully, the scene fades out. It then fades in on the rival and the girl, back in the house. The camera slowly tracks forward, and the movie fills the frame . . .

Buster's phantom sleepwalk is a miraculous, shocking moment in a film that—for the past eighteen or so minutes—has been an essentially levelheaded comedy of manners. Then the ghostly Buster rises from his stool and *Sherlock, Jr.,* begins to soar. The projectionist's dream sequence was the film's raison d'être; the rest was just window dressing.[4] And while the bit would seem to fall under the category of the impossible gag, Buster's was an accommodating dogma. In dreams, you see, all bets are off.

The sequence was the kind of technical challenge Keaton lived for. The effect might be effortless and whimsical, but the execution was anything but. The two Busters were created through a flawless double exposure. (Buster sleeps; the film is rewound; Buster wakes.) That was the easy part. For the projectionist's initial leap into the picture—to save his girl—Buster and Gabourie built a raised, recessed stage in the theater where the "movie screen" was to be. They outfitted the interior and lit it brightly; in the darkened theater, the action on the stage appears to be projected. To cross the celluloid curtain, Buster simply hopped onstage. (And "cutting" between the interior of the house and the front steps entailed only stopping the camera and switching the scenery.) Buster's frenetically edited filmic romp—which begins with him tumbling off the pedestal—was much more involved. The outdoor scenes, with their lions, trains, seas, and snows, were shot separately on location, then spliced together. Before each "cut," Buster froze in place. He was measured from multiple angles using surveying instruments. Then the crew moved on to the next setting and—using the measurements—started Buster in the same posture in the same spot in the frame. The cross-shot consistency is astounding. Relative to the camera, he doesn't change at all; only the background differs. In its day, the projectionist's dream cost many a director and his cameraman their afternoon as they sat through screening after screening, trying to figure out just how Keaton filmed the impossible.[5]

Back in the dim theater, as worlds overlap and we are swept into the dream, the villain has stolen the pearls. (The butler helped him do it, naturally.) The father phones for a detective—the world's greatest, in fact—Sherlock Jr. Immediately a gloved hand rings the bell. The thieves wince. The door opens to reveal Buster, dressed to the nines, dashing in formal eveningwear. The villain and his accomplice are no match for the detective, who casually foils their assassination attempts

21 The great detective at work. Publicity photo from *Sherlock, Jr.* (1924). From left: Kathryn McGuire, Joe Keaton, Buster, Jane Connelly, Ward Crane, Erwin Connelly.

(an exploding billiard ball, a poisoned drink, and a booby-trapped chair)—in each instance nearly hoisting the crooks with their own petards. The game of pool is a work of art. The thirteen ball is a bomb; it will detonate on contact. The rival flubs his shot, then scurries out of the room, leaving the table to Buster. A dozen innocent balls loosely surround the deadly one. In a single table-length view, we see Buster hit a shot that strikes every ball in the cluster but number thirteen. The dastards listen for the blast, but Buster proceeds—impassively, impossibly—to clear the table, hitting shot after death-defying shot. Then, when it finally comes time to sink the immobile thirteen, Buster jumps the cue ball over it and into the pocket—a scratch. After his rattled opponent miffs his turn once again, it looks like the end of the line. Buster draws a bead on the final ball—puts it away with authority, drops his pool cue, and strolls past the two men crouched in the doorway. He switched the balls!

But how, in real life, did he make those preposterous shots? Magnets? A trick table? Anything seems possible at this point. Years later, Clyde Bruckman solved the mystery. After an hour's worth of fruitless effort—trying to wing the shot on will alone—Buster got an inspiration. He chalked all the balls in the cluster and knocked them one by one into the pockets he wanted. Using the trails left behind on the felt, Buster reassembled the balls into the correct configuration, erased the lines, and got the shot he wanted.[6] It was the oldest Keaton trick in the book: do it straight.

The best sequences in the film, however, tend to be composites, combining pioneering film effects with Buster's vaudeville expertise and prodigious physical ability. After tracking the bad guys to their hideout, our Sherlock places a large circular costume case (made of what looks like paper) in the windowsill. He allows himself to be captured. As the rival blabs on about where he has stashed the girl and the pearls, we cut to an exterior shot of the hideout. For our benefit, one of the walls dissolves, exposing the action inside. In a single shot we watch Buster snatch the pearls and jump headfirst through the window—crashing through his circular case—roll once, and come up in costume! The villains rush outside to see an old lady wobbling off. In order to melt away one side of the hideout, Buster built a house with a detachable wall. He then had Elgin Lessley dissolve from a shot of the set with the wall to one without it.[7] (Back then, fades and dissolves were done inside the camera. To fade out (or in), Lessley would keep cranking as he slowly closed (or opened) the aperture. To dissolve from one scene to another, he would fade out, rewind the film, and then fade in on the new scene—thus superimposing the two fades. As the effect was created on a single strip of film, a mistake on either fade ruined *both* scenes joined by the dissolve.[8]) After Lessley's exacting dissolve, all Keaton had to do was pull off the diving costume change.

Later in the sequence, the thugs corner Buster. His assistant Gillette comes to his aid dressed as a woman peddler in a long billowy dress. Gillette backs into a wall and points to the tray hanging from his neck. As the men scramble for Buster, he dives headfirst into Gillette's tray (and stomach)—and disappears! Gillette—still in the same shot—

steps forward, spins around, and walks away. This one turns out to be an old Joe Keaton vaudeville trick. The bit is somewhat complicated, but it involves a trapdoor in the wall, a half-horizontal Gillette, and a weighted skirt. After Buster flies through the tray (which hides the trapdoor), Gillette lowers his legs to ground and ambles off.[9]

Thus the world of Sherlock Jr.—a Richard Lester–like environment of absurdity infused with a diverting visual wit. (In his house, Sherlock Jr. walks through mirrors that end up not being mirrors and has a vault that opens onto a busy street. It is the home as sight gag, much like the Beatles' apartment in *Help!*, where the carpet is grass and secret bookshelves revolve to reveal even more bookshelves.) On the set, however, the real Keaton was up to his usual dangerous tricks. The tray-diving stunt was notoriously risky, but it went off without a hitch. Earlier, the lions almost got too friendly with him when he discovered he couldn't remember where Gabourie had hidden the door in the camouflaged jungle cage. (After Keaton found the exit, Lessley told him he would have to do the scene again for the foreign negative. Buster swore Europe would never see it. In the end, the studio made a copy from the domestic negative.)

Not only did Buster do his own stunts, but he did other people's, too. If Gillette couldn't handle a fall from a moving motorcycle, Buster put on his costume and did it for him. Later, riding the handlebars of that motorcycle—which left him in command of the throttle but not the brake—he caught a choreographed face-full of dirt but then took an unplanned off-camera nosedive into a car windshield. Buster was unhurt.[10]

The full extent of Keaton's most painful mishap was learned in a postscript. Buster runs along the top of a moving train; as he comes to the last car, he grasps a rope hanging from a nearby water tower, which lowers the spout. A torrent of water slaps Keaton to the ground. When the deluge subsides, he stands and scampers off. In real life, as Buster hit the railroad tracks, his neck cracked across one of the metal rails. He finished the take, but had a headache whiskey couldn't cure. He went to bed early. Years later, Buster's doctor asked him—as part of a routine but thorough physical—when he had broken his neck. Buster said he hadn't. The doctor showed him the X-ray.[11] Back then, it had all seemed like part of a day's work.

As such neck-breaking footage almost always made its way into the final cut, on some level a Keaton comedy is a document of genuine disaster and injury, starring one poor, bruised fall-guy. In our current TV-saturated terms, silent film is the ultimate reality show, with Buster a kind of Ur-*Jackass*. Pain will always get a laugh, and we endlessly will watch someone engage in the amazing and idiotic. But the difference between Keaton and today's mindless crotch-punishing programming is that with him you don't get the money shot: the doubled-over grab to the groin as onlookers choke back their guffaws—in short, the reaction, the back-slapping payoff, encouraging a hearty, conspiratorial laugh at the victim's expense. And so there's a funny transcendence with Keaton's work; the stone-faced man keeps on keeping on, setting the story—and the imagination—free.

Thus Keaton spills off the driverless motorbike only upon reaching his destination—feet-first in the butler's gut. The exuberant ride is over, for a moment. He whisks the girl away in the villain's car, ridding them of their pursuers by tossing the exploding pool ball to deadly effect. Distracted by the girl, Sherlock Jr. hits the four-wheel brakes just before they drive into a lake. Momentum carries the top half of the car (passengers included) skimming across the water; after floating to a stop, Buster extends the convertible top upright—making a sail. He returns the pearls to his girl and situates her in a position to marvel at the scenery with him, as they sink.

Back in his booth, Buster—sleep-swimming—topples off his stool and wakes. He looks out at the movie: it is the same as it ever was, populated by actors. Buster sags against his projector. In walks his girl. She tells him it was all a terrible mistake—they know who took the watch. She glances away, coyly. Buster, a far cry from debonair Sherlock, is flummoxed. He peers into the darkness, the projectionist's window neatly framing him and his girl. Onscreen, the leading man turns the woman to him, taking her hands. Buster, less assuredly, accomplishes the same. That done, he looks again to the screen. The man kisses the lady's hand; Buster does likewise. (His girl blushes.)

The matinee idol produces a ring and slides it on the woman's finger; so does Buster, twisting contentedly afterwards with arms clasped shyly behind his back. The man kisses the woman. Buster tentatively goes in for a peck. Now the screen couple embrace passionately, and the scene dissolves to . . . them with two babies in a nursery! Buster, deadpan, scratches his head. The End.

The dream ended with them floundering in the water; real life ends with them floundering in a quiet theater. It is one of the most touching conclusions ever to come from Hollywood. That in his big moment our projectionist emulates his screen idol—with a lesser (but somehow gentler) degree of elegance and confidence—seems sweet and funny and true. Then, because it's Keaton, this shot-reverse-shot lover's progress wraps with a zinger. The kids. Be careful what you wish for, Buster.

Sherlock, Jr., previewed poorly. They didn't laugh in Long Beach. It was a different kind of comedy. Ever trustful of his audience, Buster cut and re-cut, and the film shrunk to 4,065 feet—or about forty-four minutes. Schenck thought it an awkward length and asked Buster to add another reel; Keaton said no.[12] When the film debuted at that length, the reviews were mixed. *Variety* found it "about as unfunny as a hospital operating room." *The New York Times* reviewer noted that just as he grew impatient for Buster to *do* something (after 500 or so feet), he did—in "one of the best screen tricks ever incorporated in a comedy"—and from then on the film was a gas. (Even *Variety* had to admit the dream sequence was "clever," though everything else was "bunk.") The *Times* critic came closest to hitting it on the head, telling his readers the film would amuse them, if they let it.[13]

However, to this day *Sherlock, Jr.*, defies explanation, as most memorable films do. Watching a movie is direct, visceral, immediate; writing sneaks in the back door after the furniture is in place. That's the whole point of movies: as John Huston famously explained to James Agee, "In pictures, if you do it right, *the thing happens, right there on the screen.*"[14] So, in many ways, it's the reviewing that's bunk. Yet critics—and biographers—continue to spill ink, especially on the good ones. *Sherlock, Jr.*, is one of the best. Most aspects of the film could support a chapter of their own: the Chinese-box structure (Buster has wrapped a movie within a dream within a movie), the mixed bag of camera and stage tricks, the seductive, uneasy tilt-a-whirl of movement. *Sherlock, Jr.*, is a true masterpiece, which again, for all my protesting, has to be seen to be believed. I have never watched it—including the time at a hip downtown Manhattan theater—without hearing someone gasp. It is that kind of movie. (Those who have seen it before are marked by their erratic murmurs—to them are left quieter idiosyncratic pleasures. Like the odd way Ward Crane buffs the tops of his shoes by rubbing them against the back of his calves before entering the girl's house—the sort of strange, authentic, and inexplicably coalescing detail that reaffirms your suspicion that you're in the presence of workaday greatness.) Take, as another instance of offhand merit, Keaton and McGuire's sheepish courting. Sitting in a loveseat, each makes aborted feints for the other's hand; when Kathryn suddenly slaps her palm down on the bench, Buster grabs it with equal ferocity—they both jump, the look on their faces priceless: they are at heart determined to hold hands and terrified by that determination. It is a twelve-second primer on romance, how it is wonderful, stilted, and arrives in fearful bursts.

Like the very first title says, *Sherlock, Jr.*, is a story about being able to do two things at once: move and entertain, dream and wake, negotiate between our real and our better selves—how we are all, in the end, projectionists *and* detectives. That art inflects life and vice versa is not a new statement, but a celebration of that fact perhaps bears repeating. *Sherlock, Jr.*, is a testament to the imaginative impulse, the creative wish—the amount of ourselves that we put into the movies, and what the movies give back to us. For when the lights come up and we're shoved rudely back into our misfit selves, we find we're a little better off. Our ghostly flights sustain us. And then it's time to kiss the girl.

22 Two swells at sea—Buster and Kathryn McGuire
in a publicity photo from *The Navigator* (1924).

CHAPTER FIFTEEN

5,000 Tons of Fun

It is the audience that gives us the answer.[1]

Buster Keaton

The hot-and-cold reception of *Sherlock, Jr.*—a movie that Keaton had worked on for more than twice as long as usual—was a disappointment.[2] The film did fine financially (roughly on par with *The Three Ages*), but Buster thought he had been on to something.[3] When he made a movie that was truly great, the public would let him know—of that he was sure.

Keaton continued to receive mixed reviews at home, too. He had two wonderful boys, but in the quiet of his separate bedroom, Buster was learning that family life had little to do with settling down. Given his peripatetic upbringing, it seems natural that Keaton would be a nester; Natalie, however, kept the family on the move. After a stint on Westmoreland Place, the household had relocated to a home on Ardmore Avenue with a tile roof and yew trees—this time taking possession as homeowners. (Joe Schenck lent Buster $55,000 in cash to buy the place.) Then, after ten months and a quick profit on the Ardmore resale, it was over to Muirfield Road and into an even larger residence. Buster put up with Natalie's compulsive house-swapping for the simple reason that it made him money. California real estate seemed a sure thing. Then, in 1924, Mrs. Keaton wanted to build. The family sold the Muirfield property, again at a tidy yield, and—to better weigh their options—took up in a house Peg owned on Plymouth Street. While the women badmouthed the temporary digs, Buster purchased two Beverly Hills lots on the sly. As on any other Keaton construction, Fred Gabourie was brought in to assist. The men drafted plans and chose furnishings. On one of the lots, a ranch house took shape. Natalie knew nothing of it—it would be a surprise.

More than that, the home would be a shot at reconciliation, a domestic fantasy made real in brick and mortar. Buster just knew she'd love it.[4]

Sherlock, Jr., would be released in April. While Buster fiddled with the final cut in the editing room—en route to those wiry forty-four minutes—his crew kicked around at loose ends. Schenck and Anger couldn't bear to watch studio salaries fund paid vacations, so they hired out some of the idle hands. Already the gagmen had convened and begun noisily brainstorming the next big idea, but until they struck scenario gold, there was nothing to build. So as they dreamt of flat hats, Fred Gabourie found himself thinking about boats. Schenck had loaned the technician's talents to First National for work on one of their upcoming nautical pictures, *The Sea Hawk*. Gabourie was sent north to scout boats, and he returned to the Keaton Studio with exciting news. He had discovered Buster's next co-star.

The SS *Buford* was a 5,000-ton, 500-foot-long ocean liner docked in San Francisco that the Alaskan-Siberian Navigation Company had sentenced to the scrap heap. Gabourie felt the ship practically screamed for the Keaton treatment. At last, here was something that could top the watery antics of *The Boat*. It would be Buster's biggest comic prop yet, and it was for sale—for a mere $25,000 they could set it to sea and do whatever: sail it, sink it, abuse it to their hearts' content. The *Buford* had a cheerless past. It had ferried soldiers in the Spanish–American War and then in the Great War; in 1919, the United States government had employed the so-called "Soviet Ark" to deport 249 practitioners of suspect politics to Russia in an effort to cleanse the country of a supposedly rising Red Menace. With Keaton at the helm, the *Buford* would be reborn and redeemed, henceforth christened in comedy as the *Navigator*.[5]

Schenck agreed to the lease of the *Buford*, and the steamer made its way to Los Angeles. Now that the Keaton crew had their setting—a giant floating jungle gym, as it were—it was time for a plot. Buster would reincarnate the character he played in *The Saphead*, a filthy-rich layabout of untapped pluck and good intentions. He and his equally helpless upper-crust girl would somehow become stranded alone on the ship, left to fend for themselves on the high seas. From this humble beginning, Buster would spin the biggest hit of his career. With typical simplicity, the film was dubbed *The Navigator*.

We begin with a brief prologue about a war between two tiny faraway countries. One of them has requisitioned an American ship; now the other plots to destroy it. Spies from both nations swarm the seaport.

In the same town but a world away, impeccably rich Rollo Treadway, "living proof that every family tree must have its sap," spies a pair of newlyweds outside his window and decides he is to be married—today. After a drive to his true love's house—across the street—he shakes her hand, presents his idea, and is refused. Unfortunately, his valet has already arranged a Honolulu honeymoon cruise for two. As fate would have it, the girl and the boy—prey to various complications—come aboard the wrong ship at the wrong time, at which point it is loosed from its moorings by those warring spies. The next morning, Buster sallies forth, nattily dressed for some leisure cruising. With nary a steward or deckhand in sight, he enters a long dining room and selects a seat at one of the many empty tables. Buster claps for service. There is a pause—the silence (in our minds) is deafening.

After a few casual near-misses between the ship's only occupants, Buster drops a smoldering cigarette butt; seeing it, the girl calls out, and they begin to chase each other's footfalls around the long multi-tiered decks, like a blind dog after his tail. The choreography builds to a frenzy, whereupon Buster falls down a smokestack and lands on top of his girl. Alone, adrift, they sit up, and without hesitation Buster asks the burning question: "Will you marry me?" Still no dice.

At the end of June 1924, *The New York Times* reported sighting Buster and his ship off Catalina Island. In all, the "Honorary Admiral" would spend ten weeks at sea with Captain John A. O'Brien and his crew of sixty (half sea salts, half movie people). Buster had two generators driven onto the ship (to power the lighting) and installed an

onboard editing suite. He would shoot over 100,000 feet of film
afloat. The Keaton family visited their admiral in shifts.[6]

Kathryn McGuire again signed on as the girl. British actor-director
Donald Crisp was hired to co-direct the dramatic prologue, in which he
regrettably allowed the actors to overplay their parts; then, suddenly, he
went from straight man to gagman, pestering Keaton with unbidden
suggestions on how to improve the comedy. Clumsy flops, unfunny
gaffes—no joke was too outrageous for him. One day, Crisp came to
the set and was told the picture was finished. Of course it wasn't, and
before long Buster had re-shot the prologue and excised the melodrama.[7] He preferred his emotions underplayed.

Back on the *Navigator*, Rollo and his girl Betsy get hungry. But without
their silver spoons, they're hopeless in the kitchen, where the industrial-
grade utensils and family-size rations defeat them at every turn.
Breakfast is a wash. Nonetheless, the boat affords the hapless duo 500
feet of fancy. She swings from the lifeboat pulley; he dives over the
side. Essentially it's a joke on scale—the kitchen is too big, the ship is
too big, everything is too big!—and Buster milks it brilliantly. The
compositions are bare and striking: in one tremendous long view,
she stands at the prow, from which a line extends to Buster, in a tiny
rowboat, towing the ocean liner. It is a quick, one-shot study in the
power of visual thrift. When the sun sets, the ghost ship becomes an
eerie poetic nightscape, with the horrors of emptiness repeated ad
infinitum, most famously in a deck-length of cabin doors swinging
open and shut—in unison—with each loll of the ship. Buster and
Betsy clown their way through a restless night.

On their first day adrift, they spot another boat. They signal it by
hoisting a flag—that nice bright one, she chirps—and the would-be
rescuers head full-steam away from the (apparently) quarantined ship.
Weeks later, now sleeping in cozy his-and-hers engine-room boilers,
our crew has developed its own dippy brand of seamanship. All the
problems of that disastrous first breakfast have been solved; the
kitchen is threaded with strings running to pulleys, self-lighting stoves,
coffee-bean dispensers, hacksaw can-openers—it's cooking with Ed

Gray (and reminiscent of *The Scarecrow*). Then, out the porthole, Buster sees it; he grabs the binoculars. Land! She looks. Cannibals! Then, from crisis to catastrophe: the ship runs aground and springs a leak. It must be patched from the outside. Looking around, the girl notices a strange puffy suit, with lead boots and a shiny dome helmet. A look of resigned concern settles in Buster's eyes.

Somewhere in the cold clear waters of Lake Tahoe, Buster, in a heavy diving suit, has to surface every thirty minutes for a shot of bourbon and a warm blanket. It is early summer, and there is still snow on the mountaintops. The twin cameramen, in parkas, are submerged in a waterproof wooden box no wider than a table; there is an iron chute leading to the surface. The insides of the box are packed with 300 pounds of ice so as to keep the glass pane—through which the men shoot—from fogging. Communication between star and cameraman is difficult; they use hand signals. They have been at it for a month.

The underwater sequence has been jinxed from the start. A failure at Tahoe would make a third—and possibly final—strike. The epic began east of Hollywood, at the Riverside swimming pool. The crew fortified the tank, making it the proper depth to hold the mock hull and twelve-foot propeller of the foundered *Navigator*. But the extra water weight was too much—the concrete floor collapsed. The Keaton Studio now owed the people of Riverside a new pool. Undaunted, Buster tried the scene at Catalina, off Avalon Bay. Mating fish made the water too cloudy; with every step, Buster stirred up enough murk to blur out the action. And so it was on to Tahoe. The glacial lake was famous for its crystalline water, but it was very, very cold. They were going through a lot of ice and bourbon.

Further complicating matters, deep-sea diving was not for amateurs. In the 220-pound suit, Buster was almost asphyxiated—twice. The gag had Buster sitting on the deck, steeling his nerve with a pre-dive smoke, when out of the blue the girl plops the helmet on his head. The cigarette still hangs from his lips; the faceplate clouds; wisps of smoke curl from the unlatched neck; Buster struggles wildly (but not really) for air. However, when executing the scene, McGuire twisted the helmet a half-turn too far, locking it in place. Keaton began choking. Luckily one of the prop men recognized Buster's distress was genuine and rushed to unscrew the helmet. The gag was re-shot for the film—with McGuire's locking half-turn—and if you watch it carefully (particularly in a DVD slow-motion zoom), you see his eyes widen as the helmet goes click, and Buster seems to wonder—*could this be the final take?*

Trouble struck once more when it came time to get wet. No one informed Buster that when entering the water in a diving suit, a fixed ladder is best—not a rope one. The reason: to help keep yourself upright; otherwise, you can flatten out on your back, smushing your nose to the faceplate and making breathing difficult. Caught in such a bind, Buster released the ladder and signaled for the crew to let him sink and catch his breath. They were unaware of the danger.[8] (A close inspection of this scene in the film reveals a similarly uncomfortable look on the master's face.)

The deep-sea repair job, which lasts less than five minutes, was the most expensive scene in the movie. But the underwater photography was worth the pain; Buster glides through the clear Tahoe water, trailing bubbles, as wrinkles of sunlight play across the lake floor. Despite the presence of a sawhorse, which he brought down with him—"Danger Men At Work"—Buster's labor is interrupted by a succession of sea creatures. He puts an extroverted lobster to use (as clippers), duels with a swordfish (wielding another swordfish as his blade), and eventually knifes a giant man-strangling octopus. As Buster battles below, cannibals swarm the ship and steal the girl, severing his air hose in the process.

Audiences howled at the sub-marine shenanigans, with some of the biggest laughs coming from the simplest bits. Before setting to work, Buster fills a bucket and "washes his hands" underwater—nothing fancy, just quick old-fashioned pantomime, Keaton's surefire stock-in-trade. Moviegoers loved it. On the other hand, the most involved setup—which, looking back, Buster would claim to be his all-time favorite sight gag—had to be cut from the film. Keaton had ordered

1,200 foot-long rubber fish from his property department; the school would "swim" on unseen strings, which were cycled through the water by an enormous machine perched on telegraph poles. As Buster gawked at the wall of fish, a loner would swim up and find itself unable to cross the busy stream. Ever helpful, Buster would stick a starfish on his chest and begin directing traffic, allowing the single to pass. The sequence was featured in a trailer for the film—and audiences cracked up. But when the film was test-screened, the joke bombed from Long Beach to Riverside. Clyde Bruckman was in a snit; the bit had all the makings of a side-splitter. But Keaton knew the gag game was a crapshoot. He eventually decided that context was the key. Viewers who knew the full story resented this kind of elaborate clowning while the girl was in jeopardy—even if her peril was unbeknownst to Buster. He had hooked his audience and then failed to honor his plot—a joke for its own sake would no longer do.[9]

His air supply cut, Rollo walks ashore and saves his girl. Then the cannibals attack, and—in a great naval battle involving coconuts, palm-tree ladders, fireworks, and a monkey—he and Betsy try to defend their ship. In the hell that is war, Buster lights a tiny toy cannon, which becomes attached to his leg by a string. In a quiet, personal skirmish, he struggles to outmaneuver his diminutive rolling shadow, which is burning its fuse down at a distressing pace. We sit forward, anticipating the dreadful, but just as the cannon fires, Buster trips. The shot arcs over him and sends a cannibal tumbling from the railing. Despite Buster's crack timing, the ship is overrun. He and Betsy swing down a zipline to an abandoned canoe, which sinks. Cannibals dive off the *Navigator*. The pair swim out to open water, clutch each other, and slowly go under . . . only to rise back up atop a submarine! They scramble inside, where Buster finally gets a kiss.

Compared with *Sherlock, Jr.*, *The Navigator* is a less personal, more outdoor film; it comes with the undemanding, dependable novelties of deep-sea diving and an enormous funny prop. To love *Sherlock, Jr.*, you have to love movies; anyone can laugh at a guy falling off a boat.

To be fair, *The Navigator* has its dazzling facets—Buster's enchantment under the sea, the dance of the rope-a-dope cannon, the sweeping final battle, the unique visual investigation of the ghostly ocean liner—but it is a film of a different kind. Specifically, the kind that brought out people in droves. Less intimate, a little hammy, the feature registered with moviegoers as none of Keaton's work had ever before. It opened on Columbus Day at New York's Capitol Theater to standing-room-only crowds; there was a national ad campaign featuring the stylish drawings of the famed flapper cartoonist John Held Jr.; the film was held over at the Capitol for an extraordinary second week.[10] The *Times* called it a cure for lethargy; more reserved *Variety* admitted it could reliably carry a program.[11] In truth, the numbers coming from the box office were making Schenck giddy—*The Navigator* would be the Keaton Studio's greatest moneymaker.[12] The cry had come up from the theaters, and—finally—it was the unmistakable response Buster had dreamed of. The film was something great.

In the public eye, Keaton had joined the rarified ranks of Chaplin and Lloyd.[13] In anticipation of his breakout success, he had signed a new three-year contract that September. Schenck would pay him $27,000 apiece for the next six films, plus an extra $13,000 if he managed to begin work on three in one year. Furthermore, Buster would continue to receive his percentage of the profits.[14] To celebrate—and promote the opening of *The Navigator*—he and Natalie headed for New York.

Buster had an ulterior motive for going east. On October 4th, Buster's twenty-ninth birthday, the 1924 World Series opened at Washington's Griffith Stadium. The Senators were facing the New York Giants in a contentious rivalry: a set of grandstand seats—one ticket for each home game—was scalping for $100; fans who tried to leave a game early were booed back into their seats; President Coolidge went to the opener with his wife, his Postmaster General, his Secretaries of State and War, and a Supreme Court Justice. Two days later in New York, upwards of 50,000 people crammed into the Polo Grounds to see game three, Buster included. When the series went back to Washington—all tied up for the final game—Buster followed, showing firmly where his heart was. (It was only days before *The Navigator*'s debut.) He would be on hand to see—in the bottom of the twelfth, an inning the morning papers would call the greatest played since 1912—the ball scuttle down the third-base line and bounce over sun-blinded eighteen-year-old Freddie Lindstrom's head for the second time that day, scoring the winning run for the Senators and giving them their first and only championship.[15] Such were the spoils of stardom.

23 Keaton and his *Seven Chances* (1925).

CHAPTER SIXTEEN

Brides, Bulls, and Butlers

In the silent days we could try anything at all, and did.[1]

Buster Keaton

We open on the early, easy days of 1925. Location: Beverly Hills, California. Buster pulls the car up to a strange house. Natalie looks over at him. They are with company—Joe Schenck's studio boss, Eddie Mannix, and his wife Bernice—and this is an unscheduled stop. Before them stretches a broad lawn, newly landscaped, on which stands a stylish ranch house, with three bedrooms and a pool.

Buster: "It's yours, Nat."

She is silent as they tour the house. Mrs. Mannix, on the other hand, is making sub-verbal sounds of delight. The boy cradled in a stage trunk had designed a home for a family—and decorated it to their taste—and he's beaming. Then come the questions. Natalie wonders, Where will the governess sleep? Buster wasn't aware the family would be acquiring such. And the cook? The butler? The house, it seems, is too small; an army of live-in domestics is forthcoming. Buster sells the house to the Mannixes on the spot; smitten, they pay Keaton 110 percent of cost, and move in soon thereafter. Construction begins on the other lot Buster had purchased.[2] This time there would be no surprises.

As it turns out, Buster was not the only one who had been acquiring property quietly. When it came time to discuss a follow-up to *The Navigator*, Joe Schenck dropped a bombshell of his own. He had paid $25,000 for the rights to a silly Broadway farce; the play, which had been a theatrical disappointment, was called *Seven Chances*. Not only was the material—all fanciful crisis and stagey fluff—entirely ill-suited for Keaton, but the project came with a co-director, a man by the name of John McDermott, who had sold Schenck the rights. Buster, who owed his boss money, was in no position to quarrel.[3] He would have to make do.

The premise of *Seven Chances* is best swallowed whole. Jimmie Shannon and his financial partner have been duped into making a bad deal; they need fast money or they face prison and disgrace. Happily, in their darkest hour, a lawyer materializes and tells Jimmie he is heir to $7 million provided he is married by seven o'clock on the night of his twenty-seventh birthday, which happens to be—Buster glances at his desk calendar—today. (Buster's delivery of his date of birth is hilarious and tells us all we need to know; he hangs the ludicrous premise on his deadpan face, snapping its neck without raising an eyebrow.) Luckily, Jimmie has a girl, Mary, but he bungles the proposal. His business partner convinces him to think about the needs of others (i.e., the business partner's) and so they go to the country club to scare up a wife. Buster knows seven ladies in attendance—hence his seven chances—which fall like dominoes.

The partner, the lawyer, and Buster agree to split up and meet at the church at five o'clock with a bride, any bride. After Jimmie is rejected by a wide cross-section of the female species—our hero having proposed to passing motorists, a mannequin, and a man—an ad comes out in the afternoon paper, outlining the stakes and telling interested parties to be at the church by five.

Now comes the essential Keaton moment: the awesome gathering of the storm, with Buster as its oblivious, unblinking eye. An exhausted Jimmie enters the vast empty church, curls up in the first pew, and falls asleep. He is dressed to wed, with the ring, flowers, tickets to Niagara (the honeymoon) and Reno (the divorce). As Buster slumbers, the brides converge, coming in cars, on horses, by bike, trolley, and roller skate—young brides, old brides, first-timers and encore brides, brides big and small (including one rather obvious fellow), all in various degrees of wedding costume. The candidates fill the church, sitting patiently, quietly, checking their newspapers, settling their veils, ruffling their feathers like long-enduring lovebirds. Buster wakes to bridal gridlock. Every pew is full. The minister arrives and, surveying the crowd, kicks the lot out, saying it must have been a practical joke. Pre-nuptial jitters turn lethal. Buster sticks out like a sore thumb; the women begin manhandling their groom. In the confusion, he sneaks out the window and receives an encouraging note from Mary—he has to get to her house! But between him and bliss stand 500 jilted brides. Yes, the chase is on.

Buster was sweating in the dark. It was the second preview of *Seven Chances* and, like the first, it was deathly quiet. They had a dud. From the start, Buster hadn't liked the story. McDermott, the co-director, was gone after two weeks, sacked on budgetary grounds; he had spent unwisely in what was likely an already unsympathetic environment. Buster had shot the opening in two-strip Technicolor, hoping the novelty would improve a lackluster film. He had brought in the brilliant Snitz Edwards, a short, sulky, putty-faced comedian, to play the lawyer.[4] He had thrown in a special effect or two; in fact, Buster's favorite moment in the film was the "drive" Jimmie takes from the country club to Mary's house. Buster gets into his 1922 Mercer Raceabout and grabs the wheel; the background dissolves from one location to the other—he then gets out. (Lessley matched Buster and the car using surveying instruments.[5]) There were even a few unexpected crashes and collisions (a minor leitmotif of Buster encountering out-of-frame obstacles). But he knew the film essentially would ride on the last act—the great bridal chase, when the buttoned-up stage comedy would finally cut loose.

Buster strides down an empty street on his way to Mary's. Unbeknownst to him, a flock of brides follows, taking in reinforcements from the side streets. A succession of progressively higher camera shots reveals the massive parade of veils behind him. At the last possible minute, Buster turns around—and takes off.

The bridal wave threatens to engulf Buster. No helpless jazz babies here: these are strong, smart gals, determined as hell. Like a force of nature, they overrun football games and flatten cornfields. They commandeer streetcars and hijack construction cranes. A bricklayer is building a wall. One by one, the passing brides remove a brick, for bashing purposes; once the pack is gone, there is no wall. The sequence is a testament to indomitable female will, in all its complex glory. (The women weep when they think they've killed Buster, then—seeing him alive—leap to finish the job.) Along the way, the groom is beset by bees, barbed wire, and a bull—and almost shot by duck hunters—before being driven into the hills.

In the theater, the chase was getting a few laughs—nothing too loud, but an encouraging chuckle here and there. Keaton cut an amusing figure in his leggy sprint, coattails flying, and he had put to good use the choreographic lessons of *Cops*. (There is even a moment when Buster falls in step with some marching patrolmen; at the sight of the brides, however, they scatter like mice.) Then, just as the film was fading out on Buster being chased down a hill and into the sunset—a lame ending, if ever there was—the audience sat up and roared. What was that? Keaton and his men repaired to the studio and ran the finale in slow motion. Then they saw it. As Buster scampers down the slope, brides in tow, he kicks up a rock, which begins to roll, dislodging a few more rocks—as the scene fades, he has three small rocks tumbling after him. The audience laughed, thinking Mother Nature had joined the chase!

And so Gabourie went to work making 1,500 rocks out of wire frame and papier-mâché. Some would be no bigger than baseballs; others would weigh over 400 pounds. The biggest were eight feet around. The crew went to the High Sierras and found a long ridge with a grade greater than 45 degrees—to ensure a fast roll. At the sound of a starter's pistol, Gabourie would begin releasing the boulders in a pre-arranged sequence; once they were rolling, it was up to Buster to dodge them. Lessley would keep cranking, come what may.[6]

So instead of a fade-out, the momentum builds. The bit with the bricks and the cranes was just a prelude to what is arguably the most athletic four minutes in film. High in the mountains, the hunters and the hunted part ways, as the brides go to head Buster off at the pass.

Keaton speeds along the ridge, jumps a gap, and leaps from a cliff to the top of a thirty-foot-tall tree the moment it is felled by a lumberjack. He rides the tree down, gets up, and sprints off. He flies along another high ridge, which ends in a steep sandy slope. Without breaking stride, he throws himself down the slope, head high over heels, turning front flip-flops the whole way down. Towards the bottom, he somersaults through a clump of rocks—which begin to roll—before catching his feet under him and scampering full tilt down the hill. Now in a boulder field, the dodging begins. Tiny Buster—ever-nosing downhill at impossible speeds—is caught in a bona fide avalanche. He thinks he can find safety in a tree, then behind a giant rock, but gravity is relentless, like a freight train, and at the bottom of the hill are those brides! Buster grinds to a halt. Which is the worse fate? The rocks continue their assault, and Buster dances in and out of rolling death. Rocks fly over, under, to the left and right, as Buster hurdles, weaves, and hits the ground— occasionally getting clobbered. When 500 brides meet 1,500 boulders, the brides scatter, clearing the descent for Buster. On level ground, he is a horizontal blur as he broad-jumps a horse (pulling a buggy), dives under a truck, and crosses some railroad tracks (barely missing a train). He pulls up to Mary's house, only to get his coat stuck on the front gate, which he drags off its hinges and up to the door. Buster collapses across the threshold.

The unwavering momentum, the breathless athleticism, the symphonic pacing, the impossibly sustained thrill—the sequence is a masterpiece. Words cannot do justice to the sweeping cinematography, the fully-loaded (often rolling) frame—running hills, distant horizons, clumps of brush, shadows, and boulders, and one driven little man. Then comes the inspired ritard. Buster learns he has arrived too late; the hour has passed. Hope is crushed. The girl wants to know whether they'll be married anyway, for richer or for poorer. Doesn't Buster think they'll be happy? Buster shakes his head, no. Ha! Then he explains: without the money, he's off to jail, and he won't share that shame. He walks outside. He looks towards the church, then rushes inside. The watch is wrong—according to the bell tower, they have seconds to spare!—thus he and Mary marry just in the nick of time.

The rockslide rescued the picture—for while not as big as *The Navigator*, it was a definite hit—but for most of his life, Buster would claim *Seven Chances* was his worst effort. (In the 1960s, he didn't feel it even merited re-release; he was happy enough to let it remain unseen.[7])

The accidental brilliance of the last-minute avalanche only reaffirmed Schenck's faith in Keaton's freewheeling, freeform style. Nothing kills a laugh like a scientist—or a script. Buster and his boys were fools in the funhouse, guests by courtesy of the management, who knew jokes were best caught unawares, where you least expected. Buster kept all the funny business in his head; he never wrote any of it down—when needed, he'd just sit on the floor and give the sequence a good mental chew. Later in his life, Buster would work out gags by shuffling pennies—stand-ins for people—to the music of the radio, which helped set the tempo.[8]

But the best comic marinade, Buster found, was baseball. Before long, a suspicious number of professional ballplayers wound up on the Keaton payroll. As of *Sherlock, Jr.*, Byron Houck, a former pitcher for the Philadelphia Athletics, was running the second camera. Around the same time, a talented slugger named Ernie Orsatti went to work as a prop man. In a few years his involvement would be only part-time; in his other, in-season job, he played outfield for the St. Louis Cardinals. (In 1928, Orsatti would go straight from playing in the World Series to working on a Keaton shoot.) If the crew got stuck on a busted gag—and couldn't find a way out of the rut—there was no use crying about it: they played ball. (Everyone, that is, but round Jean Havez, who served behind the plate as umpire.) Moviemaking and ballplaying seemed very much alike; neither was a job one could take seriously.[9]

Keaton's best features have that boys-at-the-sandlot attitude—a sense of play, of athletic bravado, of rough-and-tumble one-upmanship. Keep filming no matter what: Buster will dust himself off, drain the water from his ears, bounce back to fight another day. You don't get a dry run on a dangerous stunt—accidents are too likely, and injuries make for timid participants—and so you just do it in one take, counterintuitive and impossible though it may seem.[10] These were not typical chest-beating tough guys, but guys simply having too much fun to do things any other way. They might butt heads in the thick of it—games have winners and losers, after all—but they were a team through and through. From each man's individual sense of ownership to the unit's blurry, pragmatic division of labor, the Keaton Studio was a remarkable collective. As Bruckman remembered years later, "It used to be *our* business. We acted in scenes, set up scenery, spotted lights, moved furniture—hell, today even the set dresser with paid-up dues can't move a lousy bouquet."[11]

And thus the golden age of the small, streamlined independent studio. Having a dedicated, salaried unit made for cheap, easy retakes and inserts—the essential crew was always on call—and because the studio used its own sets and equipment (as opposed to renting them), post-production tinkering was only a matter of another reel of film. Even off the lot, shooting remained relatively simple. A cop or two might be dispatched for crowd control—gratis—as would any necessary firemen. At the end of the day, Buster recalls making sure each was handed an extra's check, usually for about $10. Railroads readily lent their services and equipment, too, as long as Keaton left the company name on the side of the cars.[12] The business of 1025 Lillian Way was a world unto itself—a lost world, as Bruckman points out. Soon, industry shooting schedules wouldn't make allowances for afternoons of baseball.

Even then, in February of 1925, there were signs the center could not hold. *Seven Chances* was the last hurrah of the three great gag-men. Jean Havez never saw the film released; at home on the night of February 11th, he died of a heart attack.[13] That month, Joseph Mitchell went to work for Universal, and Clyde Bruckman was lured away to the camp of Harold Lloyd. That year, cameraman Elgin Lessley would also depart; he would begin cranking for screen clown Harry Langdon. In years to come, Bruckman and Lessley would return to the fold—for a picture here and there—but the unity was broken.[14] Buster owed his success to a number of happy factors, one of which was having talented, like-minded collaborators. Losing the gagmen was a worrisome first step towards trouble.

That dreary February, Buster was in Northern California hunting and fishing with friends. Soon afterwards, he and Natalie went to New York for the premiere of *Seven Chances*. *Variety* was calling the running of the brides perhaps the best chase ever filmed.[15] Buster was spotted walking near Washington Square and swarmed by autograph-hungry NYU students. He and Natalie posed for publicity photos on the roof of the Biltmore Hotel; Harry Brand issued press releases on the Keaton view of movie comedy. That May, back in California, Buster stood as best man while his pal Roscoe Arbuckle got remarried; the Keatons hosted the reception at their house.[16]

In Hollywood, the summer weekends rolled leisurely by. Joe and Norma Schenck threw glamorous day-long pool parties at their Santa Monica beach house. Buster would be there, lounging about in his bathing suit, as would the Talmadge girls and a mixed herd of Hollywood notables: neighbor Marion Davies, Samuel Goldwyn, Sid Grauman, a youngster named Irving Thalberg, and director Ernst Lubitsch, who liked to watch the surf. There was a buffet and night swimming in the illuminated saltwater pool, perched at the edge of the ocean.[17]

But work is work, and the Keaton family soon find themselves on a ranch fifty-odd miles outside of Kingman, Arizona. Everywhere Buster goes he is followed by a girl. Her name is Brown Eyes; she is a handsome Jersey cow, and she is to be his next co-star. No one said it would work out. Cows were even harder to wrangle than starlets, but Buster told his crew to leave that to him. A fine black thread winds from his pinkie to her neck. Originally, it was a thick halter. From the day they met, Buster has taken her everywhere, feeding her treats; in ten days, the line connecting the pair grew thinner, from rope to string to thread. Voilà—she was ready for her close-up.[18]

24 Buster and his leading lady, Brown Eyes, in a publicity photo from *Go West* (1925).

The movie is called *Go West.* Buster plays Friendless, a sad, sweet, Midwestern youth who happens to be penniless, possession-less, mother-less, and, yes, utterly lonesome (he pets a dog and even it gets up and walks away). With nothing left to lose, he leaves home and—after getting trampled by the big city—heeds Horace Greeley's famous advice and goes west, like many a brave young man before him. Buster's glum luck (to say nothing of his relentlessly appropriate and unfortunately metaphoric moniker) seems designed to steer the film into the realm of tragicomedy or, worse, Chaplinesque self-pity. But is *Go West* a parody? Fans have argued both ways. Whether one finds Buster sardonically sweet or tenderly so—whether he's mocking Chaplin or embracing him—depends in part on one's ability to swallow a bovine love story. (The melodrama will hinge on the triangulated desires of a boy, his cow, and the meatpacking industry.) But if the film

169

is a satire, it is one of the straightest and staunchest ever made. Some believe the tone is intentionally ambivalent.[19] I tend to think Buster is making fun, simply with a stonier face than usual.

As with most Keaton locations, the Arizona desert was put to both scenic and comic use. A stowaway on a westbound boxcar, Friendless has secured himself inside a barrel, which falls out the cargo door and rolls down a long hill before bursting apart and depositing its freight in the middle of the great western expanse. Buster surveys the limitless empty horizon—sand and sagebrush as far as the eye can see—walks a few feet left of frame and suddenly there's a horse! (When you are named Friendless, the West is a suitably evocative landscape.) Soon Buster finds work as a cowpuncher. The ranch is in danger of financial ruin; there is a girl, a rival rancher, a cruel bunch of cowboys, and, at long last, a friend for Friendless—a fellow loner and true kindred spirit—Brown Eyes the cow.

Elsewhere that summer, the famous Scopes trial was underway, debating whether man might truly be a monkey's uncle. Nationwide there was much ballyhoo over the position of the species, but in Arizona it was clear that the cow called the shots. Upon arriving in the desert, Brown Eyes had gone into heat, and a cow in heat is not interested in acting. She was too unique-looking to replace with a double (which even then would be untrained). There was nothing to do but wait for her passions to cool. Shooting was delayed for almost a fortnight. At $13 a week, Brown Eyes originally had seemed a bargain leading lady.[20]

The cow wasn't the only problem. The heat in Mohave County—a blistering 120 degrees in the sun—was melting the emulsion off the film. The cameras had to be packed in ice. Housed in temporary tents, the electricians (and their gear) were in danger of overheating.[21] But for the most part the crew was used to working in difficult locations. Their boss would go a long way for a little realism.

Back at the corral, Friendless (in chaps and a porkpie) discovers he's not much of a ranch hand: he can't milk a cow or saddle a horse, he's a sure target for bulls, and he can't smile—even at gunpoint. (Despite his buffoonery, Buster does have a nonchalant moment of competence: when the wind blows off his hat, he plucks it from the air without batting an eye.) After much ado, the tenderfoot ends up riding shotgun on a runaway train, which carries him, the herd, and Brown Eyes steaming through Pasadena and into Los Angeles. Friendless knows the ranch will be ruined if the herd doesn't reach the stockyards, so he decides to finish the cattle drive on his own.

It was the race of the brides revisited: Buster and 300 steers stampeding through downtown Los Angeles. A bull will wind up in the inevitable china shop (not to mention barber shop, Turkish bath, and department store), occasioning a quick series of cameos, including Joe Keaton (in shaving cream) and Roscoe Arbuckle (in drag). The cattle in the city represent a nice inversion of the more common Keaton trope, the dandy in the sticks. (All that matters is that the fish be out of water.) In the film, the herd won't heel until Buster dons a red, bull-attracting devil costume and leads the pack (which has grown to include cattle, cops, and firemen). In real life, Keaton had difficulty creating a controlled but believable stampede. Authentic cowboys blocked off the side streets from 7th Street to Broadway. They eventually spent their time pushing the herd; the cattle were too good-natured to charge after Buster. In the final edit, however, the sequence is thrilling.[22]

The urban stampede ends with Friendless—hilarious in his full-body costume—riding a galloping Brown Eyes into the stockyards, where the father and the girl await. The day is saved; the grateful rancher offers anything that is his. Buster points and says he wants her. The girl blushes. But he's talking about Brown Eyes. The girl takes it as well as can be expected, and the four of them drive off in the rancher's car.

That October, Buster turned thirty. On the 25th, opening night at New York's Capitol Theater, *Go West* kept the audience in stitches. They loved the final chase.[23] *Variety* did not. The reviewer bashed the script, to the point of doubting whether the film even had one; the crabby summation: "The cow is the whole show."[24] Actually, there is more to *Go West* than the cow (to say nothing of the trained chickens, dogs, snakes, and rabbits)—as I have said, it is a curious blend of sap and satire. With a deadly straight face, Keaton milks pity from a cow, and perhaps in doing so, saves for himself the last laugh.

At the box office, the film did about as well as *Seven Chances*, though the expense of shooting in the desert whittled down the profit margin.[25] Buster had brought on his old Bluffton pal Lex Neal as assistant director and gagman.[26] While Neal was a cinematic greenhorn, it had been a fruitful collaboration.

Christmas 1925 found Buster and Natalie on Plymouth Street, awaiting the completion of their dream house. Peg had installed a Christmas tree. Norma and Constance were depressed and considering cutting short their illustrious careers (they didn't). Their father, Fred—who had followed when the rest of the family moved to Los Angeles—had died the month before. (The obituary reported that Peg and Constance were in New York when it happened. "An illness of several years" was cited, the euphemism concealing the pathological truth: alcoholism.) Buster kept busy, neatly dividing himself between bridge, baseball, his boys, and his moviemaking. He was dieting for his next role and, to some of his friends, seemed a little lonely.[27]

Once again, despite the lessons of *Seven Chances* (specifically those concerning the suitability of theatrical material), Buster was involved in a stage to screen adaptation. The film would be called *Battling Butler*. The musical version, a British import, had enjoyed a successful Broadway run a few years earlier.[28] Buster plays Alfred Butler, yet another upper-crust drawing-room habitué, the type who needs a valet to ash his cigarette for him. Sent camping by his disgusted father—who hopes the woods will toughen the boy—Buster roughs it like a Rockefeller, which means with fish forks and tea services, ice deliveries and newspapers, formalwear and flower vases, and a manservant at the end of a bell. While out hunting and fishing (or performing comic variations thereof), our pampered prig falls for a hearty mountain girl (played by the impish Sally O'Neil). Love blossoms among the woodchucks. The courting saphead happens to share a name with a boxer known as "Battling" Butler, and Buster appropriates the title in order to convince the girl's brawny family that he is marriage

25 Buster is the rope-a-dope, Sally O'Neil is the girl, and the sparring partner is unidentified in this publicity photo from *Battling Butler* (1926).

material. Eventually the other Butler shows up, and after some farcing about, Buster—a palooka if ever there was—is forced to lace up his gloves and begin training for his bout with the Alabama Murderer, a mean-looking pug with a cauliflower face.

After the affectations of *Go West*, the boxing scenes feel like grit in the eye. The violence is real, rough, and uncut. An undisguisably fit Keaton takes a disciplined mauling from a sequence of sparring partners. In the ring, he is beyond the help of his manservant (the glum Snitz Edwards). He stands optimistic, defenseless; the very first punch wallops him flat in the face, knocking him to the mat, and while he attempts to bob and weave we in the seats do our own version of the chuckle and cringe. Keaton takes the abuse with great aplomb, his glass

173

jaw never winning out over his stone face. In the film he floats from funny fall to funny fall, but in real life the sequence took a physical toll. After spilling out of the ring onto his head, Buster couldn't work for days; shortly thereafter, he was sidelined by strained ligaments. To make the fights believable, Buster rented out the Olympic Auditorium and consulted with Mickey Walker, friend and welterweight world champ. At the film's climax, Buster has to battle the real Butler, with the girl looking on. In the stage version, the brawl is avoided; Buster added the scene because he felt audiences would expect it. There is little amusement in watching a scared Alfred getting pummeled; the scene lasts and lasts, and even Buster's comeback—in which the mouse finally roars and in a blind rage defeats the boxer—is brutal. More than half a century later, director Martin Scorsese, himself not one to pull punches, would style the boxing scenes in *Raging Bull* after Keaton.[29]

Battling Butler ends with the memorable vision of Buster and his girl walking down the nighttime street in love, oblivious to the sidewalk crowds of well-to-dos; she in frilly flapper-wear, he in boxing trunks, a bare chest, a top hat and cane—much to the surprise of onlookers. At the Capitol Theater, the audience applauded the boxing. (As a warm up—perhaps intentional, perhaps not—the film was preceded by a European short in which a lobster battles an octopus.) The reviews were flattering of both Keaton's film and physique—*Battling Butler* was a hit.[30] The box office hadn't returned such numbers since *The Navigator*—and they kept going up.[31] *Battling Butler* was Buster's last movie to be distributed under his old arrangement; henceforth Keaton pictures would be released by United Artists, now under the control of its newly elected president, Joe Schenck. The other UA stars—Chaplin, Fairbanks, Pickford—enjoyed star-sized budgets; for his next picture, perhaps Buster could squeeze a little more funding out of Schenck.[32]

That March, outside of Merced, California, two men and their wives, out for a Sunday drive, slipped past the highway patrol and drove down a closed road into Yosemite National Park. The highway was still gravel; it was months from completion. When the joyriders were discovered, the order came from Sacramento: close the roads—do not let them drive out. The party was in violation on two counts: first, there was the illegal use of an unfinished road; second, it seems women were forbidden from traveling through the prison work camps that dotted the way. Trapped, the men chartered a train on Tuesday to ferry them, their wives, and the car safely out of the park—on the rails, they were beyond the jurisdiction of the Highway Commission. The story made the papers. It was a case of impish ingenuity, of life imitating art. The car belonged to one Roscoe Arbuckle. Naturally, Buster was with him, loyal to the end.[33] Two boys up to their old tricks.

The escape was by no means the last of Buster's railroad adventures. When Clyde Bruckman saw the end of *Battling Butler*, he was moved most by the drama, not the comedy. It was one of the best finishes he had seen. Days after the film wrapped, he stopped by Keaton's house. He was carrying a book called *The Great Locomotive Chase*, which he wanted Keaton to read. Keaton did, and the rest, as they say, is history.[34]

26 Keaton inspects a Civil War cannon in a publicity photo from his brilliant comedy of love and war, *The General* (1926).

CHAPTER SEVENTEEN

Mischief on the Oregon Express

Railroads are a great prop. You can do some awful wild things with railroads.[1]
Buster Keaton

The hot-dog man appeared a week early outside Cottage Grove, Oregon. It was just past the middle of May 1926. He had come over from Troutdale, where he had heard that famous film star Buster Keaton and a crew of 1,500 had arrived to shoot a movie. Word was that Cottage Grove was going to be the Hollywood of Oregon—for at least ten weeks—and that meant people would want hot dogs. A fellow named Wes broke him the news: he was the first to arrive.[2]

Keaton, Gabourie, and Bruckman (along with the wives of the latter two) had been in town earlier, on May 8th. Before going home, they inspected the river; they checked out railroad tracks; they looked over a logging camp, where they were reported to have enjoyed the food. The location was perfect. On May 26th, the Keaton company steamed into sleepy Cottage Grove, bringing eighteen boxcars of Hollywood freight: remodeled railroad cars, covered wagons, Civil War artillery, two old-fashioned narrow-gauge locomotives (on flatbeds), prefabricated façades, wallpaper, more than 1,200 costumes, and four movie cameras—one of which took panoramic shots. A few days later, Buster and Natalie arrived. They spent Memorial Day—and their fifth (wooden) wedding anniversary—at the Bartell Hotel. Buster was growing his hair long. Among the crew (which, rumors aside, would not number much more than sixty-five) excitement was at an all-time high. They had a blockbuster storyline, which was driven by their boss's favorite prop, and they had the money to do it right—they were sitting on a sure thing.

The town itself was no less drunk with promise. In the upcoming months, no one plans to report to work, or at least not with any regularity. The local ladies can't stop talking about the recent appearance of two makeup artists; the men have hinted they might be willing to share a few Hollywood secrets. The real fantasy, of course, is to be hired as an extra; Harry Barnes, the man responsible for such casting decisions, is an instant celebrity. Perhaps the only ones not envisioning their names in lights are the car salesmen, who have flocked to Cottage Grove; they dream of the advertising a celebrity sale would bring. The patience of the hot-dog man is soon rewarded—that is, if he chose to stay. He and his cart become lost in the flood of spectators that fills the streets; at one point, the crowds will swell to almost 4,000 people, about twice the population of Cottage Grove.[3]

The story is true. It comes from the book Bruckman gave Buster. A year into the Civil War, in April of 1862, Union spies in civilian dress infiltrate Georgia and board a passenger train. Heading north from Marietta, the train stops for breakfast in Big Shanty; everyone gets off. While the crew and passengers eat, the raiders steal the engine. The plan: sprint to Tennessee, destroying bridges, telegraph wires, and railroad track as they go. The determined Southern conductors board another engine and give chase. The raiders almost make it—just shy of the border, they abandon the train. All were captured, many were hanged.

Where was the humor in that? Buster loved the story and felt he could slim it down to comic proportions—simplify the chase (in real life the Confederates used many men and a few engines, he would need only one of each) and amplify the drama (he would add a double love story and kidnapping).[4] The final turn: tell the tale from the Southern point of view. To vilify the South would be to pick on the losers; Buster thought audiences would resent it.[5] His version would focus on a daring one-man rescue, which would end not with hanging, but love triumphant.

Keaton asked to borrow the real engine that ran the chase—still on exhibit at a Chattanooga depot—but the Tennessee owners were not keen on a Civil War comedy. Buster also wanted to use the actual route of pursuit, but he found the landscape unsuitable and the railroad tracks too wide—the vintage engines he planned to use ran on a narrow gauge, which Georgia no longer had. In April, Buster's location scout, Bert Jackson, traveled to backwoods Oregon, where he found the leafy country threaded with narrow-gauge lumber rails. The Oregon, Pacific, and Eastern Railroad even owned a pair of period locomotives, which Keaton could buy. He would pick up a third—to serve as a stunt double of sorts—at a lumber depot. Soon Gabourie and his men began restoring engines and building railroad cars. The town sets for Marietta, Georgia, were being reconstructed from war-era engravings. Buster insisted on painstaking historical accuracy—he wanted a vision so true it "hurt."[6]

They've fired upon Fort Sumter. "Aren't you going to enlist?" asks Annabelle Lee. She is sitting on the couch with her beau, Johnnie Gray, railroad engineer on the Western and Atlantic. Annabelle is one of two loves in Johnnie's life, the other being his engine, the *General.* The idea of service hadn't necessarily occurred to him, but, thus prompted, Johnnie scrambles to the recruitment office. He knows a shortcut and is first in line—but the army won't take him. (The reasoning, which is withheld from him, is that he's more valuable to the cause in his present occupation.) Worse, no one—not his girl, her father, or her brother—even saw him in line, way up in the front. Annabelle tells him he is a disgrace; she won't speak to him until he's in uniform.

A year later, the war is everywhere. Annabelle travels north to visit her wounded father. Johnnie, serving his one remaining love, continues to drive his route on the *General.* At the scheduled stop in Big Shanty, Annabelle goes to retrieve something from the baggage car. The raiders strike: they have the *General*—and Annabelle! Buster is washing up for supper when he sees his train speed off. He runs after it, charging down the tracks alone. He mounts a handcart and seesaws furiously; when that derails, he hops on a bike. Finally, at Kingston, he loads a train with soldiers and roars off—still alone, however, the engine not having been connected to the flatcar. A little more than fifteen minutes into the film, the great locomotive chase has begun.

The movie was called *The General.* Annabelle Lee was played by Marion Mack, a former Sennett Bathing Beauty who was suggested for the part by Norma's hairstylist. As Annabelle, she would take more than her fair share of licks, all for $250 a week. That July, Joe Keaton would come to Oregon to fill the shoes of a Yankee officer. He would join a slew of colorful vaudeville old-timers: "Turkey Mike" Donlin (once a famed slugger for the New York Giants), comedian Charles Smith, ex-welterweight Jimmie Bryant, Irish comic Tom Nawn, and Ed Foster (pianist and former pitcher for the Cleveland Naps). Another popular member of the troupe was Glen Cavender; a decorated veteran of four wars, he played the chief Union spy. Before it left Cottage Grove, the production would employ as many as 1,500 locals. It was an expensive shoot—*The Cottage Grove Sentinel* reported it was costing Buster twelve cents a second.[7]

The General is the kind of film that begs for maps, drawings, and diagrams (none of which I will include); the railroad choreography is as exacting as it is casual—the entire film is plotted with a Cartesian zeal. The intricate train-play was the motivation for the film: the locomotives were everything. When not on the engines themselves, the cameras were placed in moving cars—outfitted with special shock absorbers and running on meticulously scraped roads—or on engines riding along parallel tracks.[8] The tracking shots are superb, the diligence of the crew having rendered them fluid, discreet. The camera doesn't shake—the view runs smoothly on the level, and Keaton scrupulously parcels out information in each shot, using the moving frame to set up gags, compose irony, even steal our breath. Speed was ever a concern—the action traveling faster, slower, or on pace with the camera—and Buster became adept at driving a steam engine. (That an actor might have to become an accomplished engineer in order to fill a role seems amazing, impractical, severe, and utterly Keaton.) Buster, however, wasn't always the one running the train. For one gag, he wanted to be sitting sidesaddle on the great wheel piston rod while it slowly came to life; as the train rolled off, he would ride it—up down, up down—out of view. Handling antiquated steam engines, however, required a delicate touch; too much throttle and the wheels would spin out—mashing Keaton. The fireman practiced a few times, with success, and so Buster took a seat and got the take.[9]

The film's structure is rigorously symmetrical: Keaton would chase the raiders north; they would chase him south. (In the interlude, Buster rescues his girl and his train.) Onscreen, the axis of motion is relentlessly right to left, then left to right. Tricks pulled in one direction have their symmetric echoes: both chases involve downed telegraph wires, gushing water towers, cluttered tracks, bent rails, shots fired, burning bridges, and a stolen general. The integrity of the twin trips is by no means ham-handed—the jokes arrive naturally, logically— and that ease is all the more impressive given the limitations of loco- motion. Buster orchestrates a pas-de-deux on rails—shuttling through curves, overpasses, ramps, auxiliary lines—and the geometric invention of what should be a very linear chase (forward, backwards—always on track) is perhaps the film's headiest kick.

A sample sequence: In pursuit of the raiders, Buster hitches a flat- car cannon to his train. When he steams into firing range, he angles the gun and lights the fuse. As he steps back onto the engine, his foot catches the hitch, unhooking the cannon car. Losing speed, the cannon begins to bounce, each jolt lowering the barrel. Suddenly Buster is staring into a now horizontal—and still lit—muzzle. He chucks a hopeless piece of wood at it, then scampers around to the very front of the train, awaiting the inevitable. In a rear shot showing all three moving vehicles—the cannon and two trains—we see Buster's engine hit a curve just as the gun fires. In the distance, the raider's train—having rounded the curve and for an instant back in line—is nearly demolished by the cannonball. A lucky shot! But Buster is not out of the woods yet. The raiders have unhitched one of their boxcars, which now blocks his path. Buster pushes the car with his engine, then runs ahead to a junction and flips the switch, hoping to pass the car on the sidetrack. Meanwhile, the Yanks drop big pieces of lumber in their wake. Buster loses the race to the intersection—the

27 Keaton rides the cowcatcher in a publicity photo from *The General* (1926).

boxcar comes out in front—but while he isn't looking, it is derailed by one of the wooden beams. (Facing forward again, he registers his surprise with a glacial blink.) He slows the engine to a crawl and jogs down the line to remove the remaining obstacles. A length of wood is stuck in the ties; as Buster struggles to lift it, the engine catches up with him and sweeps him off his feet. He now rides in front on the cowcatcher, still holding on to that beam. There's another pole ahead, resting across a rail. Just as he's about to hit it, Buster throws the beam, striking it neatly on one end, flipping it off the track. And so it goes, right on down the line . . .

Precision pole-tossing from the front of a moving train—with real-life calamity at stake—seems like a typical Keaton endeavor. The people of Cottage Grove loved to watch him work. That summer, there were traffic jams along the river road; crowds hovered on the edge of every scene, but the movie people were polite: if a spectator was casting a shadow, Buster kindly would ask him to move.[10] He was having as much, if not more, fun than they.

Scenes from a small town movie shoot. Buster Keaton plays a lot of baseball. Within a week of arriving, he helps pay off the new backstop behind home plate at Kelly Field and arranges to have the grounds leveled. He plays third base for the Lions club against the Kiwanis club in a game to raise money for playground equipment. Overall, the town is more impressed with his ballplaying than his fishing, although the wise heads nod approvingly when he refuses to pose with another man's fourteen-inch trout. In truth, they are smitten with him and his curly haired costar, Marion, who wears caps and overalls and rides her bike everywhere to help keep off the weight. Every Thursday in July the Arcade Theater shows a Keaton film. The temperature breaks 105 degrees. There are accidents big and small on and off the set. A baseball hits Buster in the calf. A cannon blast throws him to the ground, unconscious. (He is back on the job that afternoon.) Harry Barnes almost gets shot in the face. The assistant cameraman breaks his arm horsing around at the hotel. Several of the Union raiders nearly drown in the rapids. A state guardsman gets his hand broken in a carriage wheel. A brakeman's foot is run over by a train. (Unable to get in the spirit of things, he sues for $2,900.) There are many fires. There are even more pranks. Someone hides a stuffed wildcat in Caruthers né Willie Riddle's bed. Eventually the manservant discovers the ruse; in the morning, he leaves the cat in the bed, which in turn scares the maid. There are picnics and dances and socials. The actors like to entertain. In the city park, under the light of Chinese lanterns, there are piano numbers, soft-shoes, monologues, keyboard ditties played wearing twelve pairs of mittens, Charlestons, songs (serious and comic), Shakespearean scenes, and a dance by Joe Keaton. One of the movie people marries a local girl. The couple is kidnapped on the eve of their wedding by an impatient mob, led by Buster; the lovebirds are married by a minister in the parlor of the hotel. The newlyweds are carried aloft to the Gray Goose, where the wedding party takes over a long wooden table. Impromptu speeches are given. Buster erects a screen around the couple and calls for a quarter a peek. The hilarity crests when the bride is abducted to a farmhouse and kept hidden for a few hours.[11] The next day, it is back to work.

Having stalled their pursuers—for a moment—Johnnie and Annabelle stop the *General* atop a high trestle bridge, which spans a wide river. Using the kerosene from the engine's headlamp, they douse the tracks and set them ablaze. They steam ahead into the Confederate camp, where Buster raises the alarm. The Yanks are coming! The army mobilizes; foot soldiers, cavalry, cannon, and guns are rushed towards the bridge. As the dust settles on the empty street, Buster, in uniform, picks up a sword and scabbard, straps it on—with feeling—then trips. Back at the bridge, a Union officer surveys the smoldering trestle. He believes it will hold the engine; once the train has passed, his men will ford the river. Victory is within grasp.

When he first went into movies, Keaton intuited the possibility of the new medium. It could record the remarkable—not a facsimile, but the real thing. Just pack your camera and go. Find it. Shoot it. Nine years later he stood ready to capture perhaps the most stunning—and undoubtedly the most expensive—spectacle in silent film history. The bridge, you see, would not hold.

Friday, July 23rd. Almost 4,000 spectators—many of whom have camped overnight—crowd the banks of the Row River. There are more than 600 cars parked in the woods; for those without transportation, the Oregon, Pacific, and Eastern Railroad runs special morning shuttles. The trestle, built by Gabourie and his crew, is 215 feet long; the water is thirty-five feet below. The bridge is packed with dynamite; its beams are partially split. On a signal, the frame is set alight. Six cameras are at the ready—all to film simultaneously—as is a stationary water pump that shoots four 120-pound streams. There will be only one take. Just after three o'clock in the afternoon, some four hours behind schedule, it happens.

The engine makes it halfway across the smoking bridge when the girders seem to melt, the wood slowly sagging, the rear of the trestle arching its back as the middle suddenly gives way in a fiery collapse. The train plunges into the river. Waves slap the banks. Smoke plumes climb above the wreckage. Steam from the boiler blows the whistle in a long, off-key wail. The engine was driven by a dummy—many spectators think he and the brakeman were real. Upon seeing a papier-mâché head wash downstream, a woman goes into hysterics.

The train was also a dummy; it was the stunt double Buster had found and fitted to look like the engine used by the raiders. The mangled skeleton would rest in the river until 1941, when the metal would be salvaged for wartime scrap. At about fourteen seconds, the shot of the falling train cost $42,000.[12]

The battle that immediately follows—in and around the river bottom—offers an almost equal visual thrill. To fill his ranks, Buster had conscripted more than 400 members of the Oregon National Guard; the men were fed, quartered, paid, and issued two uniforms—one blue, one gray. For many scenes, Buster ran them one way, had them change clothes, then ran them the other. The combat pictures are epic, in many ways so real they hurt—it is often said they have the authority of a Mathew Brady photograph. Soldiers advance down smoky woods backlit by a low sun. Cannons recoil, the river steams, trees topple, men and horses splash through the water, many wavering in the confusion. Above, shells arc back and forth, exploding in midair. Keaton's powder man had loaded 900 shots connected by 40,000 feet of wire to one of three detonating stations.[13] In the film, men fall around Johnnie, victims of an unseen sniper whom Johnnie unwittingly slays. In the end, he will save the day by misfiring a cannon; the errant shell explodes a dam, flooding the river and washing out the Northern troops.

In Oregon, Keaton and his crew soon had a real fight on their hands: fire. The bridge collapse had gone off splendidly, but the next day, while finishing the battle scenes, a forest fire broke out. Sparks from a train had lit the inferno. The entire 600-man crew—stars, gagmen, guardsmen alike—worked through the night to put it out.

Buster orchestrated the effort; countless uniforms were burned, as Buster commanded his troops to use their heavy coats to dampen the blaze. Keaton fought in his skivvies; Natalie, among others, served refreshments. In no way did historical accuracy come cheap— Gabourie had warned against using real wood-burning engines, but Buster had insisted. The bill would run near $50,000. The smoke would remain so thick that the company would have to go back to Hollywood until it cleared. They would return to Cottage Grove at the end of August, after a good rain.[14]

Having saved the day, our hero goes a step further and delivers the hostage he ferried south, who happens to be the Union general. (Johnnie knocked him unconscious in order to steal back his train.) As the prisoner is escorted off, the Confederate general examines this ragtag soldier—a civilian in borrowed robes—who stands before him. The general strips Johnnie of his uniform as Annabelle looks on. Buster's shame is palpable; he's won the battle but lost the war. Then the old man hands him a bundle, saying, "Enlist the lieutenant." Proud Johnnie models his new duds for Annabelle. When the enrollment officer asks his occupation, he firmly states, "Soldier."

It seems a natural beat to end on, a good place to fade—for a war movie. But this is something more. It was ever a love triangle, remember. And so Buster leads Annabelle to the *General*, where they take a seat on that piston Buster rode up and down, alone, in his most dejected hour. They cuddle. A soldier walks by and salutes the new lieutenant. Buster withdraws his arm to respond in kind. As he's turning his attention back to Annabelle, another soldier passes. Again the men salute. Looking down the line, Buster sees what looks like an entire regiment emerge from their tents and head his way. He quickly swaps places with Annabelle—his saluting hand now to the outside—and begins canoodling in earnest. He doesn't spare them a glance, but his right hand begins saluting automatically, piston-like, as the men file by. The End.

Thus the final reconciliation between love and duty, girl and machine. *The General* is a true comedy about war that for all its bluster—burning bridges and shell-shocked combat—has a pacifist's heart. Of the Great War, wandering France hungry, partially deaf in his pitiful clownish uniform, Buster would say, "It was not always possible to take that war seriously." He couldn't understand it—the sides seemed arbitrary: he knew too many Germans and Austrians in vaudeville that he liked.[15] Buster's politics never grew strident; his ideologies stayed soft (unlike Chaplin's). Never wholly convinced of anything, he could laugh at everything, even death. Johnnie is a quiet soul in loud times; when the war between the states comes between him and his girl, it is time to get off the couch and enlist. Deep within the enemy territory, having rescued Annabelle and overheard the enemy's battle plans, only when he spies his train—and can put it all together: girl, train, duty—does his will turn patriotic. He will win the battle, with heroics real and misunderstood, bumbling sweet and terrible, but in the end, all he wanted was to mend his fraying world, restore his separate peace.

Buster thought he had his best picture ever. The public, and reviewers, told him he had a flop—and, having cost a staggering $750,000, a pricey one at that.[16] The film premiered in Tokyo just before the New Year; it was in New York by February 1927, and in California a month later.[17] *The New York Times* felt Buster had overextended himself—it seemed to prefer the short *Soaring Wings* (also showing), which featured slow-motion sequences of flying birds. *Variety* thought the locomotive chase too long; there was too much Keaton; the film was unfunny, not fit for quality theaters. In *Life*, the influential Robert Sherwood accused Buster of clowning in poor taste—Sherwood found no comedy in soldiers dying.[18] Of all his films, Keaton forever would be most proud of *The General*.[19] For a long time, he was the only one.

Much has been made over the disappointment of *The General*. History has revived the film as a masterpiece; the darling of all-time-greatest lists—comedic or otherwise—*The General* is Buster's best-known film today. For the audiences of 1927, perhaps it was a case of false expectations. Keaton was becoming a clown who didn't do slapstick—while on location in Oregon he had told the local paper that that stuff was dead—and the film he turned out wasn't exactly a laugh riot.[20] It is a wickedly funny movie that has dangerously few yuks. The comedy and drama ebb and flow, the film's subtle cadence driving both, favoring neither, something beautifully new. The race of the dueling locomotives is a high-speed chase that is gentle and personal—an unexpected, intricate mix. Public accolades would have to wait.

CHAPTER EIGHTEEN

Golden Villa, Campus Clown

It all started with Schenck taking Lou Anger away from me.[1]

Buster Keaton

At long last, there was room enough for the governess. It was the dream house—take two—and Buster had gotten it right.

In the hills rising above the Beverly Hills Hotel stood 1004 Hartford Way, Buster's new home, henceforth to be known as the Italian Villa. It was cousin and neighbor to Fairbanks' Pickfair, Valentino's Falcon Lair, and Lloyd's Greenacres—one of the true Old Hollywood palaces, the kind of sparkling package that could justly contain a star. To think of the Villa conjures images of a gilded, breathless season— of dazzling parties, bold deals, illuminated nights, whispered innuendos, scenes real and rehearsed, unflappable luxury swaddling bright but determined play. The house offered life as a stage effect, with stirring backdrops and perfect lighting. The two-story, 10,000-square-foot neo-Italian palazzo swept over three acres. There were tennis courts, an aviary, a push-button stream stocked with trout, patios, pergolas, fountains, statues, mosaics, wrought-iron sconces. Cypresses dotted the lawn; the gardener responsible for the intricate, layered landscape had once served a pope. In the back, a waterfall staircase descended the terraced elevation to a thirty-foot pool. Inside, the family had use of twenty rooms, six baths, Oriental rugs, gold-leaf fixtures, and a checkered marble tango floor. Buster had a screening room. Natalie had her own wing. The pressing question of domestic space had been put to rest—forcefully. There was a three-room garage apartment (gardener, maid) and a servants' wing (chef, valet, driver, governess).

With furnishings, the mansion cost $300,000. Architect Gene Verge had drawn the plans; Buster and Gabourie designed and built much of the furniture at the studio, including beds and dressers. The place had the studied ease of a Keaton shot. The bed of the lazy trout stream was laid more than once; Buster spent $14,000 relocating forty-two palm trees from the front drive to the back. But for all its unembarrassed opulence, the Italian Villa bore the mark of Keaton's irreverent, practical wit. The little boys' playhouse was a precocious miniature of the big house. That carefully routed stream was also fished, its contemplative aesthetic often sullied by a guy mucking about with a pole. Buster toyed with model trains, booby-trapped furniture, and swung on the custom-reinforced drapes. He was fond of saying, "It took a lot of pratfalls, my friends, to build this dump," but Buster was proud of his creation—it was a dump built for comfort and fun.[2]

The Keatons would host winter costume balls. Buster, however, preferred entertaining outdoors, and every Sunday from May to October he could be found at the barbecue pit, grilling English lamb chops for some eighty or so of his nearest and dearest. The Keaton weekend barbecues were legendary. Any combination of neighbors might stop by—Marion Davies, Douglas Fairbanks, Charlie Chaplin, Harold Lloyd; screen cowboy Tom Mix had a habit of wandering through the hedge.[3] The guests made a heady crowd, and parties lasted late. Naturally there were moments of piqued social interest—say when Norma's husband, Joe Schenck, and her new lover, actor Gilbert Roland, met at the grill—but Sunday composures were generally kept. Actress Louise Brooks would remember the carefree, contented Talmadge girls mainly lounging about, when not catering to their mother. (Natalie, in her estimation, rated as a "very comfortable lump."[4]) The Keaton children, on the other hand, had inherited their father's impish ways. Sick of having to wash up before meals, Jimmy and Bobby once closed the valves to every faucet in the house. Only after the lawn was dug up—exposing a perfectly intact water main—was the prank discovered.[5]

By the late fall of 1926, Buster was ensconced in the Villa, hard at work cutting *The General*. (Compared to the rest of the property, his modest workroom looked like an afterthought. It was used by subsequent owners as a tool shed; in the mid-1950s, actor James Mason and his wife discovered a safe sitting forgotten at the back of the ramshackle structure—inside were rotting nitrate prints of many Keaton shorts, along with a working cut of *The General.*[6]) The family passed their first Christmas in the new house; to ring in the new year, Buster and Natalie drove south to a resort outside of Tijuana where Joe Schenck was throwing a party. Buster was distracted; the date for the New York premiere of *The General* kept getting pushed back. The screenings had not been promising.[7]

In theory, however, Keaton should have had much to toast south of the border. He was Hollywood royalty; his films were being knocked off in Russia (with imitation clowns pulling imitation stunts); according to a 1925 insurance policy, his life was worth $1,000,000.[8] He had a new house, loads of friends, and great kids. But something was amiss.

Buster had always been a drinker—who wasn't in the tipsy, high-hatted days of Prohibition Hollywood?—but now he began to drink more heavily, more often. Few noticed. Buster rarely was out of control; not surprisingly, he could be a subtle drunk. Buster Collier—a close movie friend of Keaton's, Jimmy's godfather, and, for a while, Constance's lover—thought his friend's indulgence stemmed from his standoff with Natalie. Keaton was trapped in a cold, sexless marriage, with ubiquitous, condescending in-laws, who sniffed at his social measure but didn't let that stop them from enjoying his benevolence. (One could drink a clown's booze and still think him a clown.) Years before, Joe Keaton's alcoholism had wrecked the family act—certainly the worrisome genetic and archetypal influences were there for the son—and with the failure of Buster's pet project looming on the horizon, there was the potential for great unhappiness and grave consequences.[9] But for now, Buster hustled back to work.

Keaton needed a safe bet. *The General* had strayed and the studio got burned; Buster's next film would bow to convention and make a buck—or so Schenck hoped. Two years earlier, Harold Lloyd's *The Freshman* had been a critical and popular hit; collegiate settings had been in vogue ever since. It was time for Buster to trade his engines and war for sweaters and coeds. No flashy stuff, just dorm rooms and track meets (which were cheap to film, by the way). As the title made abundantly clear, Buster was going to *College*.[10]

The film was part spoof, part fingers-crossed imitation of Lloyd. It is not a great movie. The generic premise must have seemed inert, a dull insult to the singular mind that had envisioned the daft clock-work of *The General*. Furthermore, Keaton found himself working with strangers he didn't like and old faces in new hats. Buster decided Carl Harbaugh, who would work gags and titles on his next two films, wasn't good at anything; his new director (or rather the man who received screen credit for such), James W. Horne, was "absolutely useless."[11] (Buster let Horne direct the scenes he wasn't in.[12]) Worst of all was the spiritual defection of Harry Brand. Publicity man Brand had been brought in to replace Lou Anger as studio manager. (Schenck had transferred Anger, who had been with Buster since that first flour-flinging day at Comique, to a position at United Artists.) Brand and Keaton had gotten along in the past, but now, burning with new fiscal zeal, Brand began to run afoul of Keaton. He took Snitz Edwards off the payroll without telling Buster, despite Buster's desire to keep his friend on the set for an additional day or two—in case further inspiration should strike, or some other such thing. Buster likened Brand to a man ripping apart a well-tuned engine, just for the sake of doing so. Feeling a statement was necessary after the Snitz incident, Keaton and his men played baseball for three days straight. But in the end it was Brand who got the last word. Months later, already on location for his next film, Keaton went to see *College* in a Sacramento theater. And there it was, staring him in the face—an addition to the opening credits: "Supervised by Harry Brand." The title had been inserted—with Schenck's approval—after Keaton had signed off on the final cut. Not typically one to care about screen credits, Keaton was annoyed first by Brand's meddling, and then by the inclusion of the relatively new (and at the time woefully overused) "supervisor" credit. (One day, supervisors would be called producers.) Buster didn't like self-aggrandizement—as he had made emphatically clear with his all-Keaton playbill in *The Playhouse*.[13]

By early April, a one-sentence outline of Buster's collegiate story had appeared in *The New York Times*. Keaton filmed the campus scenes at the University of Southern California in Los Angeles; he shot rowing sequences at Newport Bay.[14] Even saddled with a stale plot, he was giving it the old college try.

College plays out the revenge of the original nerd. Buster is Ronald, the high-school scholar who minds his mother and scorns jocks. After delivering a pretentious, ill-received graduation speech on "The Curse of Athletics," he follows Mary the popular girl (Ann Cornwall) to Clayton College, where his only hope to win her is by demonstrating his varsity prowess. He arrives on campus in the apposite sweater and beanie, lugging a suitcase full of athletic gear and a handful of helpful Spaulding manuals like "How to Sprint." But the brain can't get the brawn to comply; Ronald can't make the cut. He tries out for baseball, but he single-handedly brings down on his team the rarely seen triple play. (Grounders roll through his legs; he gets beaned by pitches—the insider irony of course being that Keaton was a great ballplayer.) Ronald fares no better on the track. Testing his foot speed, he is dispirited to find himself outpaced by two little boys. In an eloquent panning shot, Keaton races again, only to knock down every hurdle in his path, save one. (Finished—in more ways than one—he stares at it, then flips it over.) Trying his hand at field events, he throws various implements poorly (discus, javelin, hammer) and takes a few jumps that are neither high nor broad. (Meanwhile, the varsity high jumpers are delightfully dated by their face-first, pre-Fosbury flops.) Overall, the track and field scenes suffer from a visual problem: for all of Buster's clumsiness, the skimpy track uniform can't hide the fact that he *looks* like an athlete.

Ronald's labors get him hazed by Jeff the star jock (Harold Goodwin) but befriended by the sympathetic Dean Edwards (our man Snitz), who lands him a place on the crew team by administrative decree. Ronald makes a spirited coxswain and gets a chance at glory when he

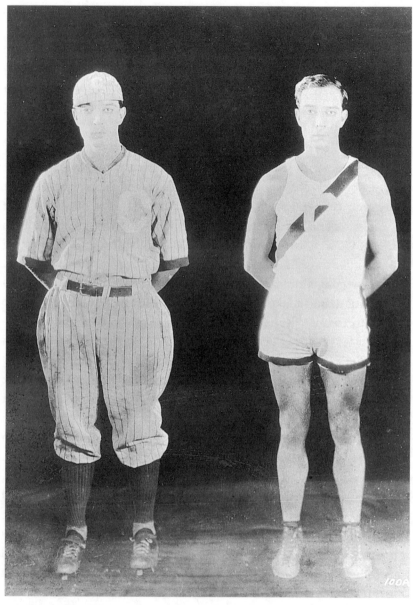

28 *College* (1927)—Buster fitted out for baseball and track, looking like the athlete that he is.

is called up for the big intercollegiate race. The sleek boats are set in the water: the rival crew will be rowing the *Bullet;* Ronald will helm the *Damfino,* which, like its predecessor from *The Boat,* sinks at the hands of Keaton before it can go anywhere. (It is replaced in time for the race by *Old Iron Bottom.*) The shots of the regatta—from above, from the side, from Ronald's point of view—are exhilarating; the sculls slip across the bay like blades on ice. With some nimble (and unorthodox) steering, Ronald wins for dear old Clayton in front of the spirited student body.

But Mary is absent in Ronald's moment of triumph. He must rescue her from Jeff, who late in the film takes a very sudden and very nasty turn. She is a prisoner in her dorm room. As he races to save her, our knight calls upon each of his newfound athletic skills. He sprints down a street, hurdling the hedges and high-jumping a privet; he (long) jumps a pond and pole-vaults through her second-story window. Inside, he puts on a sporting attack. The nerd hurls plates at the jock (with discus-like accuracy), pitches an alarm clock, shot puts a statuette, bats a projectile back at him, and—as Jeff escapes out the window and through the yard—nearly impales him with a standing lamp-cum-javelin.

For the difficult vault through Mary's upper-story window, Keaton relied on a stunt double—the first in his lifetime. At USC Buster met a student pole-vaulter named Lee Barnes; Barnes had won Olympic gold three years earlier in Paris. Buster figured he would save himself the weeks it would take to master the stunt and had Barnes double it for him.[15] It is difficult to know what to make of this fact. Perhaps the delay would have been too expensive; nonetheless, in the past Keaton always had relished a challenge.

After Ronald's hyper-athletic display, he is caught alone in the room with Mary. Dean Edwards and the prudish housemother discover the couple in a chaste embrace—the matron asks the girl if she knows the import of this, meaning expulsion. Mary says yes she does—marriage. Ronald slings her over his shoulder and hops down the fire escape. As the pair run up to a church, the scene cross-fades to them walking out, hand in hand. After such an insistently triumphant climax, we finally get a chance to catch our stirred breath and enjoy our cathartic just deserts; it seems a natural place to break—time to drop the curtain. But not to Keaton. The ending is capped by three swift dissolves that burst the happy bubble like blasts from a tommy gun. First, we fade in on our future mom and dad at home with the kids. Then, a dim view of the couple in their dotage, wrinkled, fussy, bundled before the fire. Finally, a bright outdoor shot—adjacent plots in the cemetery. The End. It is an open-hand slap to sentiment, to the promise of young romance, to basic storytelling convention. While they were living happily ever after they got old and died—so what? Ha! Fade out.

The cheeky, dark coda seems a last-ditch effort to maneuver the film into satire. But it isn't enough. Despite the strange and funny send-off, *College* remains an essentially stodgy, formulaic enterprise. Playing it safe hadn't paid off. *The New York Times* found the comedy forced and the film lowbrow; the reviewer took special offense at the sport scenes, which he felt were unforgivably idiotic—a child could have achieved better.[16] At the box office, *College* brought in even less than *The General*; while it cost much less to make, *College* was clearly a flop.[17]

As Keaton spoofed the notion of fairytale forevers, perhaps he had in mind real-life marriages that didn't last. His own was going, if not gone; so too was his parents'. The exact date is unclear, but sometime after seeing their son hit movie stardom, Joe and Myra would separate. Joe took up at the Continental Hotel, the Elysian Fields of old-time vaudeville, where Buster would pay his monthly rent. In one of his real-estate campaigns, Buster bought a nine-room house on Victoria Avenue for his mom and siblings. Over the years, the original Two Keatons remained friends. Joe would date—and be sobered by—a Christian Scientist; on the night of their 50th wedding anniversary, Myra would ride the downtown bus to invite Joe to dinner. They would never divorce.[18]

At the end of June, Buster headed to Sacramento to begin his next feature.[19] Earlier that month, there had been reports of a pair of unique shooting stages installed at the new Vitaphone studio. The footage taken there would change movies forever. The film was called *The Jazz Singer*; that October, wild ovations would threaten to drown out the miraculous sounds of Al Jolson talking and singing onscreen. It wasn't the first time the pictures had talked, but it was the loudest—at last a major feature had integrated synchronized sound into the drama. The next month, the East Coast film cabal—men from Paramount, Fox, Loew's—would meet with their Hollywood counterparts for two weeks to discuss the industry-wide ramifications of the arrival of sound. Theaters would have to be wired. Pictures re-thought. In a little over a year, more than fifteen sound stages would be up and running.

And so as Buster went upstate in the summer of 1927, an air of abeyant panic was settling over the industry. Profits were down—even without a talkie revolution in the wings—and nerves were starting to run raw.[20] But for Keaton, there were more immediate, less foreseeable challenges ahead.

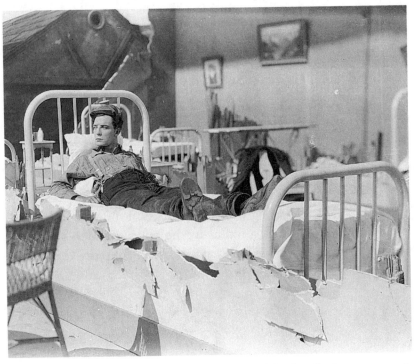

29 Buster wakes to feel a draft in a publicity photo for the stormy comedy
Steamboat Bill, Jr. (1928).

CHAPTER NINETEEN

The Fall of the House of Buster

Sunday, Labor Day weekend, 1927. This is real life, not a movie but a movie set. You're standing in front of the façade of a two-story house that's about to fall— on you. Your heels are planted on your mark: two nails driven into the ground. Wind gusts from airplane propellers attached to huge Liberty motors; one alone can lift a truck—six are blowing. It's a cyclone. This summer they've been saying that sound—when it comes—will kill the silent movie; you drink too much; your marriage is essentially over, your career could be next; yesterday you received some of the worst news in your life. So you stand in the eye of the man-made storm—winds howl in the foreground and background, but where you are it's calm, so as not to disturb the downward arc of the two ton façade. The gag has been carefully measured: if all goes right you will be left standing, unscathed, in an open window on the second floor. You have two inches of clearance for your shoulders, your head, your heels. The director (who can't bear to watch) is rumored to be off in a corner of the lot with a Christian Scientist, praying. You signal that you're ready for the cameras to roll. You lower your head. It's a one-take scene. When the house comes down, you don't even flinch.[1]

The premise came from Chuck Reisner, a beefy actor turned director who had worked with Chaplin and knew Buster from the vaudeville days. (On the set, Reisner called Keaton, thirty-one, "Little Buster.") The story was a heartwarmer about the reunion between a wimpy East Coast son and his estranged father, a salty Mississippi skipper named Steamboat Bill. Reisner signed on to co-direct. The Keaton corps, under Gabourie's watchful eye, spent $100,000 building a three-block town set, complete with boat landing, along the banks of the Sacramento River. Ernest Torrence was hired to play the father. For the girl, Buster found an unknown stage actress named Marion Byron. The sixteen-year-old, 4'11" spitfire (who went by "Peanuts") didn't know how to swim; Louise Keaton would serve as her water double. By mid-July, the crew was ready to shoot *Steamboat Bill, Jr.*[2]

Which is he? Big Steamboat Bill had rushed to the station as soon as he got the telegram. It was from his son; the boy, whom he last saw in diapers, arrives from Boston today. His timing is perfect—there is trouble in River Junction. Bill is being muscled out of the steamer business by J. J. King, the stuffed town tycoon who has his name on the bank, the hotel, the fish stand, and now a floating river palace that puts Bill's old paddlewheel to shame. Bill could use a sturdy hand to help him run the *Stonewall Jackson*—surely by now Junior dwarfs his old man! Which of the young toughs getting off the train could he be?

The truth sends Bill's grumpy heart through the floor. The apple has fallen far from the tree, then sprouted legs and walked a mile. Willie is, well, *short*. And wearing a jaunty beret, a striped jacket, a polka-dot bow tie, and an argyle vest. It gets worse: he's carting a ukulele, and above his lip crawls a moustache like a starved Parisian caterpillar. The boy's a dandy. While Bill tries to get him shipshape— clean his lip, get him an honest hat and a man's clothes—Willie bumps into Kitty from Boston, a darling slip he'd like to impress. The two are typically inconvenienced, caught between warring parents— her father turns out to be the dastardly King. Even still, Willie tries to win his old man's affection, but it is to no avail—he's a worthless shipmate. Junior is on his way back East when he sees his father snatched by the police. (King has the law in his pocket.) A storm brews as the son ponders his duty.

By the waters of Sacramento, things were getting thorny. The production had suffered the ordinary delays (one thanks to an eighth-inning fastball that broke Buster's nose), but recently the crew had come to an unprecedented impasse. Buster wanted a flood; Brand did not. That year, the Mississippi River had overrun its banks: homes were lost; people had died. Supervisor Brand convinced Schenck that a flood—in addition to being expensive—would be in poor taste. Buster posited other disasters, and in the end the men allotted him a cyclone. Keaton wasn't bothered—he would work in his flood gags anyway. (He did pause, however, to confirm a suspicion that in past years windstorms had claimed more lives than floods. He reportedly held his tongue.) And so Gabourie rebuilt the sets while Buster rerouted the comedy. The adjustment cost almost $35,000, which raised the question: Who was the true wastrel, Buster or the bean-counter?

For his storm, Keaton shipped in six enormous wind machines and rented a 120-foot crane that floated on a barge. The destruction would be biblical. The scenes were difficult and the water cold. Willie Riddle served Buster and Louise brandy between takes. But the crew was upbeat. They had a superstition: dunk Buster at least once a picture—for good luck.[3]

Willie wakes in a receiving hospital. He had gone to rescue his father—bringing him tools (file, chisel, wrench) baked inside a loaf of bread—but the jailbreak failed. He had struggled to make Dad understand what the bread was concealing. (To drive home his point, Willie "sings" a prison ditty, coolly, cleverly, as he pantomimes the loaf's true purpose. It is perhaps the film's funniest, and most under-stated, bit.) For his efforts, Willie had been clobbered by the sheriff.

Outside, the storm is raging. Cars gust down the street; the wind shears off the corner of a building. The hospital roof is blown away, revealing a startled Willie in bed. When the public library collapses next door, he dives under the covers. The bed-frame skids through a barn and down the street. When Willie crawls underneath it, it sails away. As he staggers to his feet, the façade of an enormous two-story house falls on him—leaving him standing in that open window. More buildings collapse. Buster clowns against the storm, struggling to get up the block: he leans forward at a full 45 degrees; he crawls, slides, and jumps into the wind; he goes nowhere. He seeks safety in the ruins of a vaudeville theater; he is hit by a sandbag, scared by a dummy, and dropped through a trapdoor. (The interlude pays homage to specific acts and memories of Buster's youth.[4]) Doorways topple while he stands in them—twice. A house lands on him, then disintegrates. He clutches to a tree, only to have it uprooted—he rides it, flying above the docks and into the river.

Steamboat Bill is washing downstream, locked in a sinking jail; Kitty passes by, clutching the side of a house! Willie rescues her, then spots his dad. He must man the giant paddleboat by himself. He crashes through the jail at full throttle, just in time. Evil King needs a rescue too. With everyone safe on deck, Kitty embraces her savior. To her chagrin, Buster leaps overboard. But it's okay. Having saved his father and her father, it is now time for Willie to save a holy father—floating by in his frock—so that he and Kitty can be married. The End.

Years later, Buster would remember standing under that falling façade and not caring whether it hit him or not. Shooting had wrapped in Sacramento. He was back on a Hollywood lot, working over a holiday weekend. The scene was the logical extension of a career-spanning gag—one that had started with Arbuckle in *Back Stage* and stretched from Keaton's first solo release, *One Week*, to this very film (where it occurs not once but thrice). The stunt had grown with each attempt; the stakes now were as high as they could be. The front of the house swung on a hinge; it was built solid so as to fall flat and straight—a deviation of more than two inches would crush Keaton. Another one-chance take. Few of the crew had the stomach to watch. It was a lot of drama for a mere beat in the film's climax—only one of many disasters to befall Willie, rapid-fire, in the storm. It was just a joke, but Buster felt he had nothing to lose. The day before he had gotten the news: the Keaton Studio was shutting down.[5]

Schenck told Buster he was getting out of the independent production game for good; henceforth he would dedicate his time to overseeing United Artists. That meant curtains for 1025 Lillian Way. Buster was dumbstruck. He had come to Schenck to complain about Brand; instead, he had lost his studio.

With Schenck's desertion, the movie business lost one of the few remaining independent producers. Picture budgets were getting bigger; if sound stuck, it would only drive up costs. The big studios

ran on economies of scale. The future was conglomerated. Indepen-
dents were a dying breed; only the preternatural moneymakers—
the Chaplins and Lloyds—could afford autonomy. Everyone else
had to join a shop.

Joe wasn't simply abandoning his star-in-law. He had a plan.
Buster's September 1924 contract was expiring. Joe already had lined
up a deal—he had arranged for Buster to join Metro-Goldwyn-Mayer,
which was owned by Loew's, Incorporated, whose president was his
brother Nicholas Schenck. Buster would simply trade one Schenck for
another. It was that simple.

But not to Keaton. He went east and informed Adolph Zukor, head
of Paramount, that he was in the market for his own studio. Zukor,
who had just agreed to distribute the films of Harold Lloyd, declined
on the questionable ground that a deal with Keaton would steal
Lloyd's thunder. (Buster later claimed the Hays Office was pressuring
Zukor to leave him to MGM.) After a few before-lunch whiskeys,
Keaton called on Nicholas Schenck. He wanted to hear it from the
horse's mouth. Schenck considered it a done deal—MGM would give
Keaton the finest directors, the biggest sets, the wittiest writers, and
money, money, money. It was an offer he couldn't refuse.[6]

And so another house had fallen. The dust was still settling, but
from where Buster stood, it seemed fate had placed him, unharmed,
in the open window once again.

30 Buster and the inimitable Josephine on the set of *The Cameraman* (1928).

CHAPTER TWENTY

The Company Man

His mind was too orderly for our harum-scarum, catch-as-catch can, gag-grabbing method. Our way of operating would have seemed hopelessly mad to him. But, believe me, it was the only way. Somehow some of the frenzy and hysteria of our breathless, impromptu comedy got into our movies and made them exciting.[1]

Buster Keaton on Irving Thalberg

Steamboat Bill, Jr., was released in May 1928. The reviewer for *The New York Times* said the film was long, tired, and made him more sad than happy; watching it, his face mirrored Keaton's—never a good thing.[2] Indeed the film starts slowly (it deliberately crescendos to the cyclone), and while the final tempest offers yet another astonishing example of Buster's comic velocity—at once fierce and fanciful (with those Oz-like flying houses)—*Steamboat Bill, Jr.*, doesn't hum with the usual Keaton current. It was a dud, earning the least of all of his United Artists releases.[3] But by that time, Buster was otherwise occupied. His old life seemed a world away.

The date on the contract was January 26, 1928. It was good for two years, during which Buster Keaton would receive $3,000 a week from Metro-Goldwyn-Mayer, the studio that soon would own "More Stars Than There Are in Heaven." Keaton was obligated to make two pictures a year; titles beyond that were worth $50,000 apiece. He could bring over Fred Gabourie and some of the old crew; Joe Keaton would get $100 a week. In addition to Buster's generous pay schedule, the studio would hand over a quarter of the Keaton profits to the still-intact Buster Keaton Productions, whose shareholders continued to dole out a percentage to their star. The undeniably cushy deal made Buster the third most expensive light in the MGM sky. There were, however, some unsettling provisions.

Perhaps the most worrisome clarified that while Buster had consultation rights on script and direction, he did not have the final say—that power ultimately resided with a "producer."[4]

East of Santa Monica and south of Beverly Hills, in sunny Culver City, stretched MGM's 180-acre lot, a fully integrated dream factory that churned day and night, shepherding pictures from synaptic glimmer (originating deep within one of the many wits on payroll) to post-production (with its inevitable retakes)—and from there into the great public beyond. It was the early days of the fabled studio system, when the movies met mass production. The goal was to release a picture a week—many lavish, many not, all put over with a carny's flair. The machine was run by a cast of thousands—writers, builders, directors, publicists, editors, artists, engineers, tailors, photographers, grips, designers, electricians, actors, wranglers, cooks, producers. It was the kind of place that splashed on 200,000 gallons of paint a year (who said pictures were in black and white?) and could chew through 350,000 feet of lumber in three weeks. There was a police station, a hospital, and a barbershop. In 1928, MGM had the money, the prestige, and the stars; the trademark lion roared and John Gilbert jumped—along with Marion Davies, Greta Garbo, Lionel Barrymore, and Norma Shearer. Soon Joan Crawford, Marie Dressler, and Clark Gable would add to the luster. Buster was the company's first dedicated funnyman—looked upon by the studio heads as a prized, if not somewhat puzzling, acquisition.[5]

As president of the New York parent company, Nicholas Schenck was the absentee landlord. On the lot, two vice-presidents held the reins: general manager Louis B. Mayer and head of production Irving G. Thalberg. Hollywood legend plays Thalberg as the gentleman prince to Mayer's vicious troglodyte: Mayer, forty-two, was conniving, crass, and feared; Thalberg, twenty-eight, was a romantic boy-genius who suffered from a feeble heart. A former beau of Constance's, Thalberg was celebrated as an industry prodigy, a man with razor instincts and a poet's soul; he was also a willful, driven businessman who slept five hours in twenty-four and often is credited for the rise of the producer. (At the expense of the director, note—thus settling the age-old battle between the accountant and the artist, for a time.) Buster held Thalberg in great esteem—the two were longtime friends—but he found his boss untutored in the vagaries of comedy, forever searching for a formula that wasn't there. Not long after the contract was signed, Thalberg handed supervision of the new Keaton features over to Lawrence Weingarten, a young producer who recently had married Thalberg's sister.[6]

Buster had had doubts about moving to MGM. He ran it by his friends—Chaplin said it was a bad idea, and so did Lloyd. Unfortunately, Buster's last three films had bombed; he was in no position to wheel and deal. In the end, he decided to trust Joe Schenck, the man who had made him, and sign the contract. Buster forever would call it the biggest mistake of his life.[7]

The studio brass had promised their new clown that he would be able to work with his old team—which was true, to a degree. Keaton's first MGM picture would feature the gags of the good prodigal son Clyde Bruckman; Elgin Lessley would return to handle the cameras; Fred Gabourie was on the studio payroll as technical man. The reunion turned out to be a one-shot deal. After that first picture, the talented Gabourie was promoted off Buster's crew; in short time he was running MGM's entire technical department—a nice promotion, but one that robbed Keaton of his best mechanical mind. Before long, Buster would find other members of "his" team unavailable to report for duty. It wasn't malicious or underhanded; there just was no downtime for crewmembers—they were put to work on other sets, with no guarantee of when they would be free. In their absence, Keaton was required to use other MGM staff. No more outside contracting—that was the point of the studio system.[8]

But if an unstable, unfamiliar crew was an inconvenience, the mandatory story scripting was a crime. To the MGM creed, Keaton's tried and true working method was pure blasphemy; the system was designed to streamline production, not throw it upon the mercy of the comedy gods. There was no room for harum-scarum. And so while the idea for Buster's Culver City debut was his own, the execution of it was something else altogether. Before his very eyes, Buster's old penny postcard—the one carrying a good comedy plot—would grow into a telephone book. The picture would be called *The Cameraman.*

Buster is a humble sidewalk tintype photographer eking out a living at ten cents a portrait. He has staked out an empty street; amazingly, a man walks by and becomes a customer. As Buster composes the shot, a lone piece of paper drifts down from above—trash, it seems. Soon it's a whiteout—nothing less than a ticker-tape parade. (Apparently a lady has swum the Channel.) The street is flooded with spectators; newsreel cameramen jostle Buster out of the way. But he doesn't mind. The crowd shoves him into a girl and it's love at first sight (his, not hers—she's with the newsreel guys and doesn't see him). Buster lets himself smush dreamily into her. When the parade dissolves, he gets her picture but not her name, leaving him to search for his tintype Cinderella.

It turns out she is Sally, secretary in the newsreel office of MGM. She isn't overly impressed with his magic tricks, and tintype is a distant fiddle to newsreel pictures, so Buster buys a gawky archaic pawnshop movie camera and tries to join the ranks on a freelance basis. They'll buy any good film, she tells him, so it's good film he's hunting. That and a date with her.

That was as far as Keaton had broken the story in his head. There was ample premise to ride. Now enter the MGM team, in the form of twenty-two writers assigned to flesh out the script, each hack eager to make his or her narrative mark. The plot swelled to make room for mobsters, jewel thieves, politicos, dockworkers, and the Salvation Army—or so Buster recalls. It took months to finish off the bloated script, a process further complicated by meddlesome studio money-men-turned-gagmen—even the executives were sticking their fingers in the pie. (A temptation that Joe Schenck, for the most part, wisely had resisted.) In May of 1928, a crew went east to film the convoluted caper.[9]

Even the director was being micromanaged; he carried with him instructions on how to shoot the script—despite the fact that he, an industry veteran, always had managed fine without them. His name was Edward M. Sedgwick Jr., formerly of the Five Sedgwicks, a Texan ex-vaudevillian who loved baseball and eventually learned to sit back and let Keaton handle his share of the directing. Sedgwick's name would be on most of Keaton's MGM features; the two men would get along famously. But that was after New York.[10]

Keaton couldn't cross 23rd Street at Fifth Avenue without being mobbed. A trolley driver had spotted him trying to shoot an inconspicuous street scene; the man shouted, triggering a traffic snarl. Streetcar gridlock stretched for three blocks; buses and cars jammed in every direction. There was no way to continue filming. (Buster took the opportunity to point to a line in the script describing his character as just an anonymous face on the New York streets. Of course Keaton was anything but—Chaplin might have been the king of comedy, but Lloyd and Keaton were close seconds, and MGM had paid top dollar for their wildly popular star.) The crew snuck downtown to the Battery, but again crowds swarmed the shoot.

From his room at the Ambassador Hotel, Keaton called Thalberg. The script was no good; New York was no good—they should scrap everything but the essential story, shoot what few exteriors they could get in three days, and fake the rest on the studio lot. The crew was shut-in on the other side of the country, burning money in a hotel; Sedgwick had taken to bed with ice and bromides. What choice did Thalberg have?[11]

With the script of many months out the window, Buster had a relatively cleaner slate to work with. And while enough of the old plot would remain to make *The Cameraman* noticeably more scattershot than a typical Keaton comedy, Buster was free to improvise some of the best moments in the film. Such a scene takes place at Yankee Stadium, one of the few New York locations that worked out.[12] Our cameraman's quest for footage has taken him to the ballpark; he heard the Yankees are playing, and they are—in St. Louis. The stadium is empty. Buster walks onto the diamond, sets his camera down, and— after a glance over his shoulder—takes a spot on the mound. He proceeds to pantomime an entire inning of baseball by himself, sans bat, sans ball, just a guy in baggy pants and a newsboy cap. Keaton is all business, shaking off his catcher's signals, keeping runners on base with the threat of a pick-off, adjusting his outfield. He dives for a grounder and makes the play at second; he tags a runner at home. Soon it's his turn to bat. He's sent to the dirt and complains about the brush-back. He digs in and swats one—he rounds the bases at top speed, just barely sliding out the throw to home. A homer. He dusts himself off, a hero for the first time that year, and salutes his fans. Then the spell is broken, the applause cut short by the appearance of a groundskeeper. It is an enthralling interlude—convincing, athletic, inventive, magical—Buster goofing about in the dust, outside of time or plot, as an old elevated subway trundles past in the distance, a quiet reminder that the game cannot last. Still, for a moment, an empty stadium holds its breath.

Another brilliant bit of improv was the famous changing-room scene. Sally (played by the winsome Marceline Day) has granted Buster a date. He takes her to the municipal pool, paying their way with a fistful of his dimes. The romance will have its setbacks: Buster loses his trunks after a fancy belly flop; Sally's striped suit attracts a bevy of tall admirers; at the date's end, the couple are forced to catch a ride home with rival suitor and snooty cameraman Stagg (Harold Goodwin, the loathsome Jeff from *College*). But before all that, Buster has to put on his bathing costume. The dressing room is barely wide enough for one; there are two—it has been double booked. As Buster hangs his hat, a dumpy balding crab of a man pushes his way in. Neither fellow is willing to relinquish the space, and so the stubborn struggle begins. It is full-contact stripping. Buster gets an elbow in the neck, a fist in the nose; for an instant, he's on the other man's back. They flail away like dueling strips of flypaper, grimly entangling themselves in each other's shirts, suspenders, suits. Eventually Buster emerges in his companion's swimwear, which fits him like a muu-muu. It is a simple bit—a slow burn, shot in long claustrophobic takes. Thalberg loved it. The peevish roommate was Ed Brophy, the unit manager who just happened to look the part. He and Buster got in the cubicle unrehearsed, and the camera simply started rolling.[13] For a little while, it was as if they were back at Lillian Way.

The rest of the story was hardly so straightforward. Our tintyper's first footage is ruined by his technical incompetence—in the screening room, the other newsies (with their sleek modern cameras) get a good laugh at his double-exposed and reverse-action gaffes. Battleships navigate Broadway; busy streets scenes accelerate and splinter like some kind of hyper-real Soviet Montage. Feeling for the underdog, Sally gives him a tip: there's a tong war brewing in Chinatown. On his way there, Buster knocks down an organ grinder, occasioning the gently bigoted, perfectly unforgettable line, "You kill-a de monk!" A cop makes Keaton dispose of the body, but the tiny monkey is not dead, only stunned. Buster and his new friend head downtown in time to capture the outbreak of war. Keaton and pet fend off attackers, fearlessly

31 Buster and Josephine pose for a publicity photo for *The Cameraman* (1928).

cranking amidst the chaos. The legs of the camera get shot off; Buster climbs a scaffold that is toppled—as he films, the platform slowly falls forward, affording him a dramatic "crane shot." (The fortunate fluke calls to mind such real-life, on-set Keaton occasions—just keep filming.) Our brave cameraman even goes so far as to stage a few shots, intervening in the action to offer one grappling combatant a knife, for better dramatic effect. (It is interesting to see the newsman's complicity in the violence made explicit by a visual pun equating the cranking of a machine gun with the cranking of a camera—that rascally monkey confuses the one with the other.) When Buster goes to turn in his Pulitzer footage, he finds there is no film in the camera. Now Sally is in hot water over the tip, and their chance as a couple is kaput.

Buster and his monkey cast off in a rowboat—they're giving the news game one last shot at the yacht club regatta. They land and set up the camera on the beach. Sally is joyriding with Stagg in his powerboat; he makes a reckless turn, throwing them both overboard. Cowardly Stagg swims ashore, while Buster dives in to rescue his unconscious love. He stretches her out on the beach and runs off for aid. While Buster is gone, the girl comes to, allowing Stagg to take credit for the lifesaving. Buster returns to see them stroll off in an embrace. He crumples to the sand.

Luckily, the monkey was filming the whole time! Buster doesn't know that, but he does discover that the little imp had removed the film after the tong war. Buster drops off the newfound reel (which contains both battle and waterfront footage) before returning to his tintypes. In the projection room, the cameraman's bravery is revealed to all. Sally finds him on the street—he's won himself a job and a girl! The office wants to throw a big to-do. Suddenly, we've come full circle: a crowd appears; tickertape falls. A parade—for him? With no groundskeepers in sight, Buster salutes his fans, one and all, including that man they're calling Lindbergh over there.

For Keaton, one of the greatest pleasures of the film was creating the mangled footage submitted by the rookie cameraman.[14] He was always up for a technical project, and the ghostly double exposure of a ship cruising midtown and the fractured, fly's-eye-view of midday traffic are the kind of marvelous, striking errors only an artist could make. *The Cameraman* also incorporates actual newsreel footage, such as Channel-swimmer Gertrude Ederle's reception at New York's City Hall and Charles Lindbergh's triumphant 1927 tickertape parade. (Buster claimed the film was designed to benefit from a bit of corporate synergy: MGM could promote its newsreel outfit, which distributed films from Hearst, which in turn would give the film good press.[15])

However, the historical celebrities are eclipsed by an even more remarkable supporting player—little Josephine the monkey.[16] Any furball can look cute in a sailor suit and cap, but few monkeys can act, let alone emote. The amazing Josephine has operatic range: pain, fear, confusion, joy, deceit—she does them all. Flattened by the organ grinder, she woozily comes to with a shake of the head (and a hand to the brow). Josephine will cover her mouth in dismay; she celebrates good fortune with understated pint-sized applause. Not your usual scene-stealing simian, she steers boats, fires machine guns, and shoots pictures with the indifference of a pro. (To be fair, half of the footage that lands Buster his job is hers.) In flawlessly funny, endlessly charming Josephine, Keaton had at long last found a worthy successor to his great canine co-star Luke.

And yet, one magnificent monkey does not a masterpiece make. *The Cameraman* has some original gags and some beautiful photography (especially of Buster standing on lonely paper-strewn streets after the parade has passed); it is generally a good film. But one feels a formulaic chill creeping into his work. For example, repetition is only humor when served with a dash of wit; here, there is a running gag—about Buster breaking and re-breaking an office window—that's run right into the ground. The titles offer off-key wisecracks and dopey love lines. (After the disastrous date, a real flincher: "It was worth it . . . to be near you.") For the first time, there are multiple soft sappy close-ups dripping with moony glances—sentimental, unnatural, formerly completely out of bounds. Buster's character is more of a bumbling dope than before; he is aggressively endearingly simple, as if to ensure the "sweetness" of the love story doesn't drown in the Byzantine plot.

Despite the broad strokes and mawkish sentiments, *The Camera-man* was a huge hit. At long last, the reviews glowed and the seats filled—the film would double the gross of *Steamboat Bill, Jr.* At New York's Capitol Theater, there was a promotional appearance of "Our Gang," whose short *School Begins* (distributed by MGM) shared the bill. The film's final review came decades later, in the 1950s, when a friend of Buster's asked to have it run for him at the studio. He was told the print could no longer be projected—it was completely worn out. For years, *The Cameraman* had been used as a primer picture, a blueprint for faultless comedy—it had been required viewing for incoming studio comedians. One imagines that the sound of those MGM newcomers—Abbott and Costello, Mickey Rooney, Red Skelton, the Marx Brothers—laughing in the dark might be the film's finest tribute.[17]

Unfortunately, what the studio honchos didn't realize was that the film was a success in spite of the system, not because of it. That *The Cameraman* had brought Keaton out of a three-picture nosedive seemed to validate their faith in the assembly line. Thus when Buster asked Thalberg to allow him his own unit within MGM—just a few men and Sedgwick—the mogul said no: Keaton would use available in-house talent just like everyone else. Buster argued that a constant crew would in fact save money; familiarity breeds efficiency, not to mention quality, when it comes to team comedy. No dice. From now on, production schedules were to be followed, budgets projected and kept to, shooting scripts drawn up in advance and followed—not tossed out the window.[18] Gone were the days of clowning on the fly.

In many ways, Keaton's decision to go to MGM—whether by choice or necessity—marked the subtle demolition of a golden era. The industry had gone a long way in the twenty-five years since the debut of the first popular American screen narrative, which, curiously, had concerned itself with a great train robbery—it was a short span for a world to emerge. For more than eleven years, Buster had gamboled down the side streets of comedy, blazing impractical, incomparable detours in his own peculiar way; now he was forced into lockstep with an indomitable production system. Keaton had limned the human failures and visceral thrills of a modern age; the story of him against MGM was the oldest one he knew: the misfit against the mob. It is a typically American fixation—the gauntlet of Huck, founding fathers, and Thoreau—and for that, Keaton is a decisively American comic. But while Buster would fight the good fight, his kind of ending usually bartered Yankee idealism for its bleaker national cousin, pragmatism. Buster was quiet in the face, but never doe-eyed. The savvy, bold-by-necessity one might butt up against the impressive, well-organized many and win, but sometimes numbers rule the day, the romance doesn't last, and dreams—ha, ha—don't ever come true. Some cops you just can't outrun.

The crushing hegemony of the studio system was guaranteed by the advent of sound. It was a question of economics; only the richest could evolve. Buster would prove a fearless, if not eager, convert to the new technology; he had a good strong voice and funny things to say. But with sound, the dignity of silence was lost. Once the movies talked, they never shut up. As was predicted at the time, the imagination suffered. The hushed distillation of a Keaton silent draws you in in singular ways. I will never forget, after having seen each of his independent films over and over, the disconcerting thrill of hearing Buster talk. It was a 1937 short. He entered a room whistling; then he spoke. His voice scratched my ears. It was deeper, huskier—not at all the voice I had heard in my head, which, I realized, was modeled (in a cheerfully narcissistic way) after my own internal monologue. But that's the point, the solipsistic strength of silence—something takes place inside: we cast ourselves into the film, we make it ours. And as is often pointed out, that interior work is half the fun. Think of the 500 brides thundering after Keaton at the end of *Seven Chances*. As the poet Charles Simic put it, "All of us who saw the movie can still hear the sound of their feet."[19]

The movies would suffer visually, too. There is a fluidity to the silent camera that is lost once it acquires the bulky trappings of recording. Pictures moved indoors and settled down for a while. To mask the whirr of the motor, the camera and its operator were confined to a booth—severely limiting the range of motion. Gone were the days of that old Keaton joy: hook the camera up to some whizzing speed demon—be it boat, train, or cycle—and go, go, go. The static camera put an end to the visual music—the eloquent comic staccato—that gave Buster's movies their giddy drive. Eventually cameras would be encased in soundproof "blimps," and the pictures were free to roam again, but for a while the industry forgot what it had learned about space and scope and the unique gifts of film and took its cue from the theater, offering little more than chatty farces and drawing-room dramas.[20] All those glorious, arduous real-life locations—icy depths, endless deserts, thick backwoods—were discarded for the predictable, antiseptic sound stage.

As the studio shoehorned Keaton into closeted, all-talking affairs, Buster's beloved screen self had to change. The funny absorption of a sober little clown—curious and knowing, honest and shrewd—was broken once Buster opened his mouth. Words betray a stone face. And it had been those curious inner-workings—ever hidden, as single-minded as they might be—that had made people laugh.

And so the studio system began grinding up Keaton. As Buster points out, Thalberg failed to grasp the importance of the Keaton free-wheeling method—to the man in the green eyeshade, spontaneity seemed like an acceptable casualty of the new economics.[21] Scripts and schedules were there to curb ever-growing budgets; otherwise, where would the madness stop? Allow no time for baseball brain-storming or lengthy gag polishing—no winging a hunch or acting on an accident. All hail the tyrant script. Of course, there is a certain attractive logic to the system—a fantasy of control, of precision, of having your ducks pleasantly in a row. Get the story right the first time, then follow it. But Buster simply didn't work that way.

The system was inherently cautious. Not only did it refuse to bet on Buster's on-the-spot ingenuity, but it began to second guess his physical dexterity—something few had ever called into question. Buster represented an investment; the studio did not like investments to stand under falling houses, break their necks, or nearly drown—there were to be no more dangerous spectacular stunts. Keaton learned this right from the start. While shooting scenes for *The Cam-eraman*, he heard complaints coming from Lew Cody's set. A pratfall was needed—some risky business about falling down some stairs—but neither Cody nor the stuntmen could make it funny. Happy to lend a hand, Buster put on Cody's outfit and nailed the stunt in enthusiastic fashion. He thought nothing of it. The next day he was called into Mayer's office and given an earful. That was the end of such extracurriculars.[22] And when comedy became safe—or even simply safer—it lost a measure of its rough-and-tumble vitality, its athletic bravado, its daredevil thrill. No more runaway engines or driverless motorcycles—no more real fear. As the famous line suggests, the pictures were getting small.

Buster's losses at MGM were many and great. Ease, speed, freedom, singularity of vision, silence, the help of good friends—the happy confluence of factors that had allowed his genius to flourish was going or gone, depending where one stood. Buster gave MGM a fair shake. He had never been one to sit things out. Unable to quiet the chuckling in his head, Buster would pitch Thalberg the idea for a comedy—just the bare bones, say he and Marie Dressler on the wagon trail—but Thalberg would not be able to envision it, or trust Buster to make it good.[23] Between star and studio there was a failure of imagination, of faith. The seeds were sown for Keaton's downfall, and as his career careened downhill, he would lose his health to drink and his marriage (what was left of it) to adultery. There would be long dark years before a triumphant second act, the one you weren't supposed to get in America. His story would end happily yet. But before that, he had to face all that noise.

32 Buster and Elmer at MGM, c. 1931.

CHAPTER TWENTY-ONE

End of the Affair

Dumb show is best for screen people, if they must appear in public.[1]

Buster Keaton

Buster wanted to talk—they just wouldn't let him. If one read the papers, one knew it was a time of anxiety and paranoia; the silent era was drawing to an unseemly, hysterical close. Magazines reported stories of voice tests, voice lessons, and the one true horror: mike fright—a career-ending affliction. *The New York Times* ran overwrought, melodramatic first-hand descriptions of what it was like to work in the brave new Hollywood. What once had been a noisy, comfy set—with the murmur of mood music, the sputter of klieg lights, the whirr of the camera, the whisper of the director— was now deathly quiet. Stars froze on the sound stage; it was like acting on the moon, or in a crypt. The weak of voice feared their profession would be overrun by theater actors, but seasoned stage performers—playing to the galleries—boomed too loudly into the mike and spoke with unnatural, exaggerated nuance. Writers and directors had their own headaches. Comedic timing had to be rethought—must dialogue pause for laughter, and if so, for how long? The flames of speculation were fanned by studio publicity departments, eager to whet the public's appetite for sensation and scandal. The burning question: *Could the stars learn to talk?* The balconies filled to find out. Some celebrities would not make it. Sound's most famous victim would be the great screen lover John Gilbert; according to legend, his high, anemic voice made him more peevish sheep than passion's slave—at which audiences laughed their heads off. (Others tell a darker tale involving a sabotaged soundtrack and the opportunistic hand of Louis B. Mayer, who was ever at odds with the contrary star.) After two pictures, Norma Talmadge would surrender, despite having spent a fortune ironing out her diction. Constance simply retired outright.[2]

Buster had passed the vaunted studio vocal test, a prolonged exercise in pseudoscience and hucksterism. (The gang assembles outside the strange, custom-built booth; at last, an MGM employee emerges—Keaton can speak!) Buster told Thalberg it was time: he wanted to make a talkie. For a lifelong technophile, sound was just another gizmo to figure out. Buster wasn't interested in quips or puns—he didn't go for uncharacteristic, undignified blather—but synchronized effects would increase the film's realism, something for which Buster always went to great lengths. At last, audiences could hear the crash, the bang, the sweet music of a pratfall. The answer came from on high: sound stages were for musicals and dramas, not clowns. Keaton's time would come.[3]

While Buster pitched story ideas that went nowhere, he got word from Weingarten that his next premise was already prepared. It came readymade with a title: *Spite Marriage*. The script was completed by the MGM writing corps—there would be no outside help from Bruckman. Sedgwick was back, but Gabourie was gone, as was Lessley. The new crew would assemble for the picture, then part ways— division of labor at its finest. Buster found these studio specialists narrow-minded, obligated to please their department supervisors— not their star—and more invested in their area of expertise than the greater life of the picture. The lighting guy didn't mind a terrible story, as long as it was well lit.[4] Gone were the days of pitching in, of blurred responsibility—in a way, it was every man for himself.

The plot of *Spite Marriage* was a doozy. Buster plays Elmer, a pants presser who goes gaga over an actress named Trilby Drew. The unblessed union of the title is theirs—she weds him to arouse the ire of her errant boyfriend, Lionel. Add bootleggers and a daring sea rescue and eventually love emerges triumphant. Perhaps the film's greatest significance was that it threw Buster in with a talented dark-haired Alabama divorcée named Dorothy Sebastian. The former showgirl, practical joker, and inveterate good-timer was known by a handful of variations on the nickname "Slam Bang Sebastian," due to her tendency

33
Poster for *Spite Marriage* (1929).

to topple after a few cocktails. Warm, beautiful, and popular, she played Buster's wife; offscreen, she became his mistress. The light-hearted, accommodating affair would run for two years. Sebastian was a sport. When she discovered that Buster had arranged a Palm Springs get-away with another woman, she didn't make a fuss. Instead, she secretly rented the adjacent love nest and—once the couple arrived—made such a ruckus in her kitchen by clanging the cookware that Buster and his guest fled the decidedly unromantic scene. Back in Hollywood, Sebastian revealed herself as the noisy neighbor. Keaton appreciated the joke.[5]

Spite Marriage wrapped on Christmas Eve 1928. While not a talkie, the film featured a synchronized score and some sound effects. When it premiered the following spring, the reviews were charitable; interestingly, many celebrated the lack of dialogue. At New York's Capitol Theater, the film came on the heels of a disastrous, short-lived talkie—

the *Times* declared silence the winner. (In a subsequent dispatch from London, the paper cited further supporting evidence: *Spite Marriage* had outsold its talking competitor at the box office.) The film's best scene involved the groom struggling to put his soused spouse to bed on their wedding night. Buster's well-intentioned maneuverings inevitably backfire, as her limp body flops everywhere but snuggly under the covers. Producer Weingarten hated the drawn-out bit—he thought it cheap. Buster fought tooth-and-nail to keep it in. The scene stayed, and practically every review singled it out as a corker. Over the years, the gag would appear in more than eight films, including *Roman Holiday*, with Gregory Peck manhandling Audrey Hepburn; decades later, Buster would reprise it at the French circus and on American TV.[6]

Score one for Keaton and his boffo bride. But while Buster won that fight, he would lose many others, including the battle of the bungalow. When he had signed with MGM, Buster had rented a small house just outside the gates, despite the fact that the studio offered dressing rooms on the lot. Mayer had been miffed; he preferred to keep his property within view, but he let it slide—for a while. Keaton was the only big name not to reside within the walls; even Marion Davies' $75,000, fourteen-room Spanish bungalow (built by W. R. Hearst) was on the lot. Keaton's outside digs offered him a measure of independence; rather than dining at the MGM commissary, he had Willie Riddle cook for him and anyone else who happened to be around. The Keaton Colony did not last long. As part of Mayer's campaign to bring Buster in line—meaning under his thumb—he insisted that Keaton move into one of the free studio bungalows. It was prime real estate, next to Davies and John Gilbert; the place came complete with kitchen, bar, and white picket fence. Keaton, of course, did not go quietly. He hung a sign in front—KEATON'S KENNEL—which he maintained was simply in honor of Elmer, his new St. Bernard. In truth, Keaton seemed to prefer his kennel to his Villa—he often spent the night on the lot. (As for Elmer, he enjoyed long walks with Greta Garbo.) The bungalow would become an anti-establishment watering hole. It was furnished with handsome glass-enclosed bookcases, which Louise Brooks remembers Buster—silent and drunk late one summer night—smashing in with a baseball bat.[7]

The Cameraman had been silent; *Spite Marriage* had featured sound effects; now Buster made an appearance in a talkie, but it wasn't his film—he was being eased into the fray. The talkie in question was a glittery trifle called *The Hollywood Revue of 1929*. True to its billing, the film was a plotless mishmash of vaudeville-style episodes, the insistently cheery vanity project of a studio anxious over the sound revolution. Essentially every MGM star took part—Marion Davies, John Gilbert, Joan Crawford, Laurel and Hardy—showing the world that the studio's stable could hoof, croon, and crack wise with the best. Buster revived his old army-surplus "Princess Rajah" belly dance; the finale had the whole cast in slickers for "Singin' in the Rain," twenty-three years before Gene Kelly and the Technicolor pinnacle of the singing, dancing blockbuster.[8]

A train readies to leave a small Midwestern depot; a crowd has gathered to wish the travelers bon voyage. Speeches are called for. The studio brains had taken about a year to settle on a story for Buster's first talking feature—surely these will be choice words.[9] After some yakking by the guy from the Chamber of Commerce (and Keaton's two companions), Buster moves in to speak—he opens his mouth . . . but it's nothing more than a whisper, which no one hears! Subsequently, he manages only to begin—"Friends . . ."—before being drowned out by the band. After three tries, he finally delivers his address. The jokey vocal debut is one of the few funny bits in the film (and then only funny for reasons external to the plot). Buster plays another dolt named Elmer, a homespun talent manager who accompanies his charge, Miss Gopher City, from Kansas to Hollywood, where she hopes to get her big break. Naturally the pair will make it on to the MGM lot, and what follows is little more than a studio love-in, featuring leaden dialogue, labored situations, and awkward cameos by the likes of Fred Niblo, Jackie Coogan, Lionel Barrymore, and Cecil B. De Mille. Elmer romps his way through MGM, wrecking sets and dodging guards, until his clownish screen potential is discovered and he's put in the movies. There are big, show-stopping numbers—yes, the film is a musical—and Buster (in tights and makeup) sings and dances his way through the inanity. Elmer's celluloid debut is a comic opera; one song ends with him dressed as a clown, suspended from wires, a film star and yet a hapless marionette—a no-doubt unintentional, but nonetheless biting comment on behalf of the studio writers. (Then again, the story concerns a man who goes to MGM, is made into a misunderstood clown, then has his heart broken.) Ultimately, Miss Gopher City chooses another suitor, and the film ends on Elmer's sad-clown face as he closes his eyes, overwhelmed by the pathos of love unrequited.

The film was a misguided exercise in wasted talent. While Buster—a child of vaudeville—was an amusing singer and a fantastic dancer, he almost never gets to let loose; called *Free and Easy*, the movie was anything but. The titular song is matched with a charmingly wonky dance, but to get there we have to endure unimaginative, overdetermined bits flayed within inches of their comedic lives. (See Elmer's inability to say his line, "The queen has swooned"—and thus, "the quoon has sweened," and so forth, ad nauseam.) There are long dance numbers, sparkly costumes, a few silly songs, and the worst ending of a Keaton film, bar none. Audiences loved it. (As did *The New York Times*, which happily reported that Buster had a suitable voice.[10]) The film came out in the spring of 1930; earlier that October, the stock market had plummeted, ending a decade's worth of prosperity and optimism. Perhaps people wanted it "Free and Easy" once more—who could blame them? It was Buster's curse that some of his lamest duds would be his biggest moneymakers.[11] Depression audiences devoured the high-gloss, low-plot spectacles, which only reinforced the studio's desperate embrace of noise—leaving us with all-singing, all-dancing, all-talking, but no laughing, today.

Buster claimed L. B. Mayer was so pleased with his box-office success that the mogul gave him a $10,000 bonus and a three-month vacation. Other versions assign the beneficence to Thalberg. Still others claim the vacation was a good-will gesture designed to allow Keaton a cooling-off period after he stormed off a set. Regardless, all Buster had to do was finish his current picture, an army comedy called *Doughboys*, and he and Natalie could head to Europe for the honeymoon they never had. The film sends Buster, a rich playboy who mistakenly enlists, into the trenches of the Great War; again there were bad gags and some music—mostly from a ukulele—but this time Buster was able to work in many of his own wartime routines, and the film sometimes is cited as a breath of fresh air. *Doughboys* wrapped in early June, and that summer the Keatons set sail. In Spain, they were joined by Norma Talmadge, still married to Joe Schenck, and Gilbert Roland, still her lover. The Mexican-born movie star took Buster to bullfights, which Natalie declined; one afternoon Keaton was carried home on the shoulders of local fans. Buster enjoyed his European tour, but a honeymoon it was not. By then, he and Natalie were hardly speaking.[12]

While Buster was abroad, two things of note happened. First, Dorothy Sebastian got together with future Hopalong Cassidy cowboy Bill Boyd; they would marry in Las Vegas within months of Buster's return. Second, Lawrence Weingarten saw a play, which he determined would be the basis for Keaton's next film. Before leaving town, Buster had signed another lucrative two-year contract with MGM. When he returned to Hollywood that October, he was dismayed to learn—once again—that he had been saddled with a preposterous stage plot.[13] This time, there could be no late-breaking rescues or last-minute rockslides, à la *Seven Chances*; he would go down with the farce.

Parlor, Bedroom, and Bath opens on the Italian Villa's beautiful backyard, which slopes to a pool filled with frolicking bathers. Buster is a dimwitted sign tacker who gets buffeted about by unmarried, Amazonian socialites, then discovers his libido and carries on with too many of them. There is the typical bedroom nonsense, some good physical bits, some dreadful physical bits, and one happily familiar gag. (Buster destroys a beautiful American Austin roadster in the same manner as he did the portable house in *One Week*—stranded across the tracks, the car is smashed by a second, unforeseen train.[14]) Nonetheless, the theatrical material—frantic, door-slamming mix-ups and tedious verbal buffoonery—was unbecoming to the screen's most

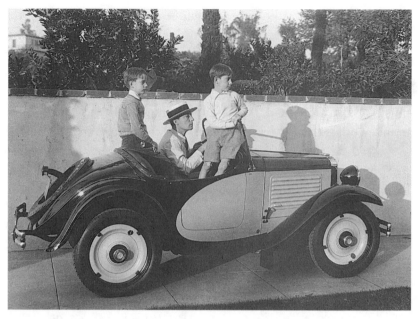

34 Jimmy, Buster, and Bobby at the Villa, sitting in the American Austin roadster fated for destruction in *Parlor, Bedroom, and Bath* (1931).

subtle, economic clown. There was a further, more personal incongruity: the idea of Keaton as an incompetent lover was becoming harder and harder to sell.

February 6, 1931. On page eighteen of *The New York Times*, the lower-left headline read: "Ex-Film Beauty Claws Keaton, Movie Clown." The less-reserved *Los Angeles Times* printed doctored pictures of Keaton and his female assailant on page two, plus a fanciful cartoon (all adjacent to the smaller item, "Deputies Hunt Reds' Arsenal"). According to the papers, the squabble erupted over a friendly wager. Keaton said he had bet actress Kathleen Key $500 that she couldn't lose twenty pounds in ten days. Key lost, but Buster gamely paid her anyway; later, he agreed to loan her money. As Buster was handing over a $5,000 check, Key suddenly demanded an extra $20,000. When Buster refused, she went mad, attacking him and wrecking the bungalow. The police dragged her off. Key refused to tell her side to the papers; two days after the incident, she was nowhere to be found. In his autobiography, Buster skipped the story of the bet, saying simply that an unstable unnamed actress appeared one day and insisted that he support her. He declines; she assaults him; he socks her in the jaw when she tries to stab him with a pair of scissors. (Cops on the scene get a black eye and a kick in the groin.) Buster says the MGM honchos insisted he give Key $10,000 to keep the matter out of court, regardless of his innocence. The truth: the weight-loss story was the studio's concoction. Angry lovers made bad press. Key, a namesake and great-granddaughter of star-spangled lyricist Francis Scott, was a feisty MGM contract player whose career had stalled. After the payoff—$10,000 to buy her silence—she left town. There are some who claim Mayer sent her abroad after putting out word that Key was never to work in pictures again. She never would.[15]

The damage control continued. The studio publicity department drafted a waiver for females to sign before entering the Kennel. MGM was not responsible for "broken limbs, loss of virtue, etc." Friends teased Keaton in telegrams, which were leaked to the press; signs appeared over the bungalow door (Danger: Women at Work!).[16] The end of May marked the Keatons' ten-year wedding anniversary. Natalie told him she was only in it for the kids, who worshipped their father.[17] Soon she would put aside such concerns; public humiliation had never been part of their agreement.

And so the Villa remained an unhappy home. There were affairs and drinking; money went out as quickly as it came in. Both Keatons could spend: she outfitted herself like a screen goddess; he played bridge for stakes he couldn't afford. (Louise Brooks later laid the blame for Keaton's downfall at the feet of his wealthier card-playing friends, studio bigshots who pressured Buster to live the million-dollar life.[18]) Buster also supported his sister, brother, father, and mother; he lent freely to his friends.[19] And so while the pranking and drinking, shopping and gambling, fighting and cheating continued as usual, the day of reckoning was drawing near.

Sedgwick was busy on another picture; he couldn't work on Keaton's latest. Buster was assigned a pair of youngsters eager to direct their first feature. Jules White and Zion Myers were known for recreating popular films using talking dogs; the "Dogville" oeuvre includes such shorts as *Love-Tails of Morocco*, *Hot Dog*, and *So Quiet on the Canine Front*. Buster didn't take well to instruction from animal handlers. While shooting a harbor scene, Keaton jumped off the side of the boat (as scripted); he continued swimming, not to return for a week (an ad lib). The film was called *Sidewalks of New York*. The plot involved a millionaire who mentors a band of downtown urchins in order to charm one of their sisters. Buster felt it was his worst effort at MGM; it would outgross every one of his independent silent features.[20]

The next release, *The Passionate Plumber*, featured the talents of Keaton, Sedgwick, Gilbert Roland, and the big-nosed, motor-mouth comedian Jimmy Durante. MGM had picked up Durante that June on a five-year contract. From the very first scene of the French farce, Buster—nominally the star—is thrown into the background by Durante's signature, manic schnozzing: an insidious torrent of mugging, catchphrases, and malaprops. Keaton was insulted; he believed MGM was exploiting him to promote Durante. The misadventures of Elmer, a brain dead beret-wearing gun-toting plumber in Paris took a mere nineteen days to shoot. The film was released in February 1932, to good reviews. *The New York Times* gave Keaton and Durante roughly equal ink.[21]

That April, the Keaton family dirty laundry made the papers again. It was a story more convoluted than the dressing-room brawl, involving borrowed airplanes, absent spouses, kidnapping, and an ill-fated jaunt to Mexico. Buster wanted to fly Jimmy and Bobby with him on a long-promised trip to a resort owned by Joe Schenck outside of Tijuana. Natalie refused to let the boys go. On Friday, she and Buster had a fight, which ended with her walking out; she was gone all weekend. On Monday, Buster, Willie Riddle, Jimmy, Bobby, and a governess took off in a plane belonging to a screen cowboy friend of Buster's. The plane touched down in San Diego, and while the group waited to clear customs and return to the air, the governess escorted the boys to the bathroom. They didn't come back. A squad car had taken them to the San Diego police station; the boys were being held to foil a kidnapping. Natalie had gotten a district attorney friend of Constance's to put the kibosh on the trip. She claimed her children were in danger; she was afraid of flying and didn't want the boys on a plane—she also thought there was a chance Buster was smuggling the kids to Mexico, never to return. The next day, the runaways went home to a still-vacant Villa. On Wednesday, April 6th, the story ran above the fold on page one of *The Los Angeles Times*. There was a large, staged picture of Buster and his boys, kneeling on the lawn, eyes downcast, awaiting mother's return. Buster jokes his way through the interview, pointing out the lamp kept burning in the window for his wayward wife and playing one of the three records he sent over to Constance's house, where he assumes Natalie is staying (the title track: "Can't We Talk It Over?"). Buster admits he went ahead with the trip to prove a point, but despite his bemused, apologetic posturing, there is a moment of real bitterness when he admits several Beverly Hills police are on hand to prevent anyone from taking his children away from him. The story ends with Buster summoning an agrarian fantasy: he says the family has not found happiness in the Villa—he wishes they were on a ranch, and he a farmer. The next day, Natalie came home.[22]

Buster returned to work on April 14th. L. B. Mayer had been demanding his presence at the studio for some time in telegrams and registered letters, which Buster had ignored. During the shooting of *Speak Easily*, Buster's next film, the star's haphazard attendance wasted eleven days of scheduled production, costing MGM some $33,000. Buster, once a compulsive worker, had developed a bottle-a-day whiskey habit. His alcoholism notwithstanding, *Speak Easily* is considered Keaton's best talkie, which perhaps says more about the poverty of the bunch than the excellence of the particular. Buster liked the story, which involved a classics professor who finances a Broadway show with money he doesn't know he doesn't have; when the blundering academic botches opening night, the crowd is in stitches and the show is a hit. Durante is back, playing himself, with Sedgwick directing. The film was Keaton's most expensive production at MGM; it too was a hit.[23]

Speak Easily finished shooting in June. Perhaps to celebrate his commercial success, perhaps to drown his artistic sorrows, Buster bought a boat. The five-bedroom, ninety-eight-foot yacht, dubbed the *Natalie*, was a gift to his wife. He and the crew sailed it from Seattle to San Pedro, just south of Hollywood. It is unclear what Natalie, not the seafaring type, thought of her $25,000 boat. It was on that vessel, in the dark morning hours of early July, that Buster would awake next to a naked stranger at the sound of banging on the cabin door. He fumbled for the light, opened the door, and saw Natalie, Constance, and a detective.

It was a mean, drunk day that had started badly and had gotten worse. There had been a row; Natalie had left, again. Late that afternoon, Buster made it down to the studio half-cocked, where he spied a pretty extra idling outside the casting office. Back at the Villa, he offered her the run of Natalie's enormous closet, tossing shoes and furs at her feet. Unable to figure the angle, the girl accepted the wild bounty, hoping to appease Buster. When she mentioned she wasn't sure where she would stash the growing pile before her, Keaton knew just the place—on the high seas. The captain of the *Natalie* refused to cast off; doing so required authorization from the owner, who clearly was not aboard her namesake vessel. The drunken pair could, however, sleep on the boat. Buster passed out and woke to that knocking. The detective and the district attorney—also present—gathered evidence, including the clothes. Natalie had only one thing to say: in the morning, Buster would hear from her lawyer. The divorce papers were filed July 25th. Buster did nothing, not even hire an attorney. On August 8th, Natalie was granted an interlocutory decree of divorce. Though legally entitled to half, Buster gave her everything: the Villa, the boat, the cash, the real estate, the insurance, two cars. He simply gave up—Natalie had gotten the boys, whom Buster had been teaching the pratfall. That autumn, she would put Jimmy and Bobby in an exclusive military school filled with Hollywood brats (there already were two Chaplin offspring and Shirley Temple's brother). In two years, she would have the boys' names legally changed from Keaton to Talmadge.

Buster would be crushed. But he did nothing—Talmadge heirs would inherit a family fortune, and by then Keaton was broke.[24]

In the August of his divorce, Buster found himself left with the family's third car. He quickly borrowed money and bought another one. It was no ordinary vehicle, however. A Depression-era bargain at $10,000, the so-called land yacht had been designed for a railroad tycoon. It was a Pullman bus with drawing rooms, galley, and deck; it had beds for eight. Buster and his guests would tool around the state in nautical costumes borrowed from the MGM wardrobe department. He would park in hotel lots, ask the staff to run a phone line to the bus, and order room service. He would go hunting and fishing. He learned he was not allowed to take his boys on overnight campouts. For a while he stayed in Harold Lloyd's driveway, then in the studio parking lot. The yacht was a party on wheels run by a man trying hard to forget. When not abroad in his motor home, Buster stayed in a small house he bought in Cheviot Hills, a few miles south of his former Beverly Hills Villa.[25]

MGM gave Keaton a less-lucrative one-year contract that October. Before he could work on his next picture, he needed to dry out; the studio sent him to an aversion therapy program, where he was forced to drink until sick, and to a private retreat in Arrowhead Springs. Through his rehab efforts, Buster met a divorced nurse named Mae Scriven. She was retained to keep him sober. She failed. At the MGM Christmas party, he misjudged a drunken pratfall, conked his head, and blacked out; the next day, he didn't remember a thing. A few days later, he and his nurse flew to Tijuana on a New Year's bender; on January 8, 1933, a judge married them in Ensenada, Mexico. Buster would never recall the wedding. The nuptials caused a stir—his divorce with Natalie would not be final until August. In October, he and Mae married again.[26]

The south of the border elopement interfered with production on Buster's latest MGM feature, another Durante yap-fest called *What! No Beer?* Buster, sallow and drawn from drink, plays a taxidermist who buys a brewery with annoying pal Durante. Buster can hardly get a

35 Buster and his second wife, Mae Scriven.

word in. And at this late date, watching Keaton pour a beer is a kick in the gut. There is some sudsy clowning, a stripping moll, a drunk horse, a gang of angry bootleggers, and a barrel-dodging downhill race that is a pathetic reprise of the *Seven Chances* rockslide. The film is a giddy hymn to booze, aimed at a country anticipating the repeal of Prohibition, which would be finalized that December. Of all his MGM talkies, this one embarrassed Buster the most—a strong statement, given the fact that Keaton often starred in the same bad movie more than once. He was the only big name on the lot who routinely acted in his own foreign-language remakes; Buster would finish the film in English, then have to relive the tragedy in Spanish, or German, or French (reading his lines off phonetically translated cue cards). Thankfully, there would be no foreign versions of *What! No Beer?*, despite its box-office success. *The New York Times* and *Variety* reviewed the film well;

both noted Durante upstaged Keaton. By the time the reviews were printed, the matter was moot. Buster was no longer at MGM.[27]

At noon, February 2, 1933—about a week before the release of *What! No Beer?*—two studio men delivered a one-sentence letter to Buster from Louis B. Mayer. Keaton was fired. The decision was final; there could be no appeal—Thalberg was absent from the studio, recovering from a heart attack he had suffered in the after hours of that unlucky MGM Christmas party. A day after receiving the letter, Buster announced his retirement from the screen, citing a physical breakdown.[28]

36 Buster and his third wife, Eleanor Norris, arriving at New York's
LaGuardia Airport from Paris, 1947.

CHAPTER TWENTY-TWO

The Little Boy Who Couldn't Be Damaged

I've had few dull moments and not too many sad and defeated ones.[1]

Buster Keaton

For Keaton, 1933 through 1935 were the rock-bottom years of his life. He was no longer a star; he could barely work. When he was drunk there were blackouts, when sober the DTs (which came with hallucinations of creeping ant armies and blood-thirsty squirrels). There were stories of Buster trading pratfalls for swigs of hobo wine, of Houdini-like escapes from straightjackets and sanitariums, of late-night arrests. Buster stopped paying his income tax; despite declaring bankruptcy, he would owe the government $28,000. With the money gone, so was valet Willie Riddle, and nurse Mae took over the care of Buster. Word went around that Keaton wasn't fit for the screen. And the pictures went on without him, for a while.

In some ways, Buster's collapse seems the result of a personal, very human failure; in others, the fall seems inevitable, written in the economics and technologies of a shifting industry. It is worth noting that Chaplin and Lloyd, both that rare breed of star whose box-office caliber grants him fiscal independence, chose to remain above the fray. The two backed off for a while, hoping to return in a more level-headed climate. Thus Lloyd was able to stagger on, self-financing his films until 1938 at a rate of about one release every two years. Chaplin's first true talkie was *The Great Dictator*, which came in 1940. Lloyd and Chaplin could wait. Keaton had no such luxury.[2]

The dismissal from MGM made Buster a Hollywood untouchable. A few months later, an offer came from Florida. A group of optimistic financiers had hopes of establishing a landmark production company in St. Petersburg, southwest of Tampa. They were going to shoot a picture called *The Fisherman*; the veteran director was an

MGM castaway (and Mayer-basher, to boot), as was the writer, who was an old friend of Buster's who had worked on *The Cameraman*. Keaton went east in May; he received the key to the city, visited Havana, collected $3,000 a week for nine weeks, then—with production stalled by rains, mosquitoes, and heat—left the Sunshine State. The St. Petersburg company fell apart. While Buster was still in Florida, Roscoe Arbuckle died of a heart attack in New York. Now Keaton seemed the broken one; he did not even go to the funeral of his greatest pal.[3]

Back in Los Angeles, Buster and Mae settled into their Cheviot Hills home, a low-slung, six-room Spanish residence on Queensbury Drive not far from a golf course. Earlier that spring, Natalie had sold the Villa; the yacht was long gone. Natalie (and the boys, when not in school) lived in a beach house Constance had bought her; the former Mrs. Keaton dated the likes of Howard Hughes and actor Larry Kent, who moved in.[4]

Buster began making two-reelers for an outfit called Educational Pictures, which—if the slogan was to be believed—provided "The Spice of the Program." Shot in three to five days, the low-budget films paid $5,000 each and, despite what the diehards tell you, are really just for diehards. From 1933 to 1937, Keaton would make sixteen shorts for Educational. Later titles like *Palooka From Paducah* (1935) and *Love Nest on Wheels* (1937) would feature combinations of Joe, Myra, Jingles, and Louise, the latter film being a Keaton-family take-off on *The Bell Boy*. Between stints in rehab, Buster churned out his first two Educational shorts. Then, in June of 1934, he and Mae went to France. Buster had received a $15,000 feature-film offer, which did not cover transportation; he cashed in some forgotten war bonds and booked two tickets on a Glasgow-bound freighter. En route to Paris, Buster received a good-luck note from Joe Schenck containing $1,000—ostensibly Keaton's cut from the auction of some over-looked studio equipment. *Le Roi des Champs-Elysées* took twelve days to shoot; Buster played two roles—the film ends with him breaking into a smile, a closing gimmick Keaton had been avoiding his whole life. From France, Buster went to London, where he had agreed to star in a deeply under-funded movie, *The Invader*. It was an early effort from the one-day legendary producer Sam Spiegel (*On the Waterfront, Lawrence of Arabia*)—running at about an hour, it too was a turkey. That fall, Buster and Mae had no choice but to return home. Spiegel was deported for forging checks.[5]

Buster returned to making Educational quickies, or "cheaters" as they were known in the business. Mae set up a beauty parlor, attempting to cash in on the Keaton name. (A large sign announced Buster Keaton's Beauty Shop, the preceding mini "Mrs." all but unnoticeable.) Buster's "marriage of inconvenience," as he called it, lasted less than three years. Some biographers have insinuated that Mae turned tricks for cash. Whatever the case, it was she who found Buster warming the sheets with fellow hotel guest Leah Clampitt Sewell while vacationing in Santa Barbara on the Fourth of July 1935. (Recently named in a wife-swapping scandal, Sewell and her husband apparently were high-society swingers.) Buster continued seeing Sewell, a friend of Louise's. Mae divorced him that October, on his fortieth birthday. She walked out with half their possessions, including Elmer. Buster would engage a private detective to search for the dog, but to no avail—Mae had sold him. Keaton went on a bender. By the end of the month, he lay in a hospital. The papers cited a nervous breakdown, precipitated by the flu. On October 23rd, *The New York Post* ran a picture of a contrite and helpful-looking Mae. She had shown up at the Veterans Hospital seeking reconciliation; she asked that a note be delivered to Buster—she and Elmer were waiting for him. She spoke of dropping her $200,000 lawsuit against Mrs. Sewell. Buster, in the psych ward, refused her admittance.[6]

That January, Mae again would marry in Mexico; this time she was the bigamist—her divorce to Buster would not become final until the following October. She would wed a few more times before being committed to a mental hospital in Queens, New York. In the fifties, she was recommitted and received shock therapy. She sued a studio responsible for a Keaton biopic (libel), then took on the state and city of New York (negligence)—the suits went nowhere. At the end of the decade, she disappeared completely.[7]

Back in 1935, on Halloween day, after more than a week in the hospital, Buster returned to his again-empty home, walked his back-yard golf course, wound up in the clubhouse, knocked back two Manhattans, and didn't drink again for five years.[8]

By 1938, Buster had clawed his way out of the abyss. The year before, Educational Pictures had gone bust; Keaton's agent (and industry friends) got him hired by MGM as a comic advisor, a spot gagman and on-lot resource for actors, writers, and directors. The once $3,000 a week megastar was reduced to a wage of $100 (later to become $350), but he never complained. When not dispensing advice or directing one-reelers (of which he shot three), Buster sat in his small office, not far from the now-quiet Kennel, playing cards, picking a ukulele, and toying with Erector sets. Keaton would serve his old studio intermittently until 1950, working with such talents as the Marx Brothers, Abbott and Costello, and Red Skelton (who would make versions of *Spite Marriage*, *The General*, and *The Cameraman*). He would become a close friend and mentor to Lucille Ball, a screen actress who MGM had decided—by the forties—was on her way out. She would hang around his office, which soon filled with fantastic machines like the two-foot-tall Cigarette Lighter, the three-foot Nutcracker, and the Venetian Blind Raiser, which reportedly involved a set of blinds, a .32-caliber handgun, the anthem "Hail to the Chief," and a portrait of L. B. Mayer. Despite such diversions, Buster took his position seriously. He was unimpressed by most of the MGM comics, whose distracted work ethic disturbed the down-and-out clown. To a man who once wrote, directed, cut, and starred in his own pictures, a former full-time prankster who demanded all-consuming attention to detail and obsessive commitment from his friends and co-workers— who usually were one and the same—these new stars seemed intoler-ably uninvolved in their work and, worse, wholly unconcerned to be so. Abbott and Costello wouldn't warm up to him. The Marx Broth-ers scoffed at Keaton's suggestions, though they never had been above recycling his bits. Buster claimed to have gotten along better with dramatic stars such as Clark Gable and Lana Turner, though he felt his best collaboration was with his good friend (and compatible co-worker) Red Skelton. The early years of the MGM homecoming were lean. There was not much money, especially as he continued to support his family, who had moved in with him (Jingles took the couch). For a while, his life outside the studio consisted of little but bridge—but he was working, and he was in love.[9]

In 1938, a friend of Jingles' brought over a beautiful blond eighteen-year-old MGM dancer named Eleanor Ruth Norris. Norris wanted to learn bridge; there was always a game at Cheviot Hills. After a more than six-month progression from quiet observer to shy participant, she yelled back at someone who had abused her for making a poor play. That was the day Buster first took note of her. (As for Norris, she had never seen a Keaton film, though she had noticed him around the studio.) For the past two years, Buster had been back in the arms of Dorothy Sebastian; it took him a while to extricate himself from the relationship—he began inviting over a good-looking wrestler and eventually finagled the bait-and-switch.[10]

In December of 1938, Buster began making cheaters for Columbia Pictures. Heading the studio's shorts department was Keaton's old Dogville director, Jules White. Memorable mostly for their titles—*Pest from the West* (1939), *Pardon My Berth Marks* (1940)—the dreary two-reelers were distributed gratis with Columbia features. They paid only $2,500 apiece and typically took three days to shoot. Buster made ten before swearing off them in 1940. He was starting anew that year, which had included a wedding.[11]

Eleanor had asked Buster to marry her. His friends worried over the age difference—his forty-four years to her twenty-one—but the couple shrugged off objections and tied the knot on May 29, 1940. Their courtship had evolved from bridge to a supper-club first date on Sunset Boulevard to a private screening of *Battling Butler*. The City Hall nuptials had the usual Keaton complications. The judge—a first-time officiant and son of supervisor Harry Brand—almost married Buster to Eleanor's mother (who perhaps looked a better match); he then mistook Eleanor's maiden name as "Morris." There was a fire nearby, and Judge Brand was forced to shout the pronouncement over earsplitting sirens. The couple drove off in a station wagon for a fishing honeymoon on June Lake.[12]

With another world war underway, Buster and Eleanor sold the Cheviot Hills home and moved in with Myra, who refused to leave Victoria Avenue. A few years before Buster sold the bungalow, he received the visit of a lifetime. Jimmy, newly turned sixteen and in command of a brand-new driver's license, took Bobby on his first drive—right over to their father's house. Opening the door, Buster was floored. He had tried to gain custody, unsuccessfully, two years earlier. Natalie had prohibited contact, but after that maiden summer drive, Buster's children were back in his life. In October 1942, Keaton returned to his consultant post at MGM. Eleanor, still a studio dancer, was earning the lion's share of the household income; every day, the couple rode to work in the family car. In 1940, Buster had begun drinking again, though not as desperately as in his dark years; still, there were periodic episodes, which caught Eleanor unawares. Buster's third wife, by all accounts, was a gracious and loving companion; strong and capable, she had supported herself since age fourteen (four years after her father died hanging lights at Warner Brothers). She could handle Buster. During the war, Jimmy and Bobby graduated high school and joined the Coast Guard. Jingles got married, had a son, and took a job in Las Vegas, one of his first. Indomitable old Joe Keaton grew senile; he died on January 13, 1946, not long after the war's end. On Victoria Avenue, Myra would point out boot-marks on the doorframe—well above her head—that he had made with his high kicks in the years before he died.[13]

With peace in Europe and Jingles and family back from Vegas, Buster and Eleanor went abroad in September 1947. A French circus, Paris's one-ring Cirque Medrano, had invited him to perform at their postwar reopening. In Paris, Buster learned he was still a celebrity. Fans, remembering his glorious silents, begged for autographs; French clowns hovered around the ring, studying his technique. For the high-paying gig, Buster dusted off a dueling skit he had worked out for *The Passionate Plumber*. He and Eleanor would return to the Medrano in

1952 and again in 1954. He soon worked Eleanor into the act; she would serve as his drunk wife in the famous putting-the-wife-to-bed bit from *Spite Marriage*. The Buster that went to France in 1952 was a different man than the one in 1947; by then, there was something of a Keaton renaissance underway.[14]

Two happy events had occurred at the end of the 1940s. Over the decade, in part thanks to his appearance in cheaters (proof he was sober and working again), Buster had begun getting small roles in various features. In September of 1949, the legendary critic and writer James Agee published an elegant, elegiac essay in *Life* magazine titled "Comedy's Greatest Era." He lamented the bygone art of Chaplin, Lloyd, Harry Langdon, and the Mack Sennett crew, but on the subject of Keaton he seemed to argue for genius most eloquently and passionately. Agee regarded Buster's stolid countenance as a national archetype along the lines of Abe Lincoln's.[15] The widely read article helped erase the memory of the bored-looking second fiddle playing alongside Jimmy Durante and replaced it with a lithe, dignified craftsman whose clowning had once captivated the world.

The other pivotal moment had come about a year earlier, when Buster walked into his son Jimmy's living room and saw the new ten-inch GE appliance that aunt Norma had given him. Keaton watched television all afternoon and by dinner declared it to be the future. In the closing days of 1949, he made his first TV appearance on *The Ed Wynn Show*, recasting a routine from *The Butcher Boy*, his screen debut of some thirty-two years ago. In two weeks he was given his own show on a local CBS station. Los Angeles audiences tuned in to KTTV Thursdays at 8 p.m. to watch Buster spin pratfalls and jokes for half an hour; the rest of the country caught up with Keaton in the pages of *Life* magazine again, this time as he compared the bustling spontaneity of the new medium to the electric, slaphappy salad days of film. *The Buster Keaton Show* ran for four months, and even with Keaton making up most of the comedy as he went along (in front of a live audience), he soon grew exhausted. There was a syndicated thirteen-week series in 1951 that also ran out of gas; most episodes featured rapid-fire silliness and a bald Keaton being adored by younger, nubile women. Still, television saved Buster. In its youth it was an intensely vaudeville-friendly medium; stations had countless hours of programming to fill, and who better to fill them than a clown trained his whole life to improvise toppers, corkers, and gaffes? Buster could be relied on to assemble a show on short notice, or simply show up and do it. Over the next seventeen years, he would make a lucrative living out of TV guest spots, appearing with such small-screen stars as Ed Sullivan, Steve Allen, Johnny Carson, and Donna Reed. There were countless commercials (Alka-Seltzer, Kodak, Ford, Phillips 66, Simon Pure Beer), a 1957 episode of *This Is Your Life*, game shows (*What's My Line?*, *Truth or Consequences*), and a part-silent 1961 *Twilight Zone* caper in which he goes time traveling in boxers and a kooky helmet.[16]

In some ways, Buster must have felt like a chronic time traveler. He was a journeyman performer whose visionary career ran the course of popular American entertainment; he had gone from the vaudeville house to the silent screen to the talking picture, and now, to television—a vertiginous span. (Ever undaunted, Keaton looked forward—in 1958—to the day when the television and movie industries would unite.) With the passing of each epoch, a few more of his compatriots fell by the wayside. (Chaplin, for instance, refused to let even his children watch TV.) But television kept Buster adventurous and young. One Easter, in 1956, he attended a Hollywood reunion at Pickfair; Mary Pickford presided over her 200 guests, including Marion Davies, Hedda Hopper, Harold Lloyd, and Ramon Novarro. Buster was eager to catch up with old friends, but after making the rounds, he found them distressingly out of touch—none of them listened to rock and roll.[17]

Keaton was now working on the stage, screen, and TV. From time to time, he and Eleanor would take roles in summer stock productions, such as *Merton of the Movies*; in 1960, they embarked on a seven-month national tour with the musical *Once Upon a Mattress*. His return to the legitimate screen—in a sizable MGM part—commenced in 1949 with the release of the film *In the Good Old Summertime*. A year later he was seen in Billy Wilder's Hollywood tragedy, *Sunset Boulevard*, as one of

37 Keaton and Chaplin in *Limelight* (1952).

Norma Desmond's bridge-playing wraiths (Buster's shadowy refrain: "pass . . . pass"). At the end of 1951, Charlie Chaplin offered Buster a part in his film *Limelight*. The melodramatic vanity project was deeply un-Keaton—ham-handed and pretentious—but the dramatic finale in which Buster and Charlie took the stage as a reunited music-hall act marked the only time the two friends ever would work together. When Keaton showed up on the set, Chaplin marveled to see him so fit; much to Chaplin's highbrow dismay, Buster credited his spryness to television. Buster would appear in many films, including *Around the World in Eighty Days* (1956), *It's a Mad, Mad, Mad, Mad World* (1963), and *A Funny Thing Happened on the Way to the Forum* (1966). During the hot New York summer of 1964, Keaton starred in the high-concept twenty-two-minute Samuel Beckett film *Film*, which Buster neither understood nor liked. He followed it up in typical democratic fashion with four beach movies: *Pajama Party* (1964), *Beach Blanket Bingo*

(1965), *How to Stuff a Wild Bikini* (1965), and *Sergeant Deadhead* (1965). Each was shot in Malibu in about two weeks; three of the four featured Frankie Avalon and Annette Funicello, plus songs, surf, and sandy oversexed teens. (The fourth compensated with a space chimp.) To Keaton, work was work, be it Beckett or beach blankets, and he had a high time making the B-movies. Some say he maintained such a break-neck schedule to ensure Eleanor's comfort after he was gone, but part of his drive was a simple love of performing.[18] Since those childhood days of vaudeville trunks and off-stage poles, no one ever had been able to keep him from an audience.

Buster's classic films—long lost to the general public—were begin-ning to resurface as well, thanks largely to the efforts of an LA movie theater manager named Raymond Rohauer. Much of the Keaton revival leads back to Rohauer, a compulsive collector, sometime bully, and slightly odd duck, who met Keaton in 1954. By 1958 Rohauer had reinstated Buster Keaton Productions and began acquiring neg-atives and clearing copyrights with ruthless abandon. From Denmark to Czechoslovakia to the Villa's long-forgotten cutting room, if there was a Keaton film secreted away, he would find it.[19]

In November 1955, Buster traveled to Rochester, New York, to accept an award from the George Eastman House. The prestigious film and photography center was honoring a handful of silent-era filmmak-ers for their contributions to the industry. Mary Pickford was the keynote speaker; awards went to Chaplin, Lloyd, Gloria Swanson, and Norma Talmadge, among others. Because it was a one-time honor, Buster valued his George Award more than the surprise Oscar he received in 1960. The unannounced special Academy Award—for "having made pictures that will play as long as pictures are shown"— was given to him at the after-show dinner by Bob Hope; Buster accepted it with a short thank-you and a deadpan face. Keaton could be cripplingly shy and, despite his popular resurgence, remained forever loath to discuss his own genius. In the winter of 1962, the Cinémath-èque Française paid tribute with a Keaton retrospective. After a screen-ing, Buster took one look at the encroaching, enthusiastic mob and dashed out of the theater; Eleanor found him in an alley, vomiting.[20]

Not all of Buster's old friends would witness his victorious second act. After parting ways with Keaton, Clyde Bruckman had enjoyed distinct but fleeting success, directing such films as Harold Lloyd's *Movie Crazy* (1932) and W. C. Fields's *The Man On the Flying Trapeze* (1935). He had worked on Buster's Columbia cheaters and both Keaton TV shows, but by then a prolonged alcoholic plunge was ending his career. In the winter of 1954, Bruckman was severely down on his luck. Sometime after Christmas, he borrowed a Colt .45 from Buster, saying he was heading out on a road trip and wanted to take along some peace of mind. A few days into the new year, he walked into the bathroom of a Wilshire restaurant—so as not to sully his home, the note said—and put a bullet through his skull.[21]

In July of 1955, Myra died. After going on a chiefly all-bourbon diet, she contracted pneumonia and was hospitalized. Jingles attended to the burial. Buster was in England with Eleanor, working on a TV pilot. When the telegram arrived, he went on a five-hour walk. He stepped up his drinking, and a few months later, at the award ceremony in Rochester, he was plagued by a vicious cough. Back in California, he ruptured veins in his esophagus and began hemorrhaging. In the hospital, Keaton bled for twenty-seven hours; he was put on death-watch. Three weeks later, Buster was discharged from the hospital, committed never to drink again. Aside from the occasional beer before dinner, he never would.[22]

With the death of Myra, Buster and Eleanor concluded it was time for them to live on their own. Keaton sold the rights to his life story to Paramount for $50,000. He used the money to go house-hunting with Harold Goodwin—the evil Jeff in *College* was now a realtor. In June 1956, Buster and Eleanor moved into the ranch house Buster had always wanted. The one-and-a-half acre home was in Woodland Hills, northwest of Hollywood in the San Fernando Valley; Buster added a pool, a cabin for grandchildren, and a homey chicken coop complete with flagpole. (The colors were raised in the morning and lowered in the evening, with hens Zsa Zsa, Marilyn, and Ava clucking at various degrees of attention below.) To better serve his guests, Buster laid model train track from the kitchen to the pool, where the line ended atop a table. The poolside express carried hot dogs, drinks, and watermelon. When not playing bridge in his den, Buster was outdoors. There were fruit trees, grapevines, an artichoke bed; Buster would amble the grounds with his St. Bernard, Elmer III, looking for four-leaf clovers.[23]

Paramount released *The Buster Keaton Story* in 1957. Buster had been a consultant on the film, though he had no say over the script. Donald O'Connor was cast as Buster; Ann Blyth would play the amalgamated three-in-one love interest. From there, the Paramount hacks rewrote Keaton's life. The movie was a lurid, boozy Hollywood fable, stocked with the usual high and low clichés. While Keaton had enjoyed helping O'Connor with the clowning, Buster and Eleanor desperately wanted to flee the first screening.[24]

The film—however painful—gave Buster his dream house, which he outfitted with prizes from his TV appearances. Soon it was a comfortable place for entertaining. Some of the most frequent faces at Woodland Hills would be various youngsters Buster met through his later projects. While touring with *Merton of the Movies*, he and Eleanor befriended actors James Karen and Jane Dulo, with whom they became very close. As the years went on, though, Buster found himself with fewer and fewer old friends to entertain. His parents were gone, as were Bruckman and Sedgwick. With Myra's death, Jingles, now divorced, was forced to move out on his own; he stayed at Victoria Avenue until the moving men arrived and ultimately ended up in the border town of San Ysidro working behind a bar. He would die there in 1988, after a fall. Louise, on the other hand, stayed close; she found a modest apartment and visited Woodland Hills regularly. After some years in a rest home, she died in 1981 of lung cancer.

Jimmy had four children; Bobby had two. They often brought the grandkids to see Buster and Eleanor. In the 1950s, Jimmy ran the publicity-stills division of Twentieth Century-Fox. Bobby, who lost an earlobe to a sniper during the war, would operate a string of garages. Both boys were mechanically inclined, like their father; Bobby liked boats and Jimmy liked cars. Today, they live in California. None of the grandchildren are involved in film.

Natalie and Buster never reconciled. In the years after the divorce, she only became more bitter. Natalie lived alone in a house on the beach, where she painted and guzzled whiskey—visitors were forbidden to speak Buster's name. She died in 1969 of heart disease. As for the others, in a strange twist of fate Kathleen Key, Dorothy Sebastian, and Viola Dana would all draw their last breath at the Motion Picture Country House and Hospital, not more than a mile and a half from Buster's Woodland Hills ranch. Buster didn't like to visit; he said talking to his peers—many of whom had never heard the Beatles—made him sad.

As for Joe Schenck, after dumping Keaton he went on to run Twentieth Century-Fox; he would go to prison for a few months (taking the fall for the industry in a widespread 1941 extortion scandal) before receiving an Oscar in 1952. For a while, Marilyn Monroe inhabited his guesthouse. He died, speechless and senile, in 1961, leaving behind a long will that didn't mention Buster. Irving Thalberg died in 1936, after a falling-out with Mayer. Mayer lived to be ousted by Nicholas Schenck, and died in 1957.[25]

In the fall of 1964, Buster made *The Railrodder*, a whimsical twenty-minute ad for Canada sponsored by the country's National Film Board in which Buster rides coast to coast in a rail cart. Much to the discomfort of the director, Gerald Potterton, Keaton insisted on doing dangerous stunts, such as blindly crossing a 200-foot trestle with his head swaddled in a map. In the summer of 1965 he went to Italy to film *War Italian Style* (1967), in which he played a general. On his way to join Richard Lester and the cast of *A Funny Thing Happened on the Way to the Forum* (shooting in Spain), he stopped in Venice, where Beckett's *Film* was screening at the celebrated film festival. A month before his 70th birthday, Keaton walked into a room and received a five-minute standing ovation, a quarter the length of *Film* itself. When asked later about the wild acclaim, Buster said, "Sure it's great, but it's all thirty years too late." After finishing the Lester film (in which

Buster plays a man seeking his children), Keaton flew to Toronto, where he was engaged to make a half-hour short on industrial safety. He had been troubled by severe coughing fits; before going overseas to Italy, he had been told he had bronchitis. Buster finished the Canadian film, but he was not in good health. On the flight from Toronto to Los Angeles, Keaton began wheezing; the attendants administered oxygen. At the hospital, Eleanor learned her husband had advanced lung cancer. The doctors gave him a week to three months.

Buster never knew he had cancer. No one told him, and he assumed it was the bronchitis revisited. (Even in Canada, he had continued to chain smoke—at the time, he was down to half a lung.) In one of the final interviews he would ever give, in that fall before the flight, the hospital, and the cancer, Buster had bragged he was so busy—"I work more than Doris Day"—that he just might never die. Indeed, Keaton convalesced that winter, managing to do a TV spot, but on January 30, 1966, he took a turn for the worse. After brunch with Jane Dulo and thirty minutes of solitaire, he passed out. The cancer was in his brain. He was taken to the hospital but released the next morning. Eleanor and a nurse tried to make Buster comfortable, but he was irrational and belligerent. He was given a nighttime sedative at seven o'clock. Joseph Frank Keaton died in his sleep at 6:15 Tuesday morning, February 1, 1966. Eleanor died in 1998, a widow and tireless champion of her husband of twenty-five years.[26]

38 Buster in *A Funny Thing Happened on the Way to the Forum* (1966).

Coda

He had gone from the vaudeville show to the beach movie, hitting all points in between, but Buster Keaton's indisputable legacy will always be his work from the twenties. At his greatest, Keaton created a silent poetry of camera and limb, reminding us how misfits find love, swells make good, civilians win wars, and would-be big-business men sometimes die trying—and that the only sane course is to laugh at it all. The ships sink, the trains crash, but you keep running the big race and somehow—with wit and humor and a little bit of luck—you're able to keep the modern demons at bay. For a decade, the country was transfixed by the high-wire antics of a matchless little clown—equal parts auteur, innovator, prankster, and daredevil—whose quest for redemption was at once savvy and innocent. And in the end, it was a brand of innocence that hastened his downfall.

When Keaton signed with MGM, in January of 1928, it heralded the end of a brilliant era. The unforgiving world Buster had captured in his films—brash, baffling, ever in a hurry—would be gone before he knew it. In the six years between Keaton's *The Cameraman* (1928) and Frank Capra's *It Happened One Night* (1934), there was a sea change in movie comedy—as evidenced by the latter film's five-Oscar sweep. Acrobatic comedy was giving way to screwball comedy, with its madcap scenarios and bantered innuendo. The new comedians battled, bragged, and won the girl with their mouths, not their feet, the sparks coming less from bold stunts than snappy repartee crackling with slang. (In those six years, the screen witnessed the verbal pyrotechnics of the Marx Brothers, whose first talkies—*The Cocoanuts* (1929), *Animal Crackers* (1930), *Monkey Business* (1931), *Horse Feathers* (1932), and *Duck Soup* (1933)—fall neatly into the gap. Meanwhile, chatty Jimmy Durante talked and sang his way to fame.) Nineteen thirty-four was the year Nick sparred with Nora in *The Thin Man* and

Carole Lombard proved she could lick John Barrymore throughout the *Twentieth Century*. The dames were getting tougher, a little dizzier, and a whole lot sexier, with their long legs and barbed tongues. The sometimes bruised but ever pale roses of Keaton—the Annabelles, Betsys, Marys, and Sallys—would have been no match for, say, the *Gold Diggers of 1933*. Furthermore, Buster's storylines had remained faithful at heart to Victorian melodrama, that longtime staple of vaudeville, relying on the basic triangle of determined young man, sweet young girl, and dastardly villain—Buster then goes looking for love in the machine age. But sometime during the depressed, more cynical thirties, the tenor changed in America. The machine age had lost its shine—having produced breadlines, not bounty—and the double-edged thrills of modernity became old news. The war between the sexes had a new cock-eyed battlefront: the screwball misadventure, with its foibles of class, sex, and lunatic circumstance. At MGM, Buster was left behind, forced to play the clumsy, dimwitted sap—he was never so guileless in his silents, which were infinitely more knowing about the moral cracks in modern life. (Buster's ends were pure, but his means were cunning.) It is difficult to say what Keaton would have done if left to his own devices; perhaps he could have given Claudette Colbert a run for her money. For sure, he would have relished the chance. But instead, Keaton was exiled to a no-man's-land, left to churn out films that had neither the brilliance of the past nor the punch of the future. And so one of the screen's brightest and bravest clowns bowed out for a while, lowering the curtain on a golden age of film, going out the way he came in, without a word.

Buster Keaton rests in Forest Lawn Memorial Park–Hollywood Hills; in one pocket is a rosary, in the other, a deck of cards. His obituary in *The New York Times*, sandwiched between "Vietnam Protest Snarls Times Sq." and "New Midwest Storm Moves Into the East," waxes inaccurate about custard pies and two-reel quickies like *The Cameraman* and *Sherlock, Jr.*[1] Buster's grave is an unremarkable plot marked by a small bronze plaque, set at the foot of a wall, at street level. It reads simply, "Buster Keaton, 1895–1966," the nickname having stuck to the end. He is flanked by strangers. A larger sidewalk marker commemorates the old Lillian Way studio, but it sits on the wrong corner. The great Villa lot has been subdivided. Schenck's Colony Studio on Manhattan's East 48th Street—once home to Norma, Constance, Roscoe, and Buster—is now a parking garage.

But before you can despair, you spy a Keaton video in a chain store; a week later you catch that singular stone face flickering on the big screen. In the theater next door, there's martial arts superstar Jackie Chan channeling Buster, not Bruce. A wall falls—who is that standing in the open window? You spot more stolen bits on Broadway, same as there ever was, proof that good gags never die. And just as you're seeing flat hats everywhere, one bright day there's a peculiar story in the paper about a boy who was picked up by a twister and blown down the block—only to walk away, unharmed.[2] And you begin to wonder.

Notes

SOURCE ABBREVIATIONS

Agee: James Agee, *Agee on Film: Criticism and Comment on the Movies* (2000)
Allen: Frederick Lewis Allen, *Only Yesterday: An Informal History of the 1920's* (1964)
Blesh: Rudi Blesh, *Keaton* (1966)
Brownlow: Kevin Brownlow, *The Parade's Gone By . . .* (1976)
Dardis: Tom Dardis, *Keaton: The Man Who Wouldn't Lie Down* (2002)
Dragga filmography: Jack Dragga, *Buster Keaton Filmography* (1997)
Eleanor Keaton & Vance: Eleanor Keaton and Jeffrey Vance, *Buster Keaton Remembered* (2001)
Keaton & Samuels: Buster Keaton and Charles Samuels, *My Wonderful World of Slapstick* (1982)
LAT: *The Los Angeles Times*
Louvish: Simon Louvish, *Stan and Ollie: The Roots of Comedy: The Double Life of Laurel and Hardy* (2002)
Meade: Marion Meade, *Buster Keaton: Cut to the Chase* (1997)
NYT: *The New York Times*
Oldham: Gabriella Oldham, *Keaton's Silent Shorts: Beyond the Laughter* (1996)
Shepard: Jim Shepard (ed.), *Writers at the Movies: Twenty-six Contemporary Authors Celebrate Twenty-six Memorable Movies* (2000)

INTRODUCTION: FOUR-THIRTY IN THE AFTERNOON IN MUSKEGON, MICHIGAN

1 "A good comedy story . . ."; Blesh, p. 133.
2 *LAT*, October 29, 1995.
3 Keaton & Samuels, p. 126.

1 CYCLONE BABY

1 *NYT*, October 4, 1895, and October 5, 1895; Keaton & Samuels, pp. 15–16, 20; Dardis, p. 7; Meade, p. 15; Eleanor Keaton & Vance, p. 45.
2 Eleanor Keaton & Vance, p. 45; Meade, pp. 9–10; Keaton & Samuels, p. 17.

3 Meade, p. 5; Eleanor Keaton & Vance, p. 45, Keaton & Samuels, pp. 17–18.
4 Meade, pp. 8, 11–12; Keaton & Samuels, p. 19.
5 Meade, p. 13; Keaton & Samuels, p. 18.
6 Keaton & Samuels, p. 16.
7 Meade, p. 13.
8 Ibid., p. 18.
9 Eleanor Keaton & Vance, pp. 46, 217.
10 Keaton & Samuels, p. 20.
11 Ibid., p. 21; Meade, p. 20.
12 Dardis, p. 4.
13 Meade, p. 21.
14 Keaton & Samuels, p. 26.
15 Meade, p. 17.
16 Ibid., p. 23.
17 Ibid., p. 24.
18 Ibid., p. 25.
19 Eleanor Keaton & Vance, p. 46; Keaton & Samuels, p. 12.
20 Eleanor Keaton & Vance, pp. 45–6.
21 Meade, p. 18.
22 Keaton & Samuels, p. 13.
23 Eleanor Keaton & Vance, p. 47.
24 Keaton & Samuels, p. 13.
25 Eleanor Keaton & Vance, p. 47.
26 Keaton & Samuels, pp. 21–3, 31.
27 Meade, pp. 32, 386; Keaton & Samuels, p. 27.
28 Meade, pp. 29–30.
29 *New York Clipper*, July 20, 1901.

2 MEET THE KEATONS

1 Keaton & Samuels, p. 13.
2 Meade, p. 27.
3 Dardis, p. 14.
4 Meade, p. 33.
5 Keaton & Samuels, pp. 32–3.
6 Ibid., pp. 24–5.
7 Ibid., p. 34.
8 Dardis, p. 12; Meade, p. 42.
9 Keaton & Samuels, p. 71.
10 *NYT*, May 21, 1903.

11 Dardis, p. 17.

12 *NYT*, May 21, 1903.

13 Meade, p. 40.

14 Blesh, p. 48.

15 Meade, pp. 41–2; Eleanor Keaton & Vance, p. 51.

16 Meade, p. 41; Keaton & Samuels, p. 36.

17 Keaton & Samuels, pp. 43–7; Blesh, pp. 48, 51.

18 Keaton & Samuels, p. 37.

19 Blesh, p. 55.

20 *NYT*, November 28, 1907; Dardis, p. 19; Blesh, p. 56; Keaton & Samuels, pp. 67–8; Meade, pp. 42–3.

21 Meade, p. 46.

22 Ibid., p. 46.

23 Keaton & Samuels, p. 40.

24 Blesh, p. 71.

25 Keaton & Samuels, pp. 40–1.

26 Clown Pole and the waking of Ed Gray: Blesh, pp. 67–8.

27 Keaton & Samuels, p. 42.

28 Meade, p. 47; Blesh, pp. 72–3.

29 Keaton & Samuels, p. 24.

30 Ibid., p. 72; Blesh, pp. 72–4.

31 Meade, p. 310.

3 STEAMSHIPS, A CORPSE, AND BROKEN FURNITURE

1 *Ladies' Home Journal*, June 1926.

2 *Variety*, December 11, 1909.

3 Meade, p. 45.

4 *Variety*, December 11, 1909.

5 Keaton & Samuels, pp. 62–3.

6 *Variety*, December 11, 1909.

7 Keaton & Samuels, pp. 62–3.

8 *Variety*, December 11, 1909.

9 Dardis, p. 19.

10 Meade, p. 48.

11 Eleanor Keaton & Vance, p. 51.

12 Keaton & Samuels, p. 51.

13 Eleanor Keaton & Vance, p. 51.

14 Keaton & Samuels, pp. 74–6; Blesh, pp. 78–80. Buster told various versions of this story; the one I include is a composite.

15 Keaton & Samuels, p. 74.
16 Meade, p. 48.
17 Keaton & Samuels, p. 80.
18 Meade, p. 54.
19 Keaton & Samuels, p. 82; Meade, p. 54; Blesh, pp. 59–60.
20 Meade, pp. 54–5; Blesh, p. 82; Keaton & Samuels, pp. 83, 87.
21 Meade, p. 55.
22 Keaton & Samuels, p. 88.
23 Dardis, p. 23.
24 Keaton & Samuels, pp. 88–9; Meade, p. 56.
25 Keaton & Samuels, pp. 89–90; Blesh, p. 83.

4 LE CIRQUE CUMEEKY

1 Keaton & Samuels, p. 281.
2 The day Buster met Lou Anger: Blesh, pp. 83–5, 87; Meade, pp. 1, 58–61; Keaton & Samuels, pp. 91–2.
3 Meade, pp. 61–2, 68; Blesh, pp. 86–8; Keaton & Samuels, p. 91.
4 Keaton & Samuels, p. 93.
5 Ibid., p. 92.
6 Meade, p. 63; Blesh, p. 88.
7 Meade, p. 63.
8 Blesh, p. 89.
9 Keaton & Samuels, p. 94.
10 Meade, p. 64.
11 Blesh, pp. 70–1.
12 Film industry data: Dardis, pp. 25, 29, 31; Meade, p. 51; Louvish, p. 59; *NYT*, May 27, 1917.
13 Eleanor Keaton & Vance, p. 52; Meade, p. 53.
14 Brownlow, pp. 294, 296–7, 338.
15 Ibid., pp. 290–1.
16 Meade, p. 76.
17 Ibid., p. 70.
18 Eleanor Keaton & Vance, p. 52; Meade, pp. 65–6; Dardis, p. 33.
19 Meade, pp. 60–1; Blesh, p. 87.
20 Dardis, pp. 31–2; *NYT*, May 27, 1917.
21 Keaton & Samuels, p. 93.
22 *Dramatic Mirror*, April 21, 1917.
23 Meade, pp. 59, 61; Brownlow, p. 496.
24 Blesh, p. 86.

25 New studio and antics: Ibid., pp. 95–7.
26 Dardis, p. 38.
27 Meade, pp. 67–8.
28 Dardis, p. 35.
29 Meade, pp. 67, 76.
30 Ibid., pp. 73, 75.
31 Dardis, pp. 41–2.
32 Natalie the script girl: Meade, pp. 73–4. "Seemed a meek, mild girl . . .":
   Keaton & Samuels, p. 94.
33 Meade, p. 68.
34 *Dramatic Mirror*, April 21, 1917, and May 26, 1917; Meade, p. 68.
35 *Dramatic Mirror*, May 26, 1917.

5 UP THROUGH THE RANKS

1 Keaton & Samuels, p. 95.
2 Meade, p. 62.
3 Eleanor Keaton & Vance, p. 213.
4 Brownlow, p. 216.
5 Ibid., p. 283.
6 Keaton & Samuels, p. 93.
7 Eleanor Keaton & Vance, p. 57.
8 Meade, p. 70.
9 Blesh, pp. 98–9.
10 Dardis, p. 44.
11 Brownlow, pp. 478–9.
12 Keaton & Samuels, p. 95.
13 Blesh, pp. 99–101; Meade, pp. 71–2.
14 Eleanor Keaton & Vance, p. 58; Blesh, p. 101; Meade, p. 76.
15 Dardis, p. 45; Meade, p. 77; Blesh, p. 105.
16 Meade, pp. 78–9.
17 Ibid., p. 77.
18 Blesh, pp. 131–3; Keaton & Samuels, p. 96.
19 *A Country Hero* and *Out West*: Meade, p. 77.
20 Brownlow, p. 363.
21 Dardis, p. 46.
22 Ibid., p. 51.
23 Ibid., p. 52.
24 Blesh, pp. 107–8.
25 Dardis, p. 53.

26 Meade, p. 391.
27 Ibid., p. 79.
28 Keaton & Samuels, p. 96.
29 Eleanor Keaton & Vance, p. 58.
30 Meade, p. 79.
31 Keaton & Samuels, pp. 98–9.
32 Ibid., pp. 97, 100–1; Blesh, p. 116.
33 Meade, pp. 80–1; Eleanor Keaton & Vance, p. 58; Dardis, p. 54; Blesh, pp. 116–17.
34 Meade, p. 81; Blesh, pp. 119–21; Eleanor Keaton & Vance, pp. 58–60; Keaton & Samuels, p. 98.
35 Meade, p. 81.
36 Keaton & Samuels, p. 105.
37 Meade, pp. 80–2.
38 Keaton & Samuels, pp. 105–6.

6 BACK FROM THE BACK

1 Keaton & Samuels, p. 109.
2 Allen, pp. 1–12.
3 Blesh, p. 123.
4 Eleanor Keaton & Vance, p. 60.
5 Meade, pp. 86–7.
6 Keaton & Samuels, p. 110.
7 Brownlow, pp. 30–4.
8 Keaton & Samuels, p. 109.
9 Blesh, p. 122.
10 Meade, pp. 83–4.
11 Buster's romantic interests: Dardis, p. 56; Eleanor Keaton & Vance, p. 106; Meade, pp. 81–2, 88.
12 Eleanor Keaton & Vance, p. 61.
13 Blesh, p. 129.
14 Meade, p. 85.
15 Keaton & Samuels, p. 109. "When the World Was Ours" is a chapter title in Buster's autobiography.
16 Blesh, p. 129.
17 Keaton & Samuels, p. 112.
18 Ibid., pp. 113–20. Buster often told the story of these pranks. All three can be found in his autobiography.
19 Meade, p. 86.

20 Comique succession and Keaton's contract: Blesh, pp. 130–1; Meade, pp. 89–92.
21 Eleanor Keaton & Vance, p. 61.

7 THE CLOWN TO DO THE JOB

1 Keaton & Samuels, p. 111.
2 Eleanor Keaton & Vance, p. 63; Meade, p. 91; Blesh, p. 138.
3 Dardis, p. 135.
4 Eleanor Keaton & Vance, p. 64.
5 Keaton & Samuels, p. 125.
6 Blesh, p. 168.
7 Eleanor Keaton & Vance, p. 64.
8 Meade, p. 93.
9 Eleanor Keaton & Vance, pp. 66–7.
10 Blesh, p. 140.
11 Meade, p. 95; Eleanor Keaton & Vance, p. 62.
12 *Variety*, February 18, 1921.
13 *NYT*, February 14, 1921, and February 20, 1921.
14 Eleanor Keaton & Vance, p. 68.

8 HIT PARADE

1 Eleanor Keaton & Vance, p. 64.
2 *NYT*, September 26, 1920.
3 Dardis, pp. 68–9.
4 *NYT*, October 25, 1920.
5 Eleanor Keaton & Vance, p. 71.
6 Dardis, pp. 88–9; Keaton & Samuels, pp. 129–30; Eleanor Keaton & Vance, p. 65.
7 Eleanor Keaton & Vance, p. 65; *Film Quarterly*, Summer 1966.
8 *Sight and Sound*, Winter 1965–6.
9 Blesh, pp. 148–9.
10 Fox: Eleanor Keaton & Vance, p. 75; Meade, p. 98.
11 Eleanor Keaton & Vance, p. 75.
12 *Moving Picture World*, November 27, 1920.
13 Eleanor Keaton & Vance, p. 76.
14 Oldham, p. 70.
15 *Moving Picture World*, December 25, 1920.
16 Meade, p. 101.

9 WEDDING BELLS AND HARD LUCK GOATS

1 Eleanor Keaton & Vance, p. 79; Meade, p. 104; *Film Quarterly*, Fall 1958.
2 Meade, p. 104.
3 Blesh, p. 154.
4 Meade, p. 100.
5 Blesh, pp. 170–1; Meade, pp. 89, 100.
6 *Variety*, February 11, 1921; *NYT*, February 20, 1921; Meade, pp. 105–6.
7 Engagement stories: Keaton & Samuels, p. 165; Blesh, pp. 156–7; Dardis, p. 74; Eleanor Keaton & Vance, p. 106.
8 *Variety*, March 25, 1921.
9 Keaton & Samuels, p. 166; Meade, p. 114.
10 Wedding details: *NYT*, May 28, 1921; Blesh, pp. 158–60; *NYT*, June 1, 1921; Eleanor Keaton & Vance, p. 106.
11 "Only Three Weeks": *Motion Picture Magazine*, October 1921.
12 Blesh, p. 161; Keaton & Samuels, p. 166; Eleanor Keaton & Vance, p. 106.

10 WELCOME TO THE PLAYHOUSE

1 Blesh, p. 163.
2 Ibid., pp. 154–6.
3 Keaton & Samuels, p. 169.
4 Blesh, p. 152.
5 Eleanor Keaton & Vance, p. 83.
6 Ibid., p. 83.
7 Dragga filmography.
8 Keaton & Samuels, p. 169.
9 *NYT*, January 2, 1922.
10 Keaton & Samuels, pp. 156–7.
11 Meade, p. 114.
12 Buster declines the Labor Day invitation: Eleanor Keaton & Vance, p. 84; Meade, p. 119.
13 Arbuckle scandal and aftermath: Keaton & Samuels, pp. 156–61, 195–6; Eleanor Keaton & Vance, p. 61; Meade, pp. 116–22, 128–9; Dardis, pp. 80–4; Blesh, pp. 178–88. "The day the laughter stopped": Buster uses this phrase as a chapter title in his autobiography, Keaton & Samuels, p. 147.
14 Ibid., p. 159.
15 Eleanor Keaton & Vance, p. 84; Brownlow, p. 485.
16 In-laws move west: Eleanor Keaton & Vance, p. 107; Blesh, p. 162; Meade, pp. 124, 130.

17 Keaton & Samuels, pp. 166–7.
18 *Motion Picture Magazine*, October 1921.
19 Westmoreland house: Blesh, pp. 204–5; Meade, p. 131; Dardis, pp. 85–6.
20 Keaton & Samuels, p. 183.
21 Meade, p. 132.
22 Blesh, p. 236; Meade, p. 118.
23 Captain the dog: Blesh, pp. 169–70.
24 Keaton & Samuels, p. 185.
25 Bridge stories: Meade, p. 115; Keaton & Samuels, pp. 185–6.
26 Meade, p. 125.
27 Fall from the bridge: Eleanor Keaton & Vance, p. 87; Meade, p. 125.

11 LOVE ON THE GO

1 *Cops* shooting dates: Meade, p. 127.
2 Oldham, p. 199.
3 *NYT*, September 17, 1920.
4 *NYT*, January 1, 1922.
5 *NYT*, June 26, 1922.
6 Keaton & Samuels, pp. 141–2; Blesh, p. 203.
7 Eleanor Keaton & Vance, p. 91.
8 Meade, p. 131.
9 Eleanor Keaton & Vance, p. 92.
10 Dragga filmography.
11 Blesh, pp. 205–6.
12 Meade, p. 130.
13 Eleanor Keaton & Vance, p. 95; Oldham, pp. 256, 263.
14 Keaton & Samuels, p. 172.
15 *NYT*, March 5, 1923, and March 19, 1923. Walter Hiers is mentioned in the March 5th review.
16 Birth of Jimmy: Keaton & Samuels, pp. 166, 185; Meade, p. 131; Eleanor Keaton & Vance, p. 107; Blesh, p. 207.

12 SIX-REEL STAR

1 Tijuana and a horse named Buster Keaton: Blesh, p. 327; Meade, p. 132; Keaton & Samuels, pp. 188–9; *NYT*, February 14, 1923, April 2, 1923, February 16, 1924, February 16, 1925, and September 22, 1929.
2 Blesh, p. 208; Meade, p. 133.
3 Blesh, p. 213.

4 Eleanor Keaton & Vance, p. 98.
5 Ibid., p. 102.
6 *NYT*, November 14, 1922, and November 25, 1922.
7 Keaton's new arrangement: Meade, p. 133; Keaton & Samuels, p. 173; Eleanor Keaton & Vance, p. 110.
8 Dardis, p. 96.
9 Eleanor Keaton & Vance, p. 110.
10 Addition of Mitchell, Bruckman, and Havez: Meade, p. 134.
11 Blesh, p. 149.
12 Margaret Leahy: *NYT*, November 14, 1922, December 3, 1922, and January 14, 1923 ("unusual comic ability"); Meade, p. 135.
13 Eleanor Keaton & Vance, pp. 111–14.
14 Blesh, p. 218; Eleanor Keaton & Vance, p. 110.
15 Meade, p. 134.
16 Blesh, p. 219.
17 Special effects: Eleanor Keaton & Vance, p. 114.
18 Blesh, p. 151.
19 *Film Quarterly*, Summer 1966; Eleanor Keaton & Vance, p. 115.
20 Keaton & Samuels, pp. 152–3.
21 Eleanor Keaton & Vance, p. 113.
22 *The Three Ages* gross: Dardis, p. 113.
23 *Life*, October 25, 1923.
24 Eleanor Keaton & Vance, p. 115.
25 *Ladies' Home Journal*, June 1926.
26 Meade, p. 396.

13 SOUTHERN DISCOMFORT, OR A FAMILY AFFAIR

1 Meade, p. 139.
2 All the Keatons in Truckee: Blesh, pp. 223–4.
3 Ibid., pp. 221–2.
4 Dardis, p. 97.
5 Eleanor Keaton & Vance, p. 118.
6 Feature philosophy: Keaton & Samuels, pp. 173–5.
7 Dardis, pp. 97–8.
8 Blesh, p. 225.
9 *NYT*, April 1, 1923.
10 Blesh, p. 227.
11 The accident: Eleanor Keaton & Vance, p. 121. Two questions: Blesh, pp. 233–4.

12 Waterfall stunt: *Sight and Sound,* Winter 1965–6; Meade, p. 140; Eleanor Keaton & Vance, p. 121.
13 Blesh, pp. 232–3.
14 *NYT,* August 19, 1923.
15 Eleanor Keaton & Vance, pp. 119–21; Meade, p. 140.
16 *Our Hospitality* reviews: *NYT,* December 10, 1923; *Variety,* December 13, 1923; *Moving Picture World,* March 15, 1924.
17 Dardis, p. 113. It is important to note, however, that the exact figures are uncertain.
18 Meade, p. 141.
19 *NYT,* December 23, 1923.
20 Meade, p. 136.
21 New Year's Eve 1923: *NYT,* December 30, 1923; Meade, p. 141; *Photoplay,* March 1924.
22 Birth of Bobby and the bedroom banishment: Blesh, p. 236 ("amateur standing"); Eleanor Keaton & Vance, pp. 107–8; Dardis, pp. 86–8.
23 Meade, p. 144.

14 THE MISFIT

1 Meade, p. 142.
2 Ibid., p. 143.
3 Co-director Arbuckle: Keaton & Samuels, p. 194.
4 Eleanor Keaton & Vance, p. 124.
5 Projectionist's dream: *Sight and Sound,* Winter 1965–6; Brownlow, p. 487; Eleanor Keaton & Vance, pp. 124–5.
6 Blesh, pp. 151–2.
7 Dardis, p. 107.
8 Brownlow, pp. 217, 220.
9 Eleanor Keaton & Vance, pp. 125–6.
10 Lion and motorcycle stunts: Ibid., pp. 124–5, 127–8.
11 Buster breaks his neck: Keaton & Samuels, p. 169; Eleanor Keaton & Vance, pp. 126–7; Dardis, p. 108.
12 Previews and re-cutting of *Sherlock, Jr.:* Meade, p. 147; Eleanor Keaton & Vance, pp. 128–9.
13 *Sherlock, Jr.,* reviews: *Variety,* May 28, 1924; *NYT,* May 26, 1924.
14 "In pictures . . .": Agee, p. 421. From "Undirectable Director," *Life,* September 18, 1950, reprinted in *Agee on Film: Criticism and Comment on the Movies.* For a more fluent reflection on Huston's quote, see the introduction to Terrence Rafferty's book, *The Thing Happens: Ten Years of Writing About the Movies.*

15 5,000 TONS OF FUN

1 *Ladies' Home Journal,* June 1926.
2 Meade, p. 147.
3 *Sherlock, Jr.,* gross: Dardis, p. 113.
4 House-swapping: Blesh, pp. 237–8.
5 The finding of the *Buford* and the ship's details: Eleanor Keaton & Vance, p. 130; Blesh, p. 252; Meade, p. 148.
6 *NYT,* June 29, 1924, and October 12, 1924; Meade, p. 149.
7 Crisp: Brownlow, p. 289; Meade, pp. 149–50.
8 Difficulties and danger in three locations: *Ladies' Home Journal,* June 1926; Eleanor Keaton & Vance, pp. 131–2; Meade, p. 150; Keaton & Samuels, p. 169; Blesh, p. 257; Brownlow, p. 494.
9 Keaton & Samuels, pp. 175–6; Eleanor Keaton & Vance, p. 132; *Ladies' Home Journal,* June 1926.
10 Meade, p. 151; Dardis, p. 112.
11 *NYT,* October 13, 1924; *Variety,* October 15, 1924.
12 Meade, p. 151.
13 Eleanor Keaton & Vance, p. 132.
14 New contract: Meade, p. 151; Dardis, p. 113.
15 Buster and the 1924 World Series: Meade, p. 151; *NYT,* October 4, 1924, October 6, 1924, October 7, 1924, and October 11, 1924.

16 BRIDES, BULLS, AND BUTLERS

1 Keaton & Samuels, p. 112.
2 The new house revealed: Keaton & Samuels, pp. 181–2; Blesh, p. 238 ("It's yours, Nat."); Meade, pp. 152–3. In some versions of the often-repeated story, Eddie Mannix is absent.
3 Eleanor Keaton & Vance, pp. 134–5; *NYT,* August 13, 1916.
4 Screening and production details: Eleanor Keaton & Vance, p. 135.
5 Car effect: Brownlow, p. 487; Eleanor Keaton & Vance, p. 135.
6 The rockslide: *Film Quarterly,* Summer 1966; Blesh, pp. 258–60; Eleanor Keaton & Vance, p. 135; Dardis, pp. 124–5.
7 Eleanor Keaton & Vance, p. 137.
8 Ibid., pp. 39–40, 172.
9 Keaton Studio baseball: Blesh, p. 149; Meade, p. 145; Eleanor Keaton & Vance, p. 172; Brownlow, p. 481.
10 Keaton & Samuels, p. 150.
11 Blesh, p. 149.
12 Shooting on and off the lot: Brownlow, pp. 480, 485.

13 *NYT*, February 13, 1925.

14 Departures from the crew: Eleanor Keaton & Vance, p. 137; Meade, p. 157; Dardis, p. 106.

15 *Variety*, March 18, 1925.

16 Buster on vacation and in New York: Meade, p. 155; Dardis, pp. 115, 126. Arbuckle remarries: Meade, pp. 155–6.

17 *NYT*, July 26, 1925; Meade, p. 158.

18 Eleanor Keaton & Vance, p. 139; Keaton & Samuels, pp. 142–3.

19 Eleanor Keaton & Vance, p. 138.

20 Keaton & Samuels, pp. 142–3; Meade, p. 156.

21 Meade, p. 156.

22 Stampede difficulty: Dardis, p. 132; Eleanor Keaton & Vance, p. 140.

23 *NYT*, October 26, 1925.

24 *Variety*, October 28, 1925.

25 Dardis, p. 133; Meade, p. 157.

26 Eleanor Keaton & Vance, p. 140.

27 Death of Fred Talmadge and Christmas 1925: *NYT*, November 15, 1925; Meade, p. 159; Blesh, p. 264.

28 Eleanor Keaton & Vance, p. 142.

29 The addition of the final fight, boxing coach, and stadium: Eleanor Keaton & Vance, pp. 142–3. Keaton injuries and Scorsese: Meade, p. 161.

30 Reviews: *NYT*, August 23, 1926, and August 29, 1926.

31 Fiscal success of *Battling Butler*: Dardis, p. 134; Eleanor Keaton & Vance, p. 142; Meade, p. 161.

32 United Artists: Dardis, pp. 135–7; Eleanor Keaton & Vance, p. 143.

33 *NYT*, March 24, 1926; *LAT*, March 24, 1926.

34 Blesh, p. 268.

17 MISCHIEF ON THE OREGON EXPRESS

1 Brownlow, p. 491.

2 *The Cottage Grove Sentinel*, May 27, 1926. This and other articles cited from *The Cottage Grove Sentinel* may be found in *The Day Buster Smiled: The 1926 Filming of "The General" by Buster Keaton as Chronicled in The Cottage Grove Sentinel newspaper, Cottage Grove, Oregon.*

3 Location details: Meade, p. 163; *The Cottage Grove Sentinel*, May 10, 1926, May 27, 1926, May 31, 1926, June 7, 1926, and July 26, 1926.

4 The true story of the *General* and Keaton's changes: Blesh, pp. 269–70.

5 Brownlow, p. 490.

6 Location scouting and prop work: Dardis, p. 140; Brownlow, p. 490;

Meade, pp. 162–3; Eleanor Keaton & Vance, p. 147. Historical accuracy: Blesh, p. 271.

7 Casting details and location expense: Meade, pp. 162–4; *The Cottage Grove Sentinel*, June 7, 1926, July 8, 1926, and July 19, 1926.

8 Brownlow, p. 491.

9 *Sight and Sound*, Winter 1965–6.

10 *The Cottage Grove Sentinel*, June 7, 1926, and June 21, 1926.

11 *The Cottage Grove Sentinel*, June 7, 1926, June 10, 1926, June 17, 1926, June 28, 1926, July 5, 1926, July 12, 1926, July 19, 1926, July 26, 1926, July 29, 1926, August 2, 1926, and September 9, 1926.

12 July 23rd and details of the bridge collapse: Meade, p. 165; Eleanor Keaton & Vance, pp. 147, 151; *The Cottage Grove Sentinel*, July 15, 1926, July 22, 1926, and July 26, 1926.

13 Filming the battle: Eleanor Keaton & Vance, p. 147; *The Cottage Grove Sentinel*, July 15, 1926, and July 22, 1926; Meade, p. 166.

14 Forest fire: *The Cottage Grove Sentinel*, July 26, 1926, and August 26, 1926; Meade, p. 166; Blesh, pp. 271–2; Eleanor Keaton & Vance, p. 149.

15 Keaton on the Great War: Keaton & Samuels, p. 98.

16 Eleanor Keaton & Vance, p. 149.

17 Ibid., p. 217.

18 Reviews of *The General*: *NYT*, February 8, 1927; *Variety*, February 9, 1927; *Life*, February 24, 1927.

19 Meade, p. 173.

20 *The Cottage Grove Sentinel*, June 10, 1926.

18 GOLDEN VILLA, CAMPUS CLOWN

1 Blesh, p. 284.

2 Description of the Italian Villa, inside and out: Meade, pp. 167–9; Eleanor Keaton & Vance, pp. 107–8; Keaton & Samuels, p. 183; Dardis, p. 119. "It took a lot of pratfalls . . .": Blesh, p. 239.

3 Parties at the Villa: Keaton & Samuels, pp. 183–4; Meade, p. 159; Blesh, p. 280.

4 Louise Brooks: Dardis, p. 129.

5 Keaton & Samuels, p. 184.

6 The editing shed and the Masons' discovery: Meade, pp. 169, 255–6; Eleanor Keaton & Vance, p. 37.

7 New Year's 1926 and screenings of *The General*: Meade, p. 170.

8 *NYT*, November 7, 1926, and February 21, 1927.

9 Buster's drinking: Blesh, p. 280; Dardis, p. 147; Meade, pp. 131, 151.

10 Dardis, p. 145; Eleanor Keaton & Vance, p. 152.
11 Dardis, pp. 147–8. "Absolutely useless": Brownlow, p. 491.
12 Eleanor Keaton & Vance, p. 154.
13 Keaton clashes with Harry Brand: Blesh, pp. 284–5; Eleanor Keaton & Vance, pp. 153–5; Dardis, p. 148; Brownlow, p. 491.
14 *NYT*, April 10, 1927; Meade, p. 174.
15 Pole vault stunt: Eleanor Keaton & Vance, p. 155.
16 *NYT*, September 18, 1927.
17 Dardis, p. 149.
18 Joe and Myra's separation: Meade, pp. 102–3; Blesh, pp. 355–6; Eleanor Keaton & Vance, p. 196.
19 Meade, p. 175.
20 The talkie arrives: *NYT*, June 5, 1927, and October 7, 1927; Brownlow, p. 571; Dardis, pp. 152–3.

19 THE FALL OF THE HOUSE OF BUSTER

1 Details of falling façade shot: Eleanor Keaton & Vance, pp. 156–61; Brownlow, pp. 492–3.
2 Story idea and shooting details: Eleanor Keaton & Vance, pp. 156, 160; Keaton & Samuels, p. 203; Meade, pp. 175, 179; Dardis, p. 153.
3 Delays and the cyclone finale: Meade, p. 179; Keaton & Samuels, pp. 204–5; Eleanor Keaton & Vance, pp. 156–8, 161; Dardis, p. 154.
4 Eleanor Keaton & Vance, pp. 158–60.
5 Falling façade: Blesh, p. 290; Eleanor Keaton & Vance, pp. 160–3; *Sight and Sound*, Winter 1965–6.
6 The Keaton Studio closes, Buster's trip to New York, and the Schenck brothers' deal: Eleanor Keaton & Vance, p. 163; Blesh, pp. 294, 298–9; Dardis, p. 156; Meade, pp. 180–1.

20 THE COMPANY MAN

1 Keaton & Samuels, p. 207.
2 *NYT*, May 15, 1928, and May 20, 1928.
3 Dardis, p. 155.
4 MGM contract: Meade, pp. 184–5; Dardis, p. 159.
5 MGM studio: Meade, pp. 184, 190; *NYT*, August 22, 1926; Keaton & Samuels, p. 201; Dardis, p. 160.
6 MGM players: Eleanor Keaton & Vance, p. 164; Meade, pp. 184–6; Brownlow, p. 426.

7 Keaton & Samuels, p. 202.
8 Difficulties with the Keaton crew: Dardis, p. 162; Keaton & Samuels, p. 205.
9 Keaton & Samuels, p. 208; Eleanor Keaton & Vance, p. 169.
10 Sedgwick: Keaton & Samuels, p. 208; Eleanor Keaton & Vance, p. 166.
11 Sedgwick and Keaton in New York: Keaton & Samuels, pp. 208–10; Blesh, pp. 302–3; *NYT*, May 13, 1928.
12 Eleanor Keaton & Vance, p. 169.
13 Keaton & Samuels, pp. 211–12.
14 Eleanor Keaton & Vance, p. 169.
15 Newsreels: Keaton & Samuels, p. 207; Dardis, p. 163; Eleanor Keaton & Vance, p. 169.
16 Monkey's name: Blesh, p. 306.
17 Success of *The Cameraman*: Dardis, p. 176; *NYT*, September 9, 1928, and September 17, 1928; Blesh, p. 302.
18 Buster's place in the MGM system: Meade, p. 187; Keaton & Samuels, pp. 212–13; Dardis, pp. 166, 170.
19 "All of us . . .": From "Cops," by Charles Simic, in Shepard, p. 245.
20 Sound technology: Brownlow, pp. 572–6.
21 Keaton & Samuels, p. 207; Brownlow, pp. 436–7.
22 Buster doubles for Lew Cody: Blesh, p. 311; Brownlow, p. 477.
23 Keaton pitching to Thalberg: Keaton & Samuels, p. 206; Blesh, pp. 308–9.

21 END OF THE AFFAIR

1 *Ladies' Home Journal*, June 1926.
2 Sound hysteria: Dardis, pp. 179–80; *NYT*, November 11, 1928, and February 3, 1929.
3 Keaton and sound: Meade, p. 192; Blesh, p. 310; Eleanor Keaton & Vance, p. 170.
4 The new premise and crew: Blesh, p. 310; Dardis, p. 171; Keaton & Samuels, p. 213.
5 *Spite Marriage* and Dorothy Sebastian: Eleanor Keaton & Vance, pp. 170–1, 173; *NYT*, March 25, 1929; Meade, pp. 189–90; Dardis, pp. 175–6.
6 Completion, reviews, and putting the wife to bed: Dardis, p. 176; *NYT*, March 25, 1929, March 31, 1929, and May 26, 1929; *Variety*, March 27, 1929; Eleanor Keaton & Vance, pp. 173, 199–200.
7 Keaton's Kennel: Meade, pp. 185, 190–1; Dardis, pp. 168–9; Keaton & Samuels, pp. 214–15.
8 *NYT*, August 15, 1929; Eleanor Keaton & Vance, p. 174; Meade, p. 192.
9 Lapse between story ideas: Eleanor Keaton & Vance, p. 176.

10 *NYT*, April 19, 1930.
11 Eleanor Keaton & Vance, p. 177.
12 *Doughboys* and the European vacation: Keaton & Samuels, pp. 220–3; Blesh, p. 315; Meade, pp. 170, 196–7.
13 Sebastian's marriage, Keaton's contract, and Weingarten's play: Meade, pp. 197, 200; *NYT*, December 19, 1930; Dardis, p. 185.
14 Eleanor Keaton & Vance, p. 180.
15 Kathleen Key incident: *NYT*, February 6, 1931; *LAT*, February 6, 1931; Keaton & Samuels, pp. 224–5; Meade, pp. 200–2.
16 Studio spin: Dardis, pp. 195–6 ("broken limbs . . ."); Meade, p. 202 ("Danger . . .").
17 Keaton & Samuels, p. 225; Dardis, p. 196.
18 Brownlow, p. 474.
19 Dardis, pp. 186, 196.
20 *Sidewalks of New York*: Meade, pp. 204–5; Eleanor Keaton & Vance, pp. 182–3.
21 *The Passionate Plumber*: Meade, p. 206; Keaton & Samuels, p. 237; Eleanor Keaton & Vance, p. 184; *NYT*, April 12, 1932.
22 "Kidnapping" incident: Dardis, pp. 205–7; Keaton & Samuels, pp. 226–7; Meade, pp. 207–8; *LAT*, April 6, 1932.
23 Shooting delays: Dardis, pp. 207, 212–13. Drinking: Keaton & Samuels, p. 240; Meade, p. 211; Dardis, p. 209. *Speak Easily*: Eleanor Keaton & Vance, pp. 186–7; *Variety*, August 23, 1932.
24 The yacht, the incident, and the divorce: Meade, pp. 208–9, 212, 223; Keaton & Samuels, pp. 225–7, 231–2; Blesh, pp. 323, 326–7; *NYT*, July 26, 1932, and August 9, 1932; Eleanor Keaton & Vance, p. 108.
25 Keaton & Samuels, p. 231; Meade, pp. 211–12; Blesh, p. 330.
26 Mae Scriven: Meade, pp. 213–14; Blesh, p. 325; *NYT*, May 1, 1933; Eleanor Keaton & Vance, p. 190.
27 *What! No Beer?*: Keaton & Samuels, p. 237; *NYT*, February 11, 1933; *Variety*, February 14, 1933. The curse of the remakes: Eleanor Keaton & Vance, p. 176.
28 Dardis, pp. 223–6; *NYT*, February 4, 1933.

22 THE LITTLE BOY WHO COULDN'T BE DAMAGED

1 Keaton & Samuels, p. 13.
2 The worst years (1933–5): Blesh, pp. 333–4, 337; Dardis, pp. 215, 219; Meade, pp. 216, 223. Chaplin, Lloyd, and sound: Dardis, pp. 184–5.
3 Meade, pp. 217–18; Keaton & Samuels, pp. 244–5.
4 Meade, pp. 210, 212, 216, 222–4.

5 Education at shorts and features abroad: Eleanor Keaton & Vance, pp. 194-5; Meade, pp. 219, 221; Blesh, p. 339; Keaton & Samuels, pp. 251-2.
6 Cheaters: Blesh, p. 340. Beauty parlor: Eleanor Keaton & Vance, p. 190. "Marriage of inconvenience": Blesh, p. 348. Mae and prostitution: Dardis, pp. 232, 241. Divorce and hospitalization: Meade, pp. 225-7; Eleanor Keaton & Vance, pp. 192-3; *The New York Post*, October 21, 1935, and October 23, 1935.
7 Mae's later life: Meade, pp. 231, 281-3, 286-7, 308.
8 Keaton & Samuels, p. 247; Meade, p. 227; Eleanor Keaton & Vance, p. 193.
9 Keaton at MGM: Meade, pp. 228, 232; Dardis, p. 246; Eleanor Keaton & Vance, p. 198; Blesh, pp. 348-50; Keaton & Samuels, pp. 260-3.
10 Eleanor Keaton & Vance, pp. 34-5; Meade, pp. 228, 234; Keaton & Samuels, p. 259.
11 Columbia shorts: Meade, pp. 234-5; Keaton & Samuels, p. 259.
12 Eleanor Keaton & Vance, pp. 35-6; Dardis, p. 253; *NYT*, May 23, 1940, and May 30, 1940.
13 The boys' visit and the war years: Meade, pp. 224-5, 229, 235-6, 238; Eleanor Keaton & Vance, pp. 36-7, 196; Keaton & Samuels, pp. 257, 277; Blesh, p. 356.
14 Eleanor Keaton & Vance, pp. 199-200; Meade, p. 239.
15 Eleanor Keaton & Vance, p. 196; *Life*, September 5, 1949.
16 Keaton and television: Meade, pp. 240-1, 247; *Life*, March 13, 1950; Keaton & Samuels, pp. 255-7.
17 Buster's career: Eleanor Keaton & Vance, p. 30. Television and the Pickfair reunion: *Film Quarterly*, Fall 1958; Meade, pp. 272-3; Keaton & Samuels, p. 271; *NYT*, October 17, 1965.
18 Stage: Eleanor Keaton & Vance, p. 204; Meade, pp. 242, 284. Screen: Meade, pp. 244, 295, 297; Keaton & Samuels, p. 271; Eleanor Keaton & Vance, p. 209; *NYT*, May 9, 1954, July 21, 1964, and October 17, 1965.
19 Meade, pp. 250-5.
20 Awards and honors: Eleanor Keaton & Vance, pp. 37, 40-1; Meade, pp. 265-6; *NYT*, April 6, 1960 ("having made pictures . . .").
21 Bruckman: Blesh, p. 365; Dardis, pp. 104, 274; Meade, pp. 260-1; Brownlow, p. 481.
22 Meade, pp. 263-7; Dardis, p. 264; Keaton & Samuels, pp. 275-6; Eleanor Keaton & Vance, p. 38.
23 Woodland Hills: Meade, pp. 263, 271-2; Eleanor Keaton & Vance, pp. 38-40; Keaton & Samuels, pp. 276-7.
24 Meade, pp. 267-71; Keaton & Samuels, p. 276.
25 Keaton's friends and family: Meade, pp. 237, 257-8, 273-4, 279-281,

307; Keaton & Samuels, p. 278; Eleanor Keaton & Vance, pp. 203-4; *NYT*, October 17, 1965.

26 The last leg: Eleanor Keaton & Vance, pp. 33, 41-3, 209-10; Meade, pp. 298, 301-6; *NYT*, October 17, 1965; *Sight and Sound*, Winter 1965-6. "Sure it's great . . .": Brownlow, p. 474. "I work more than Doris Day": *NYT*, October 17, 1965.

CODA

1 Burial and obituary: Eleanor Keaton & Vance, p. 33; *NYT*, February 2, 1966.
2 *NYT*, November 13, 2002.

Bibliography

Agee, James, *Agee on Film: Criticism and Comment on the Movies*, 1958; reprint, Modern Library, New York, 2000

Allen, Frederick Lewis, *Only Yesterday: An Informal History of the 1920's*, 1931; reprint, Harper & Row, New York, 1964

Blesh, Rudi, *Keaton*, Macmillan, New York, 1966

Brownlow, Kevin, *The Parade's Gone By . . .*, 1968; reprint, University of California Press, Berkeley and Los Angeles, 1976

Dardis, Tom, *Keaton: The Man Who Wouldn't Lie Down*, 1979; reprint, University of Minnesota Press, Minneapolis, 2002

Dragga, Jack, *Buster Keaton Filmography*, printed in *Buster Keaton: Cut to the Chase*, 1995; reprint Da Capo Press, New York, 1997

Keaton, Buster and Charles Samuels, *My Wonderful World of Slapstick*, 1960; reprint, Da Capo Press, New York, 1982

Keaton, Eleanor and Jeffrey Vance, *Buster Keaton Remembered*, Harry N. Abrams, Inc., New York, 2001

Louvish, Simon, *Stan and Ollie: The Roots of Comedy: The Double Life of Laurel and Hardy*, 2001; paperback, Faber and Faber, London, 2002

Meade, Marion, *Buster Keaton: Cut to the Chase*, 1995; reprint, Da Capo Press, New York, 1997

Oldham, Gabriella, *Keaton's Silent Shorts: Beyond the Laughter*, Southern Illinois University Press, Carbondale and Edwardsville, Illinois, 1996

Rafferty, Terrence, *The Thing Happens: Ten Years of Writing About the Movies*, Grove Press, New York, 1993

Shepard, Jim (ed.), *Writers at the Movies: Twenty-six Contemporary Authors Celebrate Twenty-six Memorable Movies*, HarperCollins, New York, 2000

The Day Buster Smiled: The 1926 Filming of "The General" by Buster Keaton as Chronicled in The Cottage Grove Sentinel newspaper, Cottage Grove, Oregon, Cottage Grove Historical Society, Cottage Grove, Oregon, 1998

See Notes for newspaper and magazine articles.

Acknowledgments

I owe an immeasurable debt to the following people for their friend-
ship, counsel, and good cheer through the writing of this book and
beyond: Tod Lippy, Stacy Cochran, Jim Shepard, Shawn Rosenheim,
John Irving, Janet Turnbull Irving, Taylor Hamra, Beth Butts, and the
true experts, The Damfinos.

I would like to single out my editor, the incomparable Walter
Donohue, for his wit and patience.

Most of all, love to my parents and sister for their wise and unflag-
ging support, and to Heather, for going to the movies, reading first
pages, and putting up with Buster and me.

Index

All films in which Buster Keaton appeared are indexed under Keaton, Buster, films of.
Bold location references are for photographs.

Edward McPherson is a writer who has contributed to such publications as *The New York Times Magazine, The New York Observer, I.D.,* and *Esopus.* He grew up in Texas. He saw his first Buster Keaton film in a class at Williams College, but the obsession didn't bloom until he moved to New York to work for *Talk* magazine. For this, his first book, he spent more than a year and a half repeatedly watching and admiring more than 60 Keaton films in his apartment. He lives in Brooklyn, New York.